Madame Claude

Lorem ipsum dolor sit amet, appellantur conclusionemque per eu, te pro tamquam omnesque delicatissimi. Ea sit velit sadipscing. Qui ea equidem nominati petentium. Sea ad consetetur adipiscing, te nec salutandi periculis conceptam, alia scripserit ne pro. Ei ius elit singulis.

In mea nominavi dissentias. Cu habeo graece constituam cum, propriae adipisci volutpat eu nec. Mei ne minimum rationibus, pro no stet etiam pertinax. Minim scripta quaeque mel cu, case admodum has an. Per malis philosophia id.

Putant regione quaerendum mea id. recusabo efficiantur ut pri. Denique appellantur vituperatoribus et vis, tacimates mnesarchum honestatis ei cum. Ne sea decore omnesque, luptatum conclusionemque est id. Id quo case quas velit, menandri antiquam eu duo. Nam id postea temporibus, et splendide intellegam pro, id atqui ancillae vim. qualisque ne mea.

Cu his modo definitiones. Ne duis dolore eos. Accommodare concludaturque pri no, sale inimicus electram ne pri. In nec quando possim efficiantur, id etiam mollis conceptam duo, eos in wisi aeterno.

Ne ius ceteros accommodare. Eius efficiantur necessitatibus at duo, cum cu error definitiones. Qui epicurei persecuti instructior id, fierent incorrupte quaerendum nec an. Usu an minim

Adipiscing Augue

Le Sexe, C'est le Vrai Pouvoir par Madame Claude

Cu his modo definitiones, amet, appellantur conclusionemque per eu, te pro tamquam omnesque delicatissimi. Ea sit sadipscing. Qui ea equidem nominati petentium. Sea ad consetetur adipiscing, nec salutandi periculis conceptam, alia scripserit ne pro. Ei ius elit singulis.

In mea nominavi dissentias. Cu habeo graece constituam cum, propriae adipisci volutpat eu nec. Mei ne minimum rationibus, pro no stet etiam pertinax. Minim scripta quae mel cu, case admodum has an. Per philosophia id.

Putant regione quaerendum mea recusabo efficiantur ut pri. De appellantur vituperatoribus et vis, tacin mnesarchum honestatis ei cum. Ne decore scripta omnesque, scripta lupt

Voulez Vous Epouser un Milliardaire?

lis dolapiae officit et oritenia ex everum, sin pro blaut ratia ipsum aperapieut erro molore imi, sam, offic tem voluptassiti re moloribus, celeste euitate nosam lis dolapiae et officit et accus sollandis magnis eut repratenpor modit expelli caboreptur, quis estempo rionsed issinctium facepudit acest fugia.

MADAME CLAUDE

ALSO BY WILLIAM STADIEM

The Auctioneer: Adventures in the Art Trade

Jet Set: The People, the Planes, the Glamour, and the Romance of Aviation's Glory Years

Moneywood: Hollywood in Its Last Age of Excess

A Class by Themselves: The Untold Story of the Great Southern Families

Too Rich: The High Life and Tragic Death of King Farouk

Marilyn Monroe Confidential

Mister S

Dear Senator

Daughter of the King

Madam 90210

Everybody Eats There

Don't Mind If I Do

Lullaby and Good Night

MADAME CLAUDE

Her Secret World of
Pleasure, Privilege, and Power

WILLIAM STADIEM

St. Martin's Press

New York

Author's note: This is a true story, though some names and
details have been changed.

Endpapers © Michel Gangne / Staff / Getty Images;
newspaper clippings © Shutterstock.com

Design by Donna Sinisgalli Noetzel

www.stmartins.com

Library of Congress Cataloging-in-Publication Data

Names: Stadiem, William, author.
Title: Madame Claude : her secret world of pleasure, privilege,
  and power / William Stadiem.
Description: New York : St. Martin's Press, [2018] |
  Includes bibliographical references and index.
Identifiers: LCCN 2017055116| ISBN 9781250122384 (hardcover) |
  ISBN 9781250122407 (ebook)
Subjects: LCSH: Grudet, Claude. | Prostitutes—France—Biography. |
  Prostitution—France. | Businesswomen—France.
Classification: LCC HQ194.M28 S73 2018 | DDC 338.4/730674092
  [B]—dc 3
LC record available at https://lccn.loc.gov/2017055116

Our books may be purchased in bulk for promotional,
educational, or business use. Please contact your local
bookseller or the Macmillan Corporate and Premium Sales
Department at 1-800-221-7945, extension 5442, or by email
at MacmillanSpecialMarkets@macmillan.com.

First Edition: May 2018

10 9 8 7 6 5 4 3 2 1

For my mother

CONTENTS

MADAME CLAUDE

INTRODUCTION

*I*f the measure of a person's power is the magnitude and amplitude of the secrets he or she keeps, then Madame Claude was surely one of the most powerful people in the world when I met her in Los Angeles in 1981. From 1957 to 1977, Madame Claude had been the unofficial Madame de la République of the Old Guard regimes of Charles de Gaulle and his successor, Georges Pompidou, catering to the sexual whims of fellow heads of state, royalty, tycoons, and stars who bestrode the earth. It was her connection to Hollywood and her panoply of celebrity clients that had occasioned her relocation to the West Coast. Notwithstanding the blandishments of Beverly Hills, despite the sun and despite the stars, her loyal stars, when I first encountered the elegant French Queen of Sex, she seemed as dispirited in her exile as Napoléon on Saint Helena.

Madame Claude had fled France in 1977 in the face of looming criminal charges that she had evaded taxes on millions of dollars in undeclared income. What she denounced as a political witch hunt was couched by the new centrist government of Valéry Giscard d'Estaing as an effort to show the world that France's commitment to American-style modernity was more than allowing a few McDonald's to open on the Champs-Elysées. Giscard was waging an antiprostitution campaign against the supermadam who was considered the embodiment of France's decadent ancien régime. Claude herself detested the *p* word. She vehemently maintained that her famous clientele wasn't paying for *sex*; they were paying for *an experience,* a spectacle. Claude wasn't in the sordid business of putting bodies in beds. She was in the rarefied business of making the dreams of the world's biggest dreamers come true.

If Paris was the capital of sex, Madame Claude was the *capitalist* of sex. In her late fifties, as chic and slim and blond as the most high-toned Paris socialite, Madame Claude held court at the high tables of Hollywood's power restaurants as filmdom's leading actors, agents, and moguls compulsively table-hopped to kiss the hand that had answered the magic telephone that could turn any celluloid fantasy into reality. For her alchemy, and for basically creating and perfecting the concept of the call girl, Madame Claude had become rich, one of the richest entrepreneurial women in the world of her time. She was to eros what Coco Chanel was to fashion, elegant, imperious, and entirely self-made. If she weren't trading in sex, she could have been a beacon of feminism, a genuine role model.

Ever since I had first discovered Paris as a student, I had been aware of Madame Claude. She was as French as the Eiffel Tower. A date with a "Claude girl," as they were known, was one of those pinnacle Paris experiences, like staying at the Ritz or dining at Maxim's or wearing a Lanvin suit, that I never expected to have, an apotheosis of luxury that the French do better than any other nationality. Yet here I was in Beverly Hills, hanging out with the woman who knew more about the private lives of the world's brand names, names like Kennedy, Rothschild, Mountbatten, Agnelli, Onassis, Pahlavi, Saud, Sinatra, Brando, than anybody else. My mission was to convince her to collaborate with me on a book about those names and about those lives, as well as the lives of the women she called her "swans," the

Cinderellas to whom she played the role of the most outrageous Fairy Godmother who ever existed.

I had a simple title for the book: *Sex and Power.* Nobody could tell it better than she. I thought it was a project that, aside from its potential pecuniary rewards, might help relieve the entropy of Claude's American displacement. Because Claude's initial affect was that of a banker, a woman of high finance, I fell prey to the image of her as a James Bond villainess, a lady Auric Goldfinger. But as I got to know her, I saw that Madame Claude did not love only gold. Even more, she loved to *talk,* to tell stories, to provide the lowdown on the high-ups. She was as acute as William Buckley, as incisive as Joan Rivers and Don Rickles combined.

In short, Madame Claude was great fun, though you didn't want to be on her bad side, as was the current French government and the Establishment that had reneged on a collective promise to always protect her, as she had always protected them. Now that this unique social contract had been breached, it seemed that the act of telling the truth, the awful truth, might set Madame Claude free. She certainly enjoyed telling it to me. I often asked her if she were afraid of reprisal. This—she waved around at the movie stars and the foie gras and the vintage wines of the restaurant where we were dining—this was the reprisal, her own gilded cage.

As for the reprisal of a more corporeal sort, Madame Claude was one of the most fearless people I had ever met. She fused the politesse of an avenue Foch doyenne with the sangfroid of a Mafia capo. Claude knew exactly how weak male flesh could be. She had catered to the flesh of rulers, of despots, of dictators, of arms merchants, of wielders of immense, deadly power. She knew what they needed and wanted and was utterly confident that her unique ability to provide femininity on its ultimate level would be her perennial protective shield. As for the swans who were her trademark, to believe the politically correct party line that Madame Claude had relocated to the epicenter of American beauty to retire from the sex trade and open a pastry shop would have been beyond naïve. With stunning actresses and models to groom and perfect and rich and famous men to introduce them to, how could Madame Claude possibly resist the siren call of Alexander Graham Bell to seize the line and make the match? It would have been like inviting Michael Jordan onto a basketball court and not expecting him to take a shot. Madame Claude was truly the Nijinsky of the fix-up.

I spent several months talking and talking with Madame Claude in Los Angeles, during which we somehow became friends. I was a good listener. Then again, with the adventures she could recount, who wouldn't have been? In the course of our unlikely relationship, I ended up meeting many of the legends of the world whose mandate was to create legends. There was a factor here of gilt by association. If I could be keeping company with Madame Claude, I perforce must be someone worth knowing. That was entertainment. I also met a number of her swans, some local, others imported from Europe, all special and all relentlessly ambitious, even for Hollywood. I got a vivid idea as to how Madame Claude played the headmistress of her very unique finishing school. Above all, I was amassing a treasure trove of material for the book she was warming to with each new story she told.

And then, without warning, Madame Claude made what is known as a "French exit," leaving without a trace, without a good-bye. I later learned that, with the French taxmen and the American immigration men breathing down on her, she had made another great escape, this time to her cattle ranch in the South Pacific. By 1985, with the Socialist François Mitterrand in office, Claude must have thought the coast was clear; she returned to France, to her country sheep farm. For the first time in her formerly charmed life, Madame Claude made the wrong gambit. She was arrested and sent to prison, not once but twice, in a tragic downhill decade in which the Queen of Sex tried to resume a throne that her ever-Americanizing country had abolished.

Between Madame Claude's incarcerations, thwarted reincarnations, and eventual relocation to the Riviera, I never was able to connect with her again. She died in Nice in 2015. She was ninety-two. She had seen it all, done it all. Few women have walked a higher wire. Although the book we had talked about doing together never got done, I decided I would have to do it myself. The true story of Madame Claude, her saga of sex and power, was a novelistic epic of self-creation, of ambition, risk, triumph, and tragedy that had to be told. Here it is.

Chapter 1

INTRODUCTORY FRENCH

*C*amelot was coming to Paris. It was their first official European tour, and the First Couple couldn't have been more excited. While Jackie Kennedy was thrilled to be meeting one of her literary idols, the new French minister of culture, André Malraux (*Man's Fate*), who was going to give her a special tour of the Louvre, the person John Kennedy may have been thinking the most about was Madame Claude, who was going to provide JFK with her own take on man's fate. It was a rendezvous with destiny that the new president had been plotting for weeks.

After the Bay of Pigs fiasco in April 1961, John Kennedy had decided that he needed to re-jump-start his presidency. The best way to get global attention as a new-world statesman and rebut his Cuban misadventure was to meet with two of the key statesmen of the Old World, Charles de Gaulle and Nikita Khrushchev, on their home turf of Europe. But just because JFK was doing serious business overseas didn't mean that he would keep in abeyance his obsessive sex drive, which was turning the White House into a cathouse of well-bred "aides" who spent more time in the swimming pool, and, afterward, the Lincoln Bedroom, than in the typing pool.

If JFK's on-the-job bed-hopping at the White House was resulting in something of a French bedroom farce, what better place to continue the production than Paris itself? And what better side benefit to such a diplomatic excursion than to sample the treasures and pleasures of Madame Claude, whom JFK had recently heard about through his jet-set playboy network of Frank Sinatra, Igor Cassini, and Porfirio Rubirosa, all of whom had regaled him with tales of this new, young (thirtyish), and elegant procuress who specialized in turning the high-propriety daughters of the postwar *nouvelle pauvre* French aristocracy into *filles de joie*.

If JFK had a type, it was the wholesome, snooty, proper, preppy girl whose flaunted untouchability, call it a cordon sanitaire, he could violate, like the girls at Miss Porter's or Ethel Walker who inflamed his adolescent lust when he was at Choate and Harvard. Girls just like Jacqueline Bouvier, whom he had to marry to have his way with, and then quickly realized that one way wasn't enough. Here was a madam who specialized in exactly what JFK was after.

Of course, the president had as many exceptions to his rule, and his type, as there were beautiful women who crossed his path. Marilyn Monroe, his latest obsession, was hardly the Farmington type. Nor was Judy Campbell, who had shared beds with not only JFK, Sinatra, and the Chicago mob boss Sam Giancana but also with his father, Joseph, whom everyone still called "Mr. Ambassador," from his stint as Franklin D. Roosevelt's man at the Court of St. James's. (JFK called his father "Big JP.") Still, Judy Campbell, for all her California nonpreppiness, was a convent school girl who exuded the same sort of pedigreed purity that Jackie offered, and that was the trademark and stock-in-trade of this new Madame Claude. JFK couldn't wait.

JFK had no aversions to prostitution, whatever its level of euphemism, nor to sharing a mistress with his father. He was a chip off the old block. Despite their Irish Catholic heritage and their roots in Puritan Boston, the Kennedys, at least the male Kennedys, were anything but bluestockings where sex was concerned, particularly commercial sex. After all, Joe, one of the biggest of American big businessmen, thought it was only natural to combine his two great passions, sex and commerce.

While at Choate, John Kennedy had lost his virginity to a white streetwalker in Harlem, an experience he recounted to his Choate classmate and best friend, LeMoyne Billings. When he was at Harvard, and Joe was ambassador to England, father took son on a grand tour of some of the legendary legal bordellos, or *maisons closes,* of Paris, which were basically deluxe hotels where no one ever slept alone. Le One-Two-Two, for example, named for its number on the rue de Provence, behind the Galeries Lafayette department store, was included on many of the more expensive guided tours for foreign visitors of the City of Light.

Sex at Le One-Two-Two, or other famous brothels like Le Sphinx or Le Chabanais, named for the *rue* where it stood, was as much a high-end Paris tradition as dinner at Maxim's or a show at the Folies Bergère. After a gourmet meal on premises, gentlemen could repair with the beauty of their choice (there were sixty to choose from) to one of the twenty-two bedrooms, each with a unique theme. There was a jungly African room, a beachy Miami room, a replica of a stateroom on the *Normandie,* a pirate's lair, a seaplane cockpit, and, as a standard feature of all of these places, a well-equipped dungeon.

Le One-Two-Two was a favorite of not only Joe Kennedy but also his many Hollywood friends, including Humphrey Bogart, Fatty Arbuckle, Gary Cooper, and Cary Grant. Women loved it, too, including Marlene Dietrich and the love of Joe's life, Gloria Swanson, who lived in Paris in the Roaring Twenties as the marquise de la Falaise. Her husband, the marquis, became Joe's employee at the Kennedy-owned Pathé Studios. The marquis introduced Joe to the splendors of the Paris night at the same time Joe was having an open affair with the marquise and producing her never-completed disaster epic *Queen Kelly,* itself the story of a colonial-era madam in German East Africa.

During the war, Le One-Two-Two and the other leading clubs

were taken over by the occupying Gestapo and turned into un-official bordellos for the Nazi top brass, These houses were shuttered forever in 1946 by a law engineered by Marthe Rich-ard, herself a prostitute turned aviatrix turned spy who, post-war, got into sexual politics. Mobilizing French wrath against the Nazis, Richard effectively branded all the bordellos with a scarlet swastika and put all the ladies of the evening (there were hundreds of thousands throughout France) out on the streets, such as the rue Saint-Denis, scene of Billy Wilder's sixties hit *Irma la Douce,* its title character a happy hooker played by Shirley MacLaine. The streetwalker soon became as much a symbol of Paris as the sidewalk café.

No law, however, could fully eradicate brothels from the French scene. Secret houses sprung up, often controlled by the Corsican Mafia. None was more exclusive nor more discreet than the sprawling nineteenth-century home of Madame Billy (now demolished), on 4, rue Paul-Valéry in the posh sixteenth ar-rondissement, which catered to major politicians, French movie stars like Jean Gabin and Yves Montand, and American tycoons like Henry Ford II. Joseph Kennedy had frequently taken Jack there for postprandial high jinks in the fifties, en route to the Kennedys' rented summer villa in Eze, on the Côte d'Azur, even after Jack had married Jackie and was elected to the Senate. The Hyannisport compound had its summer charms, but bouil-labaisse and easy access to fancy prostitutes was not among them—hence the French seasonal diaspora. Rose often stayed in Massachusetts, leaving the boys to their Riviera *divertissements.* Shame and restraint were not in the Kennedy playbook.

What Madame Billy had had was an old-fashioned brothel, with twenty pretty women on the premises, an enormous bar, and ten bedrooms. What this new Madame Claude was offering was a bespoke fantasy of a far different order. She could tailor for her clients the woman of their dreams. Her brainstorm had been to combine the fantasies of Le Crazy Horse Saloon, that shrine of ecdysis on the avenue George V since 1951, which was considered the world's most elegant striptease club, featuring the most spectacular showgirls on earth, with the realities of prostitution.

Le Crazy Horse's rule toward its preternaturally perfect specimens of femininity was look but don't touch. The same standard of hands-tied voyeurism applied to the Amazonian creatures of the Lido and the Folies Bergère, much as supermodels are viewed today. Madame Claude's genius was enabling this protective shield to be breached, to allow normal men, or at least normal rich men, to touch the untouchable. You didn't have to be Tom Brady to get Gisele Bündchen. You didn't have to be Harvey Weinstein, either. You didn't have to harass anyone, to play power games. And you didn't have to be single, either. Even if you were a head of state.

Madame Claude's special and secret service was geared, as was most of the late fifties Madison Avenue aspirational advertising, to "the man who has everything." Aside from being tall, stunning, and statuesque, Claude added another element to the mix: class. Her girls weren't mere strippers; they were from fine old French families. In France, in particular, snobbery was a great virtue, and Madame Claude played it to the hilt. Most of Claude's business was "out-call," in which she sold brains and charm as much as the sex itself. She sent her charges on dates for dinner, dancing, and a happy ending in the most glamorous venues in this most glamorous city. Time was money, and a lot of the time what was being paid for was the romance, or illusion thereof, rather than the sex alone.

Visiting moguls and stars, usually traveling without spouses in tow, would end their enchanted evenings in their luxury suites at the Ritz, the Plaza Athénée, the Crillon, or the George V. When discretion was required, as it would be with JFK, a top secret rendezvous in an above-reproach venue, and surely not one of Paris's ubiquitous *hôtels de vingt minutes*, which catered to the walk-in trade, could be arranged. Claude did maintain a

three-bedroom apartment on the rue de Marignan, in the commercial heart of the Champs-Elysées. Two or more beautiful,
invariably tall, and sylphlike model types were there on call, to
cater to the idle minds and devil's workshops of *Paris Match* journalists or photographers right around the corner, or to those of
the stars and executives from Paris's "Little Hollywood" district
of film companies clustered across the Champs on the rue de
Ponthieu and the rue du Colisée.

The Marignan flat also served the visiting English and European tycoons who stayed down the Champs at the Travellers
Club, where a naughtily conspiratorial chief hall porter had
started Madame Claude on her merry way just a few years before by passing her phone number to his most privileged members. (The club was all-male until the twenty-first century.)
Ironically, the Second Empire marble mansion that housed the
Travellers, on 25, avenue des Champs-Elysées, had been built in
1865 by Esther Lachmann, one of Paris's top prostitutes of an
era when "*les grandes horizontales,*" as the supermistresses were
known, were the equivalent of today's female rock and movie
stars and brand-name Kardashianesque celebrities.

Lachmann, born poor and Jewish in Moscow in 1819, is a
study in sexual social climbing; she would become a role model
for Madame Claude herself. Lachmann, the daughter of a weaver,
was married at seventeen to a poor Russian tailor, had a son, then
abandoned them both to go to Paris. By age twenty-one, she had
become the mistress of Henri Herz, a prominent pianist and piano manufacturer, who introduced her to the high-art world, if
not high society. When Herz refused to leave his wife for her,
Lachmann crossed the Channel to London, where a fellow courtesan lent her the low-cut gowns that would catch the attention
of the British male aristocracy on opening nights at Covent Garden. In 1851, she hit the conjugal jackpot by marrying the Portuguese Albino de Araújo de Païva, whose family fortune came
from the opium trade in the colony of Macao.

In 1852, the thirty-three-year-old "La Païva," as she became known, divorced the opium scion and found a new mark in the twenty-two-year-old German mining heir Count Guido Henckel von Donnersmarck. It took her nearly twenty years to get the young count to the altar, which she did in 1871. But it was one of the most expensive affairs in history, during which La Païva was gifted by the count not only with the grand Château de Ponchartrain, outside Paris, but also with the construction of the current Travellers Club, then considered the pinnacle of Paris conspicuous consumption, the equivalent of the Aaron Spelling mansion in Holmby Hills in the Reagan eighties. Auguste Rodin was one of the craftsmen who helped construct the mansion, and he, Zola, Flaubert, and Delacroix were regular guests at La Païva's parties, considered the greatest of a lavish era. She even inspired an 1873 play by Alexandre Dumas, *fils,* about a courtesan so successful but so ruthlessly vile that her husband, an arms-dealing tycoon, is justified in murdering her. The name of the play was *La Femme de Claude.* It was reputedly the inspiration for Madame Claude's *nom de bordel.*

Catering to the erotic whims of a visiting president was dollar diplomacy on the most delicate and demanding level. It was also a logistical nightmare, given that the eyes of the world were on the new president and his lovely wife in the first manifestation of her Francophile iconhood. That JFK could be caught with his pants down on a state visit was a possibility that couldn't even be contemplated. However, John Kennedy was so obsessed with sex, and so bold and reckless in his obsessions, possessing his father's arrogance that the right kind of bad boy could get away with *everything,* that JFK forged ahead in strategizing his French sexcapade as if it were a priapic D-day.

Most of the preliminary planning was done between Madame Claude herself and Pierre Salinger, Kennedy's trusted press secretary, who, despite so many assumptions, was only *half* French (his mother) and had grown up and been educated in San Francisco.

Still, he was fluent in French; plus, he shared his boss's penchant for naughtiness. So the assignment was literally a labor of love. At first, Madame Claude turned Salinger down. There were too many things that could go wrong and too much attention on the prospective client, arguably the most famous man on earth.

Claude was relatively new in the business, and the last thing she needed was a scandal on the front pages of the world press. Most of her clients came from show business, industry, and finance; she had few contacts at this point with the French government. If they could shut down the mighty Le One-Two-Two or the iconic Sphinx, they could shut down her little operation like swatting a fly and ship her off to Fleury-Mérogis, the brutal Alcatraz of *la belle France,* where bad madams went to die. Claude was doing fine. Why risk losing it all?

Salinger, a born salesman, turned all the negatives into positives. The French loved sex as much as they loved the privacy of their dalliances. They would avert their eyes. And, Salinger pressed, if Madame Claude could service President Kennedy, she would become a "made woman," capable of taking care of all the top men in every country. This was the stuff myths were made of. Would Maxim's have feared to serve Curnonsky, the "Prince of Gastronomes," the ultimate gourmet of the twentieth century? Rise to the occasion, Salinger exhorted Claude. Do it for your career. Do it for your country, he riffed, paraphrasing JFK's inaugural address. Think big! Weighing risks and rewards like the shrewd banker she might have otherwise been, Claude decided to go for it.

Salinger had gotten the contact information on Madame Claude from Sinatra's valet and former navy admiral's chef and aide George Jacobs, who was the Chairman's majordomo for all things sexual and culinary. Jacobs had gotten the number from Igor Cassini, the Russian-born count and now America's top gossip columnist as the Hearst newspaper chain's Cholly Knickerbocker. Twenty million people read Cassini, a charter member of the world he covered, who was married to Charlene Wrights-man, the daughter of Joe Kennedy's next-door neighbor in Palm Beach, the Standard Oil tycoon Charles Wrightsman. Igor Cassini was an inveterate rake and connoisseur of all things sexual and global. It was Cassini, more than anyone else, who had put the notion of Madame Claude onto the to-do list of JFK.

Ironically, it was also Cassini who had first "discovered" Jac-queline Bouvier at a 1947 Newport, Rhode Island, ball, and in-augurated her in his column as "Deb of the Year." There were other deep ties. Cassini's stepmother-in-law, Jayne Wrightsman, was Jackie Kennedy's style mentor, while his playboy brother, Oleg, who had been married to Gene Tierney and engaged to Grace Kelly, was Jackie's own White House dress designer, Camelot's secretary of style. Both Igor and Oleg had sampled Madame Claude's treasures and pleasures, and their recommen-dation was like a "By Appointment to Her Majesty" seal of ap-proval. Their proximity to Jackie may have been a little close for comfort, but walking the edge in matters of sex was exactly the way JFK liked to play.

JFK's initial request, a month before the trip in May, was for Anouk Aimée, who had just appeared the previous year in Fel-lini's *La Dolce Vita*. Kennedy had been mesmerized, and obsessed with her. That he would ever suggest an assignation with a ris-ing movie star seemed beyond audacious, even for a dashing young heir like himself. But Kennedy was nothing if not auda-cious, and access to stars and models was precisely what made Madame Claude different from all other madams. She could make the wildest dreams come true, even if the dreamer was the president of the United States. She was the ultimate enabler, taking the French concept of droit du seigneur to its outer lim-its of privilege and entitlement.

Despite the seeming arrogance of the president's request, it did have its own internal logic. Anouk Aimée was a mere star-let, just being discovered. She was not above the struggle, not yet. He could have asked for Brigitte Bardot. After all, he was having an affair with her American counterpart, Marilyn Monroe, who herself had not been above turning a few tricks in her own starlet days. That's what actresses *did,* for Christ's sake. Jack had learned this from his father.

"What does he want *her* for?" was Madame Claude's initial response to the JFK request for Anouk Aimée. "He's already got her." Claude was referring to the frequent comparison in looks between Jackie and Anouk. They were close to the same age, tall, dark, mysterious, and slinkily regal, though Anouk was the half-Jewish daughter of two thespians and had a background light-years away from Jackie's preppy Newport privilege. The explanation was that JFK liked the package more than the contents. He was drawn to Jackie's looks but wanted a more seductive, sexual version. Such was Anouk Aimée. JFK, a cinephile, had done his homework, or at least assigned it to one of his White House mistresses/assistants.

Anouk had been divorced from her second husband, an unsung Greek film director, and was raising their daughter. Surely she would be up for a brief encounter with the most famous man in the world. Wrong! It is not clear whether Madame Claude made her overture directly or through one of the actresses who did moonlight for her, or through one of her film-world clients. Anouk was horrified by the notion, not of a paid assignation, but with someone she viewed as a "puerile warmonger" for his Bay of Pigs invasion and, with foresight on Anouk's part, his mounting involvement in the morass of French Indochina. Claude never told Salinger what Aimée had said, only that she wasn't available, away from Paris on movie business during JFK's tiny window of opportunity. But at least Madame Claude had the idea of what JFK was looking for. There were plenty of sexy Jackie types in Paris. It was just a matter of time and place.

Of course, there was no such thing as "an easy lay," even where Madame Claude was concerned. To begin with, the trip to

Europe soon mushroomed into a huge geopolitical event. It also mushroomed into a family vacation. Because Paris had a glamour that few women can resist, Jackie's sister, Lee Radziwill, insisted on tagging along, as did Jack's mother, Rose, and sister Eunice, Jackie's two secretaries, Tish Baldridge and Pam Turnure (JFK's ex-secretary and reputed ad hoc mistress), as well as Jackie's friend Tony Bradlee, wife of *The Washington Post*'s Ben, who was covering the trip. Ben's sister, the pot-smoking artist Mary Meyer, was already flirting with JFK back in Washington and would soon begin a series of White House trysts with him.

Too many women, Joe Kennedy concluded, and he opted to stay home. How his son would figure out a way to add still another Jackiesque filly to his stable while in the glare of the world's spotlights was beyond him. However, Joe was all for such Flying Wallenda tightrope feats and, if consulted, would surely have urged his son to go for it. Meanwhile, primed by his confidant Igor Cassini about the wonders of Paris's new supermadam, Joe himself began planning his next French excursion with her firmly in mind.

Aside from all the snooping eyes, Jack Kennedy had his perpetually aching back to worry about. The condition may have been exacerbated by the president's anxieties about his upcoming meetings with two leaders who had even more contempt for him than his vanquished rival Richard M. Nixon. De Gaulle was a national treasure, a living legend, aged seventy long before seventy became the new fifty. When JFK was born, de Gaulle, already a hero and a leader, had been fighting for years in the trenches of the western front in the Great War. De Gaulle exuded tradition, heroism, gravitas. JFK exuded youth and charm, the shock of the new; his seriousness had yet to be proved. And if the world had any idea how much of his time was focused not on NATO or Algeria or Vietnam, but on a hot date from Madame Claude, the perception of history would have been dubious, to say the least.

To calm his back, and to boost his flagging confidence, Jack

Kennedy decided to make a very curious and controversial addition to his already-bulging entourage. This was his "pain specialist," Max Jacobson, MD, a Park Avenue practitioner who was the first "celebrity doctor" to become a household name to readers of the gossip columns like the one of Igor Cassini. JFK had been referred to Jacobson by both Igor and Oleg, who were patients, and by his Choate schoolmate Alan Jay Lerner. Lerner's legacy to his prep school friend was the unlikely combination of *Camelot* and amphetamines, which were Dr. Jacobson's stock-in-trade. Jacobson, known as "Dr. Feelgood," had a front-page clientele that also included Marilyn Monroe, Elvis Presley, Judy Garland, Leonard Bernstein, Maria Callas, Elizabeth Taylor, and Nelson Rockefeller, many of whom, like Presley, Monroe, and Garland, would eventually die from drug-related causes.

JFK was so hooked on what Jacobson called his "vitamin shots" that he was able to convince Jackie to shoot along with him. The trip to Europe, Paris, Vienna, and London in barely a week not only would require immense energy but also entailed the time zone recovery from the twelve-hour Atlantic crossing in the Lockheed Super Constellation that served as *Air Force One* before an impatient JFK replaced it with one of the new Boeing 707 jets that cut the travel time in half. Dr. Jacobson, then sixty, was a refugee from Nazi Germany. He represented the old Renaissance ideal wherein no gentleman, much less a head of state, would embark upon a grand tour without his trusted doctor by his side.

Jack and Jackie might have been even better served if they had taken a psychiatrist, or at least a marriage counselor, along as well. Notwithstanding their status as the world's dreamiest political couple since Anthony and Cleopatra, the president and First Lady were at each other's throats the entire trip. To begin with, in Paris, Jackie, who had been coming to France since her junior year abroad and was fluent not only in the language but also in the history, culture, and, above all, style, totally stole

Jack's thunder. Plus, she had a French name. It was nolo contendere for the president, who could see in their Simca cabriolet from the half-million-strong crowd en route to Paris from Orly Airport, waving and cheering at Jackie, that it was she, and not he, they were turning out for.

The die was further cast when the newspaper *Libération* ran a cartoon of General and Mrs. de Gaulle in their canopied bed. The general is blissfully asleep, covers pulled up to his neck, with a balloon cartoon of a photo of Jackie above his head. Madame de Gaulle is sitting bolt upright, staring unhappily at the photo of Jackie. The caption is one word with an exclamation point: "Charles!" Always Hollywood-quick with a quip, JFK self-deprecatingly introduced himself to a press luncheon of over a hundred French reporters by saying, "I do not think it altogether inappropriate to introduce myself to this audience. I am the man who accompanied Jacqueline Kennedy to Paris."

Settling in to their state apartment for visiting dignitaries at the quai d'Orsay, Jack felt trapped. How in the hell was he ever going to get to Madame Claude and cheat on a wife who had instantly become the hottest thing to hit France since Brigitte Bardot took off her bikini top in *And God Created Woman*? It was no problem to fight with that wife. Their initial presidential spat was that Jackie was way too French for America's good, and good image. This was many decades before "freedom fries" and the Francophobia occasioned by France's rejection of the war in Iraq. Still, America and France had major differences, particularly over NATO, nuclear weapons, and the coveted oil of Algeria, which de Gaulle was willing to give its independence, an act that many Americans feared would throw it, like Nasser's Egypt, into the open arms of Soviet Russia. Jackie's flaunting of her Frenchness seemed to Jack like sleeping with the enemy, even though it was he who was dead set on doing so.

Their battle focused on a dress. The second night in Paris was the highlight of the entire trip, a candlelit multicourse champagne dinner for 150 in the Hall of Mirrors at Versailles, followed by a performance of the ballet of the Paris Opéra in a theater built by Louis XV. Even for JFK, who loved a big bash, especially one with this much deep décolletage, the event seemed a little too "let them eat cake" for the Americans back home who would be reading about the ball in *Life* magazine. Jackie, he insisted, had to stand up a little for America by wearing her Oleg Cassini dress.

Never mind that Oleg Cassini was a Russian and the dress was a knockoff of a design by Jackie's favorite French couturier, Hubert de Givenchy. It was still an *American* dress, and Jack wanted her to flaunt it for the old red, white, and blue. But Jackie, perhaps emboldened by Jacobson's frequent injections, quietly staged her own war of independence and insisted on wearing her Givenchy rhinestone-studded white satin extravaganza, which she secretly had taken with her, to the palace of the *Roi Soleil*.

Jack wasn't being overly sensitive or overreacting to Jackie's obsession with all things French. A group of French women reporters, knowing her fascination with Givenchy, asked her if she were planning a visit to his atelier. Jackie snapped back, "I have more important things to do." And when a reporter from *Women's Wear Daily,* which had taken a gadfly approach to Jackie's lavish expenditures on her wardrobe, asked her if she read that fashion journal, she snapped once again, "I try not to anymore." A final question from the press corps was whether she would buy a French dress for Caroline, then three. Jackie said a terse "No," after which the reporter followed up with "Was it forbidden?" "No, it's not forbidden," Jackie snapped again. "I just don't have time."

If clothes were Jackie's "thing," sex was Jack's. Because Madame Claude's essence was the telephone (her greeting, *"Allô, oui,"* would become part of the French culture), Pierre Salinger was continually on the line to Claude, juggling the time of the rendezvous, which could be no more than one hour. Kennedy and Salinger had their own code for the transaction, which involved buying for Jackie a gift saddle from Hermès, the famed store, which had become a fashion status symbol for the rich and famous. Claude played right along, asking if the jockey (her simulacrum "Zhack-ee") had any need for riding crops, whips, or spurs.

The girl Claude had lined up was a twenty-three-year-old Sorbonne graduate from a poor but tony family of Normandy's lesser nobility. She was a trusted two-year veteran, whose older sister also worked for Claude, sometimes selling herself to the same men she had sold jewels to for their wives while working days at Harry Winston on Avenue Montaigne. JFK's blind date was a very Jackie-like sylph who was employed as a fitting model for Givenchy himself, and thus was in the perfect position to be decked out in samples of the designer couture that Jack had wanted his wife to eschew, for the glory of Old Glory.

And what was in it for the model? The thrill of meeting the president? The notion that she was representing *la gloire de La France?* The large fee? Most of Claude's girls weren't in it for the money. If they were, they didn't stay for long. Claude's was a sort of finishing school for superbeauties. They would be meeting the most important men in France, and, case in point, the world. A lot of these men weren't married. The goal Claude instilled in all of her charges was that beautiful women deserved to marry beautifully. Claude was in many ways an old-fashioned matchmaker with a modern, direct approach to cutting through the archaic courtship rituals. Her amazing track record of *beaux mariages* in the decades ahead was testament to her own vision and her finesse and her brilliance as matchmaker to the rich, titled, and famous.

Because Salinger had been filling Claude in with the continuing "America First" psychodrama, the idea to turn the encounter into a French version of Hitchcock's *Vertigo,* in which James

Stewart obsessively remakes Kim Novak into a fake image she had herself concocted as part of a scam, was Madame's idea, not the president's. Pierre Salinger was sure it would have the desired effect. JFK was known for the "quick in-and-out," but, as a man of wit and taste, he liked his quickies with a liberal dash of imagination and inspiration. Madame Claude, who would in time become a sort of Dr. Ruth, if not Dr. Spock, in the psychology of sex, understood the relationship of hostility and eros, of frustration and arousal. Dressing her damsel in Givenchy was waving a red cape at a bull; the bull was sure to charge, as was the president.

The "Claudette" had an apartment in a quiet residential neighborhood near the parc Monceau in the seventeenth arrondissement, ironically the venue where Luis Buñuel's Madame Claude–inspired *Belle de Jour* would be shot in 1967, when Madame Claude had become a household name in France, and the favorite unkept secret of the tycoons and statesmen of the world. Right now, however, she was a very recherché resource, sort of like the great one-star Michelin restaurant that has not been discovered by the trend-chasing hordes. By 1967, Madame Claude would become the sexual equivalent of those three-star temples of gastronomy, like La Tour d'Argent or Le Grand Véfour or Taillevent. Now she was a hot tip.

The challenge was, with only two days in Paris, how to find that magic hour for JFK. His first day was spent, after soaking his aching back in the marble tub of his digs at the quai d'Orsay, playing humble student to Gen. Charles de Gaulle's eminent professor in the stately halls of the Elysée Palace across the Seine. Despite all the formal cordialities, JFK later told his team of best and brightest how he could feel de Gaulle's strong anti-American vibes. De Gaulle himself wasn't thrilled when JFK brushed aside his request for aid for France's nuclear program, nor for regarding France on an equal footing with England as the joint architects of the future of Europe, a continent that in the general's view, the despised English weren't even on.

Kennedy sought de Gaulle's advice for how to deal with the wily Nikita Khrushchev in Vienna in the days ahead. De Gaulle used the term *méchanceté*, by which JFK understood in his Choate French that de Gaulle meant the Soviet premier was *méchant,* or a bad boy. De Gaulle shook his head at JFK's misapprehension, just as a typical Frenchman might put down an American tourist who mispronounced the Champs-Elysées in asking for directions. That Frenchman would give the Yank a blank stare that indicated he'd never heard of the street. Then the French president told the American president to "ask your wife to explain it to you," which was the worst sort of putdown JFK could hear, given the fact that he felt Jackie had hijacked France from him altogether and had sold her soul to Hubert de Givenchy. *Méchanceté*, JFK later learned, meant malice of a deep order. The difference between *méchanceté* and *méchant* was the difference between Adolf Hitler and Dennis the Menace.

France's deification of Jackie continued at the grand state dinner that first evening at the Elysée Palace. Earlier that day at lunch, Jackie had already curried President de Gaulle's favor by gifting him with a 1783 letter that George Washington had written (in English) to the comte de Noailles, who had fought for the colonies with Lafayette and had later been a banker in Philadelphia. Flattery had gotten Jackie everywhere, and had gotten Jack increasingly annoyed, especially after de Gaulle praised the First Lady to JFK by telling him that she knew more French history than most French women. Jack knew that Jackie had done more cramming for this trip than she had ever done for a final exam at Vassar, where she had dropped out. Notwithstanding this seeming mutual admiration society, what Jackie and de Gaulle said about each other off the record was another matter entirely. Jackie called the general "an egomaniac," while de Gaulle would famously predict to André Malraux that Jackie would "end up on an oilman's yacht."

The second day in Paris, wherein everyone was getting ready

for the big ball at Versailles, was Jack's D-day, or C-day, for Madame Claude. Jackie would be out the entire morning and afternoon with her own "dream date." Jackie admitted to having a huge crush on André Malraux, then sixty, the famous writer and de Gaulle's dear friend and "culture czar." It was on this trip that Jackie and Malraux began cooking up the plan to have the Louvre send its most important treasure, the *Mona Lisa*, on tour to the United States in 1962.

On this day, Malraux gave Jackie an inside tour of the Jeu de Paume museum, across from the Louvre, in the Tuileries Gardens, then at the height of its spring bloom. Afterward, they drove along the Seine just outside of Paris to see the Château de Malmaison, the love nest of Napoléon and Joséphine. The château had just been restored by the architect/designer Stéphane Boudin, whom Harry Winston would soon hire to redo his Fifth Avenue flagship store and whom Jackie would soon hire to redo and "Frenchify" the White House. When one of the Malmaison curators told Jackie that Joséphine had been pathologically jealous of Napoléon, with all his mistresses, Jackie replied in French, "She was quite right, and I don't blame her." Was it a shot across Jack's bow? He wasn't paying attention. Jack might have been jealous of Jackie and her intellectual-giant consort, but if he was, he was planning his own sweet revenge, and, if he wasn't, he was planning his own cultural expedition.

Whatever Jack was planning was not what the French had been planning for him. There had been talk of his visiting the war museum at the Ecole Militaire, or Napoléon's tomb at the Hôtel des Invalides. But JFK begged off, claiming he needed his own Hôtel des Invalides, for his back. Having Dr. Jacobson along provided him the perfect cover. Jacobson said he had a French medical colleague, a "pain specialist," whom he wanted Jack to see in a joint consultation. Jacobson also needed to visit a French pharmaceutical-supplies headquarters on the outskirts of Paris to assemble some more "vitamins" for the shots. He averred he hadn't realized how ill Jack would be, or how tired Jackie would be. His supply had fallen short of the demand. So off he and the president went, on their medical mission, with a Secret Service driver who was supposedly in the dark about their real objective. Even if he weren't, these were times when Americans subscribed to the "sophisticated" French philosophy that a politician's private life was not a public matter.

The idea that Dr. Jacobson was taking the president to the home, and not office, of the pain specialist (aka the Claudette) was to avoid any public curiosity and attention. The problem arose when they arrived at the appointed address on the boulevard de Courcelles. Leaving the Secret Service man outside, JFK and his doctor trooped inside and trudged up six flights of stairs (there was no elevator) to pound on the appointed door fruitlessly for five endless minutes with no answer. They tried two other neighbors in vain, one of whom, an elderly woman, seemed shocked to see someone who resembled the very famous leader of the Free World standing outside her door. Talk about double takes. The president and his doctor, nonplussed, descended from the precipice to seek out the building's concierge. But she, too, was away.

So into the waiting car and off to a neighborhood café, where Kennedy put on his fedora to disguise himself and then went quickly downstairs to find a pay phone to call Pierre Salinger to find out what had gone so terribly wrong. This was long before cell phones; furthermore, the French phone system was primitive compared to America's. At the café, filled with workingmen in dark blue smocks smoking and drinking their break time away, JFK, who went unnoticed, tried to dial Salinger's hot line at the American embassy, but he then realized the phone didn't work without a *jeton,* or token.

JFK had to slither up the narrow, curving stairwell and abashedly request a token from the grizzled bartender, who gave him the most curious and dubious of looks. Neither he nor

Dr. Jacobson had any francs. JFK had no money at all. Jacobsen fished out a twenty-dollar bill and gave it to the barman, who seemed mystified. The doctor motioned for him to keep the change. Eventually, the president got the token and made his call. Salinger, as it turned out, had written down, by mistake, "boulevard" de Courcelles, when the actual address was "rue" de Courcelles, an altogether different thoroughfare. Time was running out. Jackie would soon be back from her day tour with Malraux. The president would have to begin putting on his white tie for the Versailles gala. Should he just give up?

No way, insisted JFK, with all the decisiveness that had made him a war hero on PT-109. They forged on and found the right address on the rue de Courcelles, which, fortunately, was also in the seventeenth arrondissement and only a short distance away. The president and his physician went inside for their consultation, which, according to Madame Claude, was a complete success. When Salinger had advised her that JFK was taking Dr. Jacobson along, Madame Claude's first instinct was to offer a companion for the doctor, possibly the sister of the Jackie look-alike. That would have kept the secret in the family. But Salinger made a command decision to keep the matter as simple as possible. The doctor thus cooled his heels while the president took his pleasure.

Dr. Jacobson did offer one of his famous injections to the young lady, who was splendidly dressed in the exact same white Givenchy dress the First Lady would be wearing at Versailles. She looked like Cinderella on her way to the ball. But the only ball she would be attending was the imminent one in her simple bedroom. Dr. Jacobson tried to explain to her the aphrodisiac effects of his medicine. But her English, while sufficient for amorous purposes, was not adequate for pharmaceutical matters. Besides, one of Madame Claude's cardinal rules was "no drugs," even if the president of the United States and its preeminent cultural symbols, Elvis Presley and Marilyn Monroe, were getting high and happy on the Dr. Feelgood program. She politely declined, though she observed, with a minor degree of discomfort, as the doctor injected the president before closing the door to the bedroom. For his back, the doctor assured her. As for his libido, the doctor could see that the Claudette's own considerable charms, so splendidly displayed in the designer finery, were more than sufficient.

The president was alone with the model for no more than a half an hour; he was known to be efficient and to the point in his affairs, not to mention so excited by all the pressure and frustrated misdirection that, still possessing the hair trigger of relative youth, he could not be expected to fit the title of the seminal 1951 rock-and-roll classic "Sixty Minute Man." John Kennedy was quite the opposite.

What was notable about the presidential exit was that when he and Jackie *la deuxième* emerged from the bedroom, the model was dressed as neatly and primly as she had been when she greeted her visitors at her door. Not a hair of her Jackie style bouffant coiffure was out of place. What had the president done—or not done? As Madame Claude later explained the encounter, the president was fascinated by the dress itself, and what made his wife so prefer the craftsmanship of Givenchy over Cassini. So the fitting model, who was very well versed in the art and science of couture, gave the president a striptease combined with a seminar, so he might understand why, in couture, as in cuisine, and other pleasures of the eye and the flesh, *"Les français, ils sont meilleurs."* That night at Versailles, JFK was profusely complimentary to Jackie over her Givenchy, telling everyone in the vast entourage how fabulous she looked, with never so much of a hint of America First.

Two days later, Kennedy confidently held his own against America's greatest adversary, Nikita Khrushchev, in Vienna, notwithstanding that the Russian premier shamelessly flirted with Jackie even more than had General de Gaulle, while remaining deadly dour with the president, particularly over Berlin. Still,

JFK remained all charm, however impervious to it Khrushchev was. Was it the vitamin shots that kept Kennedy's spirits high and positive? Or was it the sweet medicine of Madame Claude?

What about *la française*? According to Madame Claude, she later learned that the reason the president wanted her to replicate Jackie in an erotic dimension was because the real Jackie and he were not sleeping together. The president complained to the model that his wife was much more interested in fashion than sex. The model did her best to show him that the two were not mutually exclusive. Claude recounted that the president was more than pleased with his afternoon "French lesson." The proof was in the paying. Normally an hour with a Claudette in 1961 would have cost a typical Frenchman the equivalent of fifty dollars. The price of a streetwalker, even a beautiful one, on the rue Saint-Denis was rarely more than five dollars, though it would not have included a high-end *défilé*, or runway show, like the president received, nor would the object of desire have been tailored as a precise doppelgänger of the most famous woman in the world.

Thus the premium for the Madame Claude experience was about ten times the going rate. A meal at Maxim's or La Tour d'Argent, the most expensive three-star temples of gastronomy in Paris of their day, would cost twenty-five dollars a person, including champagne, while a *poulet rôti, salade verte,* and *pommes frites,* washed down with a glass of Beaujolais, at a typical bistro would have cost $2.50. And a night at the Ritz might have cost the same twenty-five dollars, while a nice but normal hotel was $2.50. The moral was that the rich were indeed different. They could pay ten times as much.

But the presidential encounter wasn't for the standard haut monde. This was an affair of state, one of thousands Madame Claude would go on to cater in the decades ahead. Her price for her services to the American president was two thousand dollars, which was basically the cost of the finest saddle at Hermès, which had been the code word for the adventure. She had done such a discreetly perfect job that, endorsed by the powers that were, she became a secretly approved government "contractor" for matters amorous, the go-to madam for American affairs.

Although the "sophisticated" French claimed they had no interest in the romantic doings of JFK or any other leaders, domestic or foreign, this was not to say that JFK had pulled the wool over their eyes. The French, according to Madame Claude, were fully aware of every step JFK had taken, every call Pierre Salinger had made to her. The state apartments at quai d'Orsay had a thousand ears and eyes. And there was no such thing as too much secret information. The French authorities were so impressed with Claude's handling of the matter that soon she was enlisted by the Elysée Palace, as well as the DGER (the French equivalent of the CIA) and the DST (the French FBI), to provide them with strategic information gleaned between the sheets. Within a few years, she would become the country's worst-kept, most coveted secret, the most famous woman in France, whom everyone knew about but had never seen, Madame de la République.

Curiously, on his next visit to Paris, Oleg Cassini contacted Madame Claude and asked to meet the model that JFK had been so pleased with. The Camelot inner circle passed around mistresses like trading baseball cards, and JFK had urged his fellow lothario not to miss her. Alas, Cassini didn't care for her at all. Because Jackie was always importuning him to copy Givenchy, the French couturier had become Cassini's bête noie. Whatever lust Cassini may have felt was overcome by his regal Russian pride and fierce competitive nature. What was good for Givenchy was bad for Cassini. The model never stood a chance.

Chapter 2

THE MAKING OF A MADAM

Madame Claude had the unique achievement of turning sex into a luxury brand. Like Yves Saint Laurent to fashion, Manolo Blahnik to footwear, Alain Ducasse to gastronomy, Conrad Hilton to hotels, or even Betty Crocker to cake mixes, Madame Claude became the standard, the measure, the lodestar of what she was selling. In France, and much of Europe, she was a household name, even if that name was rarely in the press. But unlike branded people such as Coco Chanel or Frank Sinatra or Donald Trump or Dr. Oz, who are the essence of what they are selling, Madame Claude was more like the Wizard of Oz, the genius behind the scenes, Ray Kroc at McDonald's or Steve Wynn at his Vegas palaces.

Today nobody knows who Louis Vuitton was, a cobbler who made fancy trunks, or Guccio Gucci, a saddle maker, but everybody knows the brands. Madame Claude was that kind of brand, the gold standard for sex, just as Eileen Ford was the gold standard for models. The two, in fact, were intersecting sets. Now, both Ford and Claude having recently passed away, the Ford brand endures, while the Claude brand has exited into legend, perhaps because photographs, the essence of Ford, are eternal, while sex, the essence of Claude, is ephemeral, the Snapchat of the luxe life.

Madame Claude was a one-woman and onetime show, but what a spectacle it was. There was a huge mystique and a mythology behind Madame Claude. However, very few people knew much about her. Given the imperatives of her technically criminal enterprise, Madame Claude, the most discreet of criminals, was not one to leave a paper trail. She had no close friends, wrote no diaries, sent no letters, kept the lowest-possible profile, all essential to doing what she did, which was top secret and against the law, although for the first half of her career she was effectively an arm of the state, a very secret service. She was the stuff of gossip, great gossip, great stuff, but never the stuff of tabloids.

When the law did turn against her, Madame Claude had no choice but to out herself with a series of three very self-serving memoirs over two decades of battling the French system of justice. This was her charm offensive. She never flaunted herself among her clients at high-profile nightclubs like Castel or Régine's; she was much too *pudique,* or modest, which was the French term most used to describe her, for such public displays of herself. However, she did tell her story—sort of—to make herself look good, and to portray the big business she built, a business based on sin, lust, vanity, greed, into something pure and lovely. She turned her sex operation into a dreamy fairy tale. Claude thus became her own mythmaker. But how much of it was true?

"There were only five people at her cremation. Not any friends, no family, none of her famous creations, no countesses. Just five gay men—me, my partner, and three hairdressers. She loved hairdressers," recalled Philippe Thuillier, a French television producer, who was the first person to put Madame Claude on the air, in a documentary interview following her arrest and imprisonment for *proxénétisme* in 1992. "Somehow we had become friendly. I had met her at the prison when she got out, poor little old thing, walking with a cane, her hair all white, not the glamorous, imperious blonde everyone talked about. She looked pathetic. The first thing she wanted was a hairdresser. I got one for her. She liked me for that."

Madame Claude died in Nice in December 2015. She was ninety-two. She didn't have Alzheimer's, as had been widely reported. According to Thuillier, she had suffered an aneurysm from a fall at her apartment and had been in a nursing home for her final three years. She had a daughter who lived nearby and worked in a hospital in Monaco. But the daughter was estranged. She did not attend the final ceremony, after which Claude's ashes were scattered in the garden of the mortuary.

"She had left Paris in 2000. First, she lived in the suburbs, outside of Paris, for the fresh air. Then she moved to Nice, for the warmth, the sea. She had rich connections there, so she would be part of a circle. She didn't want to be alone anymore, to die all by herself. But that is what happened," Thuillier said. "She had this romantic notion of reuniting with her daughter, whom she had abandoned as a baby. Claude had left her with her mother [the girl's grandmother] in Angers. Claude sent money, but she rarely saw them. Just money.

"But now Claude wanted to see her. I helped her hire a detective to track the daughter down. He found her shopping one morning at the Galeries Lafayette in Nice. They saw each other for Claude's first six months in Nice but then no more. They had a plan to meet one day a week, but then the daughter wanted to change the day. Claude refused. She refused to take orders from anyone. They had a fight. It was over before it could even begin. The daughter had her own life. She had a husband, a doctor who was the same age as Claude. He died before Claude, but the daughter never reconnected with the mother. They had a difficult relationship, as you might imagine. Claude died alone.

"It took a long time for her to trust me. But she ended up liking the documentary, which got fifteen percent of the whole French audience. That was very big, and I made her some money, which she needed. God knows how she could have lost so much.

Finally I became more than just her producer. I was a friend, one of the few. I would see her, both in Paris and then Nice for twenty years, three or four times every year. When I would visit, she'd always greet me with platters of foie gras and the best smoked salmon and champagne, Laurent-Perrier. She was a good hostess to me.

"She liked to go out, to discover new restaurants, especially Italian places. We'd go to the theater, but she'd always say it was awful and leave after the first act. She was the biggest critic, and not just of women, of everything. Movies were easier. One of her favorites was, strangely, *The Bridges of Madison County*, with Meryl Streep and Clint Eastwood. She liked Meryl Streep. She thought she was smart and tough. Like her.

"The thing she enjoyed most was shopping. She was the queen of shopping. Furniture and shoes. She loved shoes. Then we'd have lunch. The Paris place she liked best was Brasserie Lipp. That's where all the big politicians went, stars, the biggest authors, members of the Académie Française. Lipp was the hangout of the truly powerful in France. Sometimes she'd see women she had "made," the wives of these big men, and only once did I see one say hello to her. She loved it when she was remembered, but she had become an invisible person, like in Stalin's Russia. Still she would point out her exes, in a combination of pride and bitterness. She'd talk of the past, her cars, her homes, mostly her bad investments. Funny that she had the top bankers in the world, and she made all these terrible investments."

Thuillier described how much Claude read, how interested she was in the world economy, in politics, areas where she once had been so connected, intimately connected, to the men whose fingers were on the triggers. "She'd have the TV on constantly, night and day. She was always watching the news, reading several papers. She missed being in Paris, in the action. But she always had her boundaries. If you asked her something she didn't want to discuss, she'd dismiss it with a '*pas important*' and move on.

"To my knowledge, she never had a boyfriend, nothing like that. As for women, there were very few that she would even tolerate. Her true love was her business. She was incredibly proud of what she had created. There was nothing like it. She had made sex *different*. Claude had frequent plastic surgery until she fell down and had the aneurysm. She had two male surgeons that she approved of. She was losing her hearing, and had to wear a hearing aid, which she hated. Her life had been on the phone, and now she couldn't hear it. Claude kept her perfect petit young figure. In her casket, she wore a simple classic white Chanel suit. There was no jewelry. There was no religion. Her hair looked great. That was what mattered to her at the end. Her hair looked great."

In 1975, Madame Claude, at the height of her fame and power in Paris, published her first memoir, *Allô, Oui*. The telephone had become her trademark and her anchor. In an old world of brothels and streetwalkers, only slightly modernized in Paris by the *Amazones,* the name for motorized hookers who would pick up their clients in flashy sports cars, Madame Claude became the first person to harness the relatively high technology of the telephone to the oldest profession. In a sense, she was the Steve Jobs of prostitution. She wrote *Allô, Oui* with her best male friend, Jacques Quoirez, the playboy tycoon brother of her best female friend, Françoise Sagan, the bestselling wunderkind author of *Bonjour Tristesse* and other hit novels, films, and plays. Quoirez, spurred by fraternal competitiveness, wanted to have his own bestseller, with a film version to boot, two years later, of which he coauthored the screenplay.

Madame Claude would write two more memoirs, each following prison stays, after fleeing from France and its tax authorities in 1977. She had expensive lawyers to pay, big fines to defray. Claude had fallen from the grace of the French powers that had always protected and treasured her, and created her sobriquet, Madame de la République. But once she fell, the second half of her life was an endless struggle against a *république* that pursued her on various charges with the relentless zeal of Inspector Javert in *Les Misérables.*

The second of Claude's memoirs came out in 1986, after her term for tax evasion. It was called *Le Meilleur, C'est l'Autre* ("The Other Is Better") and is the story of the pursuit of feminine perfection—by herself, by her women, by her clients. It is perhaps best described as the converse of Betty Friedan's *The Feminine Mystique,* or Gloria Steinem for call girls. The final memoir, which Philippe Thuillier admits helping Claude write after getting out of her next incarceration, this time for procuring, was the 1994 *Madam,* a revisiting of the Quoirez-assisted autobiography of 1975, again with an emphasis on the notion of "Claude-ism" (she detested the term *prostitution*) as empowerment rather than exploitation. Together these three books represent what constitutes the written record of her very secret life. The queen of the telephone did not write letters or diaries, though she did love to gossip with the few confidants who won her trust. People who knew Madame Claude, and few ever claimed to know her well, have described her as a *mythomane,* or fantasist. And how can that not be so, at least in some part? With her career built on fantasy, why should the story of her life not be equally fantastic?

About the only thing that people will agree upon about Madame Claude was that she was born on July 6, 1923, in the Loire Valley city of Angers and that her real name was Fernande Grudet. Everything else in her biography is subject to debate. If you believe Madame Claude, she herself was the *haut-bourgeois* template for the swans she created. All the girls would have to do was to emulate her to become all that they dreamed of being, or all that she dreamed they could be. The curriculum vitae of Madame Claude's privileged, idyllic girlhood may have been the biggest fantasy of all.

Angers, in the heart of château country, has long been one of

the most aristocratic cities in an aristocratic country, the home of
the dukes of Anjou and the Plantagenet kings. Its famous and
foreboding twelfth-century castle, with its seventeen striped
turrets looming over the river Maine, was the seat of Henry II's
Angevin empire, which stretched from Ireland to Spain and Italy. The city had grown rich from its vast slate quarries, which
may have provided prosperity, but also a sense of gloom. All the
houses had dark slate roofs, leading Angers to be known as "the
Black City."

After the French Revolution, the biggest business in Angers
was Cointreau, the orange-based liqueur that became one of the
world's favorite after-dinner drinks. It was a city of fine mansions, clubs, and museums surrounded by a rolling countryside
of grand estates—in short, a city of rich people. You were either
a noble or a slate worker. One could see why Madame Claude
would have wanted to belong. You could also see why someone
who didn't belong would want to escape. This was a dark, deadly
serious, somber place, the antithesis of Paris, with its boulevards,
its lights, its gaiety, its golden opportunities.

Angers was a city of art. Its greatest treasure was also its
greatest emblem. This was the famous Apocalypse Tapestry, the
finest and largest of all medieval tapestries and one of the glories of France's artistic patrimony. Commissioned by Louis I, one
of the dukes of Anjou in 1377, the ninety-scene tapestry, which
has the effect of an endless cyclorama, re-creates the horrendous
vision of the end of the world of Saint John the Divine from
the Book of Revelation. The tapestry held pride of place in the
city's looming Gothic cathedral. It has always been a major tourist destination, as well as required and repeated viewing for the
children of Angers. It makes a huge impression on anyone, and
that doubtlessly included the young Fernande Grudet.

Amid the visions of monsters, devils, and multiheaded beasts,
one of the most riveting of the tapestry's panels is *The Great Whore
on the Waters*. Here an angel leads Saint John to see the "Great

Whore," who is the symbol of all the vices and perversions of Babylon, the secular city that will be destroyed at the end of the tapestry. The Great Whore is seated atop a verdant hill. She is a sylphlike goddess, willowy and perfect, clad in a diaphanous robe, festooned with jewels, just like a Madame Claude girl-to-be. She is totally narcissistic, stroking her lush, long blond Godiva tresses with an ivory comb.

The Great Whore is riveted by her own beauty, staring at herself in a large hand mirror. However, the reflection in the mirror is not that of the serene blond goddess, but, rather, a scowling dark witch, the image of a tainted soul. Alfred Hitchcock used a similar reversal in *The Lady Vanishes*. In that classic thriller, the eponymous vanishing lady, kindly and beatific, seems at one point to have been finally discovered; however, when she reveals her face, the "lady" turns out to be the witchlike abductor, as opposed to the expected serene abductee.

The Great Whore panel has a deep blue background, on which is emblazoned multiple crests of the letter *Y,* which has been interpreted by art historians as the forked life choice between vice and virtue—either to surrender to your senses or to retain your self-control. It was a choice that Fernande Grudet would eventually make. In one of his most famous stories, F. Scott Fitzgerald called Paris "Babylon Revisited." If Angers, with all its gloomy virtues, was the New Jerusalem, Paris/Babylon, with all its vices, had to look like a wonderfully sinful, seductive alternative to Fernande Grudet.

In her second memoir, *Le Meilleur, C'est l'Autre,* Madame Claude for the first time talked at length about her youth, which had been glossed over in two pages in *Allô, Oui.* Here she created a very rosy, detailed picture. She portrayed herself as an aristocrat from an old, well-established family. Her father was an engineer/industrialist in the railway business and one of the civic and political leaders of Angers, eventually rising to be its mayor.

"The Angevins," she wrote, taking an elite perspective, "are calm, courteous, balanced. There was a sweetness to life there. I can always recognize people from the region when I travel. In Angers, you have the classic nobility from the eighteenth century and the nouveau riche. They do not mix." She didn't even mention a working class, as if she were not aware of it. She also gave her early view of the battle of the sexes, on which, as Madame Claude, she would be the ultimate peacemaker. "I talked little and observed much when I was young. When I was five I asked my father why don't men marry men and women marry women, because they both seem to prefer the company of the same sex."

Grudet *père* dispatched all his children to same-sex schools. Fernande's two brothers, she said, were sent away to be educated by the Jesuits; she and her sister by the Visitadines, or the Sisters of the Visitation. Claude described her school as a place where girls from good families like hers were sent to learn ladylike etiquette and to be protected from the harsh realities of life. The Visitadines were an order dedicated to instilling in young women like Fernande the virtues of humility and gentleness embodied by the Virgin Mary, then pregnant with Jesus, in her visit to her cousin Elizabeth, simultaneously pregnant with John the Baptist. The schools the Visitation sisters ran were considered less austere than those of other orders, which required perpetual abstinence and prolonged fasts.

In the 1986 memoir, Claude recounted how strict her convent school actually was, particularly in stifling any Sapphic proclivities. "You could not be alone with just one other girl. There had to be three or more in any social gathering. You couldn't sleep with your arms under the covers." The motto of the order was Live Jesus, but it might well have been Never Complain. Claude graduated from the convent and came home to Angers with the goal, that of all proper Angevines, to get married to a fellow grandee. But there was little time for romantic thoughts. War was looming. The Nazis occupied the city in 1940 and executed her father as an example to his fellow aristocrats who dared resist the Hitler juggernaut.

In 2011, France's TV2 released a multihour documentary on Madame Claude. One of its reporters, Meriem Lay, went to the archives in Angers to dig into Claude's past. "Everything is false," she said. There was no Mayor Grudet in Angers history. There were no brothers. There was a sister who died in 1924, when Claude was one. The closest Claude's father got to the railways was operating a snack cart at the Angers train station. He died in 1941, not before a Gestapo firing squad, but in a local hospital, of cancer of the larynx. There is no proof of a convent education, only the Jeanne d'Arc public school. However, Lay did unearth that in 1935, at age twelve, Fernande Grudet had won a prize for top grades in her class in religious studies and was also given a certificate for her "upstanding morals." She completed her education at another public school, Immaculate Conception, where her fellow students were the children not of the Cointreau industrialists, but of factory workers and estate gardeners.

"She was definitely from the wrong side of the tracks. Quite literally," noted Dominique d'Orglandes, now in his late eighties. A former photo editor at *Paris Match* in the Madame Claude sixties and seventies heyday, he retired back to Angers and his family's grand château overlooking an infinity of vineyards. The d'Orglandes clan, which goes back to William the Conqueror, bought the château in 1937, when Claude was attending Immaculate Conception. "My grandfather was in the military," he said. "We also had a city house on avenue Jeanne-d'Arc. I remember my mother warning me never to go beyond that avenue. Avenue Jeanne-d'Arc was the end of the world. Beyond it was an area called faubourg Bressigny. That was no-man's-land. That was where the Grudets lived."

The beige stone mansions of the avenue Jeanne-d'Arc have

largely been converted to banks and law offices, though the visual grandeur still remains. But a block away, the houses become dramatically more modest, if not actual shacks. Providing a personal tour through his city, d'Orglandes proceeded to a dead-end street called impasse Diderot. "This was where the Grudet house was. Now it's a garage," he said. "Monsieur Grudet didn't just have the little business at the station. He had a café down the block on the rue Diderot. He was a businessman, just not as important as she portrayed him. There were also a number of *maisons closes* in these blocks. This was the red-light district. Nothing like the Sphinx or the One-Two-Two. But brothels nonetheless. Every city this size had them. The Germans enjoyed them. They took them over and kept the French out."

Perhaps here was the genesis of Fernande Grudet's ultimate career plans. Back across Jeanne-d'Arc and the equally grand divided avenue Foch, were the fancy hotels, the Hôtel d'Anjou and the Hôtel de France, where the businessmen stayed, the kind of businessmen that Fernande wanted her father to be, the type of businessmen that she one day would cater to. Dominating one city square was the imposing statue of King René, the duc d'Anjou who became the king of Naples. In Naples, the Castel Nuovo, also known as the Angevin Castle, bears a striking resemblance to the Château d'Angers, testimony to the royal ties between Madame Claude's home city and the Italian one. Little could she have guessed as a schoolgirl at Immaculate Conception that her own empire, an empire of sex, would one day span the globe.

But first the war, and more myths. "Madame Claude despised that program," Philippe Thuillier said, referring to the 2011 television series, entitled *Madame Claude: Sex, Lies, and State Secrets*. "She said *it* was all lies, not herself. She felt they wanted to make her look bad. They were out to humiliate her. She had nothing to do with it." One of the biggest of the alleged Claude lies it tried to explode was her assertion that she had been an active member of the French Resistance.

Claude has said that she was eventually captured and then, in an assertion not made until the publication of her final memoir, *Madam,* sent to a concentration camp. In the book, the camp was unnamed, but in publication publicity and interviews, Claude identified the facility as the all-women's camp of Ravensbruck, outside of Berlin. There she allegedly began an affair with a Nazi commandant. Through that connection, she said, she was able to save the lives of a number of fellow female prisoners, including Geneviève de Gaulle, niece of Le Grand Général.

Because the horrors of her incarceration were far at odds with the joys of sex *Madam* was limning, Claude was very nonspecific about the details of her experience. One memory she did outline, though, was how the prisoners were rationed a certain amount of water each day, which could be used for drinking or washing. Claude said she was known at the camp as "the camel" because she never drank any of her water. Her fastidious family and the equally fastidious Visitadines had made her a "clean freak," an obsessive compulsion that would carry through into Fernande Grudet's transformation into Madame Claude. In that pristine operation, the emphasis was on hospital-level hygiene, as Claude groomed her girls into perfumed perfection. For the former "camel," cleanliness far transcended godliness.

Once again, TV2 reporter Meriem Lay dug into the archives at Ravensbruck and could not find any record of Fernande Grudet. More lies, the series declared, for all France to laugh at. Resistance? Ravensbruck? Never happened. However, a number of people who knew Claude had seen the concentration camp identifying tattoo on her arm. One of these was the society writer Taki Theodoracopulos. Another was playboy Porfirio Rubirosa. Another was Patrick Terrail, the proprietor of the Los Angeles überbistro Ma Maison, and nephew of the proprietor of Paris's premier restaurant, La Tour d'Argent, Claude Terrail, himself an habitué of Madame Claude. They all saw the tattoo.

The catch here was that Ravensbruck did not tattoo its inmates. The only concentration camp that did so was Auschwitz. During the war, a convoy of 827 Jews was transported from Angers to Auschwitz to be gassed. Three hundred and ninety of them were women. According to camp records, only nineteen survived. Dominique d'Orglandes suggested that Fernande Grudet may have been among them. D'Orglandes pointed out the Angers synagogue, not far from the impasse Diderot, on the rue Val-de-Maine. It had been converted from the old eglise Saint-Vincent. It served the city's current population of around fifty Jewish families. There were two main squares in Angers named for Jews, place Mendes-France, named after the fifties French prime minister, and place Anne Frank, which had been called place de la Juiverie, "the Jewish Square," until being renamed long after the war. "Angers has always had a Jewish population," d'Orglandes said. "If Madame Claude wanted to be thought of as part of the top society of Angers, it would not be something she would discuss."

Either at a camp or back at home, during the wartime period, Claude got pregnant. She had the child, a daughter, a "little redhead" she named Anne. In *Allô, Oui,* the child was said to have come from an affair with an older fellow Resistance fighter. In the Ravensbruck version, the child was the spawn of her affair with the camp's top Nazi. In the TV2 version, the child was an unattributable accident. Unable to raise Anne herself, Fernande left the child with her mother. This is the same daughter who did not attend her mother's cremation. They were never close. Fernande Grudet eventually turned her back on her family and Angers and went off to Paris, the Babylon of her youthful dreams, to make a life for herself.

In *Allô, Oui,* Claude did not discuss in any depth her supposedly powerful family in Angers. All she did recount of her supposedly charmed girlhood was one trauma of adolescence, in 1936. At thirteen and dealing with her hormones, Claude was approached by her favorite cousin, Bernard, who took her by the hand and led her to a full-length mirror. Claude was tiny, barely five feet tall, skinny, with dark hair and a hooked nose. They took a long look together. Then Bernard said, "My poor girl, just look at yourself. You are ugly and you will always be ugly, and no man will ever want you." "That comment changed my life," she wrote, describing how its terrible shock caused her to get violently sick for two days. The diagnosis of the family doctor was *une fievre de croissance,* or growing pains. "I realized that I could not be like the other girls, so I had no choice but to become the best at something else."

The journey of becoming special was a rocky road, which *Allô, Oui* recounted. Fernande's first romance came in joining the local Resistance, which she described as more of an exhilarating adventure and love story than a desperate struggle for survival. The big lesson, Claude wrote, that she learned from the war and that she would take with her in her later career as Madame Claude was that male camaraderie was far more important to men than their relationship to the opposite sex. A woman's place was on the periphery. That was a fact of life, and she would learn to work with it.

Fernande's young friends were torn between the "liberty or death" heroics of famed Resistance hero Jean Moulin and the awkward teenage collaboration depicted in Louis Malle's 1974 film *Lacombe, Lucien,* which she referred to as accurately evocative. Fernande Grudet, along with her cousins, may have chosen the good fight, though most of what her circle did consisted of the good life, sitting around, smoking Gitanes, talking philosophy, and making love. Even Fernande, notwithstanding her cousin Bernard's bleak prognosis. At seventeen, she lost her virginity to a handsome and worldly Resistance leader of forty, who had come down from Paris to organize the Angevins.

"I was not equipped to resist," she wrote. Because Bernard had insisted she would never lose that virginity, this was a major triumph for her. "The ugly duckling got the man that all my girlfriends coveted," she preened. Fernande decided she must be in love. However, the lover she calls only "J" was, she wrote, captured, deported, and executed. The concentration camp episode does not appear in Claude's first two memoirs, only in the 1994 *Madam,* which recounted that Fernande was also arrested and deported. She found herself in Ravensbruck, seduced, abandoned, and pregnant, although it is unclear if the father is the noble "J" or the evil Nazi.

Whoever, she managed to escape, or be released, and, too ashamed to return to Angers, she went to the Basque country, where she gave birth to Anne in a "ghastly" provincial clinic. Finally, facing reality, she took Anne home to Angers and her now-widowed mother and prepared to continue her Resistance work. Unfortunately, Fernande had no resistance of her own. Her immune system depleted, she came down with tuberculosis and was sent to recover at a sanitarium in Assy, in the French Alps near the Italian border, whose clear, salubrious air did not compensate for the squalor and madness of the hospital, which Claude described as a version of the Charenton lunatic asylum, where the marquis de Sade was held.

Many of the patients, whom she characterized as suspended in a limbo between life and death, were obsessed with having sex, a last fling before the ever-looming end of life. At Assy, Fernande's late teenage loss of innocence expanded into her first lesbian affair. In a literary flourish, she sometimes refers to her lover, Lucile, as "he" and sometimes as "she." Masculine or feminine, Lucile sounds like a beautiful, powerful, and insatiable character—in Claude's words, "a dog in heat." She was from Paris, urbane and sophisticated, and lorded her snobbery over Fernande, making the young Angevine feel like a provincial hick. Lucile seized the role of the dominant partner in the relationship, creating an inferiority that Fernande as Madame Claude would have been the last woman on earth to accept. Eventually, Lucile, in Claude's view, "fucked herself to death."

Fernande survived and was able to transfer to a smaller and vastly calmer rehabilitation clinic in the Pyrenees. Part of her recovery was falling in love with Antoine, a Spanish anarchist who had been living in France for years since the end of the Spanish Civil War, in 1939, to escape the fascist brutality of General Francisco Franco. For once, Fernande had a boyfriend who was more infatuated with her than vice versa; it was a big part of her healing process. "As they say in romance novels," Claude wrote, knowing the cliché but nonetheless embracing it, "he respected me." After a year of being loved, Fernande was able to make the big move to Paris.

Arriving just after liberation in 1945, Fernande Grudet was "more afraid of life than of death," which she had stared in the face, through war and disease. She moved to Saint-Germain-des-Prés, the intellectual university quarter, where Jean-Paul Sartre and Simone de Beauvoir counted as bigger celebrities than Edith Piaf and Marcel Cerdan. She set out to conquer her own existential fears. Moving into a cheap hotel filled with young people who wanted to forget the war through "white nights" of New York jazz and Hollywood movies and endless brainy Paris conversations in smoky *caves,* or nightclubs, Fernande wore the bohemian uniform of a black turtleneck and black slacks, "drank all night and slept all day." However, after a few months Fernande realized that style alone was not enough; she lacked the talent to be a singer like her new pal Juliette Greco or a filmmaker like her new pal Yves Robert. She decided to move across the Seine and up the hill to Montmartre.

The relocation may have seemed as if Fernande was just exchanging one artists' enclave for another. However, Montmartre was home to a constituency that Saint-Germain totally lacked: the Corsican Mafia, which Fernande fell promptly into, head over heels. Seduced by their hard masculinity, their warrior code of honor, and their surprising chivalry and respect for women, Claude rhapsodized about these high-rolling gangsters, soon to be immortalized in New Wave films from Godard and Melville. "They were never stingy," Claude noted. "They had their own elegance. But they were also like kids." They stole what they wanted to buy, the toys they wanted, cars, clothes, watches, rings, girls. They'd celebrate their big scores by going to the best nightclubs on the Champs-Elysées or in Pigalle—the Lido, the Moulin Rouge—and drown their girlfriends in champagne. And then they'd wake up the next morning and start planning their next crime. "Where are these splendid animals today?" Claude lamented.

Claude said that she got to know some of the big gangsters, including Pierre Loutrel, aka "Pierrot le Fou," who was famous as a Robin Hood who stole from the Nazis on behalf of the Resistance, and was killed after the war in a bloody shoot-out at a jewelry store on the avenue Kléber, in one of Paris's fanciest neighborhoods. She also proudly knew Emile Buisson, France's public enemy number one. Responsible for over thirty murders and a hundred robberies, Buisson, who had also spent five years in the Shanghai gang scene, was executed by guillotine in 1956. Claude, who noted how obsessed she was by the delicate geometric tattoo on Buisson's neck, could not contain her admiration for the *efficacité* of these superhoods. Such connections, grisly though they were, would prove immensely valuable to Madame Claude when she started her own business in 1957.

Fernande Grudet became a keen observer and admirer of this very visible underworld. Claude outlined the hierarchy of this Parisian inferno: At the top were the bosses, who stayed home and planned the crimes. Beneath them were the strongarm types, who actually did the dirty work of the holdups and break-ins. The next level down were the drug dealers, who were not the force in the postwar era that they would later become.

And at the bottom were the pimps, called *maquereaux*, in dishonor of those smelliest of fish.

During her stay in Montmartre, Fernande met the one great love of her life, another professional crook, named Hugues. She was entranced by his ability to speak five languages fluently and his consequent skill as an international criminal, committing "jobs" throughout Europe. He was also a master of disguise. Once, meeting some American friends at the Ritz, Claude noticed Hugues was there and she almost didn't spot him. Hugues's only problem was that he was too handsome for Fernande's insecurity. Claude admitted she, like most women, was drawn to good looks but only fully trusted those who were "a little ugly, a little poor, a little shady."

This grand affair was the only time in her fastidious life that Fernande let herself go. Claude recounted her happy memories of crumpled sheets ("I can only stand spotlessly clean sheets, tight, without creases") and limp, wet towels ("I have a closet full of new linen, fluffy and thick"). She was so jealous of Hugues's effect on other woman that she forced him to move with her to a small rural village in Provence, where there was no one to covet him or for her to be jealous of. But it was hard for Hugues to mastermind big jobs from a hamlet with only one phone in the local café. After two years of this self-enforced rustication, unable to fulfill their fantasy of becoming the Bonnie and Clyde of Provence, they ran out of money and returned to Paris.

Back in the big city, jealousy immediately raised its head once again. Obsessed with his infidelities, Fernande left Hugues. Unable to live with him but incapable of being without him, she decided to kill herself. For Fernande, who was obsessively methodical about everything, suicide was no exception. She wrote her will (Hugues had given her a share of his criminal lucre) and paid her debts, leaving what she had to her daughter and mother. Her gangster-girl lifestyle was so far from Angers maternity that motherhood seemed to have vanished from her mind. Her biggest problem was to find a "clean" way to exit the world. She went through the same catalog as Dorothy Parker had in her 1926 poem "Résumé," which concluded:

> *Gas smells awful;*
> *You might as well live.*

Before Fernande Grudet came to that same conclusion, she had also considered blowing herself up on a plane with a bomb, but ruled that out for killing other innocents, as well as buying a car to crash into a tree, a purchase she could not afford. She finally decided that the water of the Seine was the best way to go. She took a big dose of sleeping pills and proceeded to a desolate bridge. However, she was saved by a homeless drunk, a *clochard,* who kept importuning her for money. His obsessive panhandling made her laugh, and turned her suicide attempt into a joke. Instead, she took him to a brasserie and had a celebratory "life breakfast" of croissants washed down with *vin rouge.* You might as well live.

Now it was time to get serious. The suicide attempt behind her, Fernande realized she had a duty, if only financial, to her forsaken daughter. Without Hugues's tainted earnings, she had nothing to send home to her mother in Angers. She tried a few commission sales jobs, from renting apartments to selling Bibles door-to-door. But Paris was still in its postwar funk, and there was little market for fancy rentals, and even less for salvation. Her last option was to become a hooker, which she refers to very gingerly in her sanitized memoirs.

The biggest growth business of postwar Paris was street prostitution. Through her many Corsican evenings, Fernande had kept company with many, many prostitutes. Who else was going to consort with gangsters? Debutantes? She was almost as fascinated by them as she was with the gangsters, though Madame Claude always insisted she preferred the company of men to women, just as the men themselves did. In any event, Fernande, aided by her contacts, took to the streets, specifically the Grands Boulevards between the Opéra and the Madeleine. This was the prime tourist area, close to the American Express offices, where Yankee travelers, enticed to Europe by the postwar giveaway prices, came for their mail. The Americans loved to shop at the fancy department stores, Galeries Lafayette and Aux Printemps, where they spent their traveler's checks. They adored the Café de la Paix and the Ritz, where they went to eat, drink, and sleep in the footsteps of Ernest Hemingway. And even though it wasn't mentioned in the tourist guides, they also came for the prostitutes.

After the war, the GIs had come home with tall tales of their adventures with the streetwalkers of Pigalle, which they called "Pig Alley," and the rue Saint-Denis, where literally thousands of women beckoned down a mile-long thoroughfare of lust that terminated at a triumphal arch modeled after Rome's Arch of Titus and built by Louis XIV. These red-light districts were, like the Corsican gangsters, the stuff of legend, and of films. They constituted the "Par-ee" that, after seeing which, these GI types could not be kept down on the farm. But Fernande Grudet, through her Corsican mentors, understood the city's economic geography of lust well. She was smart enough to go where the money was, which was the area around the Opéra.

This was the deluxe sex district, where all the most famous legal brothels had been clustered, where people like Joe Kennedy and his sons had come to play. Now, after 1946, these houses of mirth were shuttered by the Richard law; all their fabled courtesans were working the same streets as Fernande herself. These women entertained their customers in the hundreds of *hôtels de rendezvous* clustered behind Paris's most famous gourmet emporium, Fauchon, across from the Madeleine. The hotel Fernande used was on the rue Godot-de-Mauroy, where customers in droves trolled the pavements night and day, eyeing the hotel entrances, seeing what beauties might emerge, "waiting for Godot" in their own lubricious way.

Fernande Grudet quickly saw that, despite all the gawkers, there was still more supply than demand. Notwithstanding her efforts to look chic, which was the lure in this part of town (sluttily *cheap* played better in the other locales), she would literally spend most of her time pounding the pavements, "waiting for the dough." She observed that the girls who got the most business were the tall ones. Size mattered here. And tall, Fernande was not. France had very few tall girls at the time, and with the food shortages and other deprivations, France wasn't growing them any bigger in the early 1950s, when Fernande took this plunge. She despised the work, describing it as "standing in front of a hotel, trying to look stylish, holding three poodles on a leash (the guise of walking the dogs), waiting for men to show up." The waiting was the hardest part, harder than the sex.

Eventually, Fernande got tired of waiting. She retreated back to Montmartre and began seeing the regular clients she had met on the gilded pavements of the eighth arrondissement in her tiny two-room apartment on the rue Damrémont in the hilly, bohemian eighteenth. Here in the mid-1950s, she might have been considered an early call girl, except she didn't have a telephone. Instead, she would troll the bars of the mid-range businessmen's hotels, often around the railway stations of the Gare du Nord and the Gare de l'Est. Even though Claude had a nice slim figure and had learned to dress alluringly on her budget, she had a severe inferiority complex because of her size. She didn't feel like she *belonged* at the Ritz or the Crillion, so she stayed away. It was that sense of belonging that she would instill in her pupils as Madame Claude. Back at the railway station hotels, a lot of local Parisians would be meeting their out-of-town clients. These men couldn't take Fernande to their homes, so she took them to hers. The personal touch was appreciated.

A victim of social Darwinsism, Fernande Grudet did not like her fate. But she was eager to do what she had to do to change it. As Madame Claude, she would employ only very tall girls, even if she had to go to Scandinavia and Germany to get them. However, while on the rue Godot-de-Mauroy, she was light-years from being Madame Claude, though the notion was simmering in her head. In *Allô, Oui,* she confessed that "I never had a great liking for women," decrying their "stupid" self-victimization. In her view, and it was a close-up one, her sisters of the streets were masochistically looking for a veritable catalog of ways of being exploited, and on places like Godot-de-Mauroy, every opportunity to be used and abused would present itself.

Claude looked back bitterly at her teenage encounter with the mirror. Despite her sexual adventures in the war, in Montmartre, and now on the sidewalks of this sex bazaar, she could find no real reassurance in the men she had seduced. Deciding she could never be attractive in conventional ways, she began to explore alternatives to traditional love and marriage. What Fernande, then close to thirty years old, which was middle-aged in those times, was conjuring up was, in effect, the Madame Claude Erotic Manifesto: "I wanted to send women out like guided missiles, women who would accomplish for me this destructive and seductive undertaking that my cousin Bernard had deprived me of that summer evening."

Just as Fernande Grudet realized in Saint-Germain-des-Prés that she did not have the talent to become an artist or an actress, her epiphany on the mean streets of the Madeleine was that she also lacked whatever it took to be a soldier in what she viewed as the war between women and men. The key part of that epiphany was that instead of becoming a soldier in the trenches of that war, she decided that what she truly wanted to become was a *général,* and one day, perhaps, commander in chief. And despite what sounded like a call to battle, Madame Claude would forge her reputation not as a bellicose feminist but as the ultimate peacemaker, albeit on terms that she believed were a total male capitulation to the "weaker" sex.

If anyone was going to exploit women, Fernande Grudet vowed to herself, it would be she. She didn't want to hurt them on behalf of men; she wanted to protect them in ways they could not protect themselves, while using them to achieve her own greater ends. Her notion of the word *exploit* was about maximizing potential, theirs as well as hers. She then explored three business possibilities. The first was a marriage bureau, or a matchmaking service, of which there were many in Paris. However, she saw that these agencies, totally legitimate and legal, were always advertising in the newspapers and magazines. They also had nice offices on streets like the Champs-Elysées, to better instill confidence in the hopeful spouses-to-be. Those ads and that rent required capital that Fernande did not have.

So she moved on to the second option, opening a modeling agency. That new field was still wide open. There were no model agencies whatsoever on the European continent after World War II, although some small agencies did exist in London. In Paris, modeling agencies were illegal, because it was considered un-French for someone to take a percentage of another's earnings. The link to *proxénétisme* was more than obvious, and the line between modeling and prostitution was a blurred one. The legitimate models at the couture houses like Christian Dior (founded in 1947), which provided the first signs of rebirth in the dark postwar economy, had to arrange their own bookings. How "legitimate" they were was a point of contention. Dior himself admitted that he had haunted the great bordellos to find his first models, who were all prostitutes to begin with.

This all changed with the arrival, in the fifties, of the Texan photo model Dorian Leigh. Leigh and her sister Suzy Parker were favorites of the leading lensmen of the era, Avedon and Penn, and would create the concept of "supermodel." Leigh saw a niche here and seized it. She delved into French law and figured out that if she took her commission from the employers, be it *Vogue* or Dior, rather than from the model herself, no "pimping" could be presumed and no law violated. There was almost a Robin Hood effect, taking from the rich corporations and giving to the (then) poor models, and the French were all for that sort of *egalité.*

Armed with comforting legal opinions as well as a French work permit, Dorian Leigh opened her first office near the Elysée Palace in 1957, around the time Fernande Grudet was contemplating a similar move. At first, Leigh was harassed by the police, who accused her of operating a clandestine prostitution ring and tried to close her down. Luckily, she found a deep-pocketed partner in the very legitimate New York model agent Eileen Ford, who was looking for a foothold in Europe. Leigh became Ford's Paris liaison, and the authorities were appeased. Fernande Grudet had no Eileen Ford to team up with. She was a poor streetwalker who hung out with Corsican mobsters, not a *Vogue* cover girl who hung out with the Rothschilds, Aly Khan, and Jean Cocteau. In short, she was intimidated by the competition. She had a good idea, but, again, she lacked the capital and connections to make it work. Ironically, many of the models of Dorian Leigh and Eileen Ford would be working for her as Madame Claude in just a few years.

Thus Fernande Grudet arrived at her third and final option, to open a third kind of agency—for prostitution. But before she took her plunge into this business, she engaged in several months of market research, just to see exactly what her options were. As curious observers were not welcome in sex operations, Fernande's "research" actually consisted of working for a while in a number of establishments where sex was being sold for money. Her first job, and surely the most dramatic where she was concerned, was in a "house of pain," where she worked as an apprentice to an experienced dominatrix, whose "passion for pain" impressed Fernande, as did the bizarre tools, whips, shackles, clamps, and torture implements that could have been in a museum of the Middle Ages.

Claude described the place as an "arsenal of damnation," noting that among the clients were judges of the highest rank, whose job was to sentence criminals in a more contemporary idiom. Others were big businessmen of the most tyrannical order, here to get a dose of their own bitter medicine. The proprietress, herself a beautiful and elegant avenue Foch type, spoke of her dungeon as a safety valve for great leaders. Never judgmental, Claude defended the place by asking, "Who among us had not had strange desires?" She admired the owner, who spoke of her clients in the most sympathetic terms, describing them as wonderful children who just happened to have this one odd idiosyncrasy. Too odd and specialized for Fernande Grudet, she moved on to sample other secret spin-offs of the bordellos that Marthe Richard had closed, to the collective distress of the rich male population of not only France but all of Europe, which looked to Paris as the pinnacle of sophisticated self-indulgence.

Fernande's next stop seemed more like a perpetual tea party than a brothel. Here, in a beautiful mansion in the sixteenth arrondissement, a woman who called herself a countess held a very formal tea, from *cinq à sept,* which was the French time for extramarital dalliances. Mozart played in the background, liveried waiters served canapés, and ostensibly happily married men and women met here for the sole purpose of pairing off and cheating on their spouses. The countess was the only one who made money here. She was paid a hostess fee by both the men and the women. There was no financial angle for Fernande here, other than a finder's fee for bringing in itchy high-society clients. But high society was not Fernande's beat. Not yet. She was still a Montmartre girl, a gangster moll. So she kept researching.

Then there was the French version of the little red schoolhouse. Here was a brothel for pedophiles, or men with "father complexes," as Claude referred to it, doing her best to be completely tolerant. It wasn't only about spanking Lolitas after spoiling them with chocolates and bonbons and talking baby talk to them. The was also a classroom where the client himself could go back to school and be forced to wear a dunce cap and be punished by a stern teacher for 1,001 variations of not doing his homework. Although Claude described the place as "*puerile et charmante*," she knew she was too old to play Lolita and thought, erroneously as it turned out, that she was not tough enough to play the schoolmarm.

The place that made the best impression on Fernande Grudet was an old-fashioned brothel, which Claude characterized as being typical of Latin American countries. It was a place where men would come after dinner, run into their friends, smoke cigars, and end their evenings with a trip upstairs with a concubine of their choosing. What these men needed, she observed, more than sex was the company of other men, but it took the girls to give them the excuse to get together. For the women, aside from the money, Claude noted that they got to spend their nights in a house "infinitely gayer than their own." Looking back, Claude noted that this ambience probably inspired the kind of operation she was to run more than she might ever have guessed when she encountered it as a working girl.

Finally, Fernande visited a *maison de partouze*, a suburban mansion where suburban couples came and paid a fee to indulge in orgies and swap spouses with people they had never met before. Invitations to these early "swinger" events were quite expensive, and enabled the host couple to live in their grand style. Theirs was the house that sex built. The key here to Claude was jealousy as an aphrodisiac. Watching your wife having hot sex with a total stranger was said to have revived many a stagnant, taken-for-granted marriage. But Fernande, who had never had any marriage, simply couldn't relate. Again she moved on.

In the end, it took two men to turn Fernande Grudet into Madame Claude, and they weren't pimps. They were Alexander Graham Bell and Thomas Edison, and she gave them total credit. Unlike in most of the modern world, the telephone in France had had a hard time catching on. In the thirties, before World War II, only 3 percent of all French households had telephones, compared to 7 percent in England and 15 percent in the United States. As late as 1968, only 15 percent of French homes had phones, though this was the year that the bells finally began ringing. By 1980, 80 percent of French homes had phones. In short, the French, slow to embrace all sorts of contemporary technology, were used to getting their sex through very old-fashioned face-to-face.

Madame Claude's innovation, and it was surely new in this land of the old, was to provide this sexual word of mouth over a previously untrusted technical device. In the 1950s, phone calls in France were like using one of the early computers, complex and unreliable. Most people would line up in post offices and wait for a long time to get a *cabine,* where an operator would connect them to a desired number. Some bars had public phones where, as JFK learned, to his chagrin, one had to engage in the very cumbersome process of purchasing a *jeton,* or token, from the bartender, then descend to an area of fetid urinals and wait one's turn while others used the phone. The *jeton* lasted only a minute or two, after which the caller was cut off and had to drop a new *jeton* and start again, much to the annoyance of the long line behind him.

Most phones in France were used in places of business. President de Gaulle once famously joked that *he* didn't have a home phone. Even for the rich, who would be Claude's target market, these were primitive instruments, often requiring a switchboard and the disturbing possibility of eavesdropping. Romance and privacy were essential bedfellows, and phones seemed anything but private. But Claude could see that the communications technology around the world, even across the Channel in England, was improving every day. She saw the ads for modern rotary phones, even some in living colors, as opposed to the funereal black, which showed how the original phones were for communicating bad news, or serious news, and were intended for anything but fun. But the world was changing, and so were the phones, even in antediluvian France.

Until Claude, sex was something men in France had to see to believe. And seeing it couldn't have been easier. All you had to do was take a walk. But Claude introduced a new approach that somehow inspired confidence in a previously distrusted American tool. She became synonymous with the very modern concept of the call girl. Linking the oldest profession to one of the newest ones was Fernande Grudet's eureka moment.

Madame Claude would make another brilliant French connection by combining her call-girl service with the other two avenues she had been exploring, the marriage bureau and the model agency. The idea that a man could *hire* a lovely, innocent, marriageable girl, a wannabe bride-to-be, or a stunning mannequin whose image he had seen in *Vogue* or *Elle* or *Paris Match,* or on the stage of Le Crazy Horse, took sexual fantasy to an altogether new and different level. Whether on the perfumed streets of the rue Saint-Denis or the satin sheets of Le One-Two-Two, the customer was entitled to whatever fantasy he wanted to conjure up, but he always knew that he was dealing with a prostitute. Madame Claude's second genius innovation was to take the prostitutes out of prostitution and replace them with either cover girls or girls next door.

At the beginning, in 1957, Fernande Grudet had nothing more than a tiny apartment in Montmartre, her own first phone, and a few other prostitutes she knew from her time in the life. She was a long way from Dorian Leigh, and the girls were a long way from *Vogue* covers. In *Allô, Oui,* Claude describes how minimal her expectations were when she opened her little *bureau.*

All she wanted was to survive and make enough money to send home to Angers for her mother and her now teenage daughter. It is not clear how often, if ever, she went home to visit.

Fernande Grudet was unable to afford advertising. She relied on word of mouth, both hers and those of the three or four fellow streetwalkers (but tall ones, always tall) she had recruited with the promise of taking them off the streets and into something much more comfortable. Each of them told their friends and clients, the barkeeps where they drank, the desk clerks at the *hôtels de rendezvous* where they worked, and, if they knew any, the concierges at the better hotels where, if they had been lucky, their higher-rolling street clients had taken them to spend an expensive night rather than a cheap half hour.

Claude estimated that she and her street companions saw, on average, thirty customers a day. She compared the frequency to the number of consultations performed by a popular doctor. She wanted to believe that the services provided were similarly medicinal and healing and referred to her team as "nurses of the soul," noting that most of their time was spent talking and listening rather than making love. If Claude, true or false, liked to portray herself as an upper-crust aristo-femme from the Loire Valley, it became a case of "You can take the girl out of Angers, but you can't take Angers out of the girl." She and her charges were nothing if not "ladies." They were offering charm, beauty, cultivation.

Sex was never referred to directly, only in the vaguest passing. Sex, Claude insisted, was not what she was selling. She called it "therapy." However, she refused to be snobbish toward the girls on the rue Saint-Denis, attacking the contempt that the press, politicians, and, above all, threatened housewives displayed toward these painted working girls as a form of "racism," long before that word became a rallying cry. Claude was a big fan of President Charles de Gaulle. She wrote with pride how he had put a snooty relative in her place after she complained to him about the streetwalkers infesting the sidewalks in front of Fauchon, that sacred gourmet mecca, like cockroaches. "My dear," de Gaulle thundered, "leave these beautiful people alone." Paraphrasing Groucho Marx, de Gaulle stood up for their honor, which may have been more than they ever did.

Fernande Grudet sat—and sat—in a dingy room at a cheap metal desk, waiting for the phone to ring. She worried about everything, particularly whether her team of women would even show up. But arrive they did, and wait they did. They studied foreign languages—English, Spanish, German, Italian—in hope of better days, and foreign affairs, to come. Each ring, Claude wrote, sounded to all of them like "celestial music." When one girl was dispatched, usually to some hotel, it was as if she were being sent on a sacred mission, "carrying with her the entire destiny of our little group."

And when the girl returned, whether in an hour or the morning after, Claude and company would embrace her like a French fighter pilot coming home from a sortie where he had shot down the Red Baron. Mission accomplished! They would toast her with cheap champagne, and the gray office would erupt into a party. Claude, who would later develop the reputation of a drill sergeant, not known for levity, described these early days as filled with "fits of giggles." And a remarkable female bonding. "We often had a hard time going our separate ways in the evening."

It took some time, several years, in fact, but the phone did begin ringing, and not just from traveling salesmen in hotels. The first callers were the people Claude referred to as the *locomotives,* the young engines of trend, the kind of men who discovered the newest restaurants, the coolest bars, the hottest nightclubs. Claude suddenly found herself on the Paris "hot list." And what was hot for Paris was hot for the world. The advances in aviation became almost as important to Claude's success as the innovations in telecommunications. In 1959, Pan Am began flying the first Boeing 707s nonstop from New York to Paris. Those

707s, and their rival Douglas DC-8s, cut the transatlantic travel time from thirteen hours to barely over six, thereby creating a "jet set" who could fly to Paris for the weekend, sleep at the Ritz, stroll through the Louvre, eat at Maxim's, dance at Régine's, fuck a Claude girl, and be back on the job on Madison Avenue by Monday morning.

Madame Claude became an international "must do." That celestial phone of hers would begin ringing from all over the globe, but, now most important, from the Elysée Palace, which knew that sex was the soft underbelly of French politics, and the quai d'Orsay, home of the Ministry of Foreign Affairs, which wanted to know exactly what all the masters of their respective universes who patronized Madame Claude were up to. The convent girl from Angers was not only becoming rich; she was also becoming an international power broker. She was right. What she was selling was more than sex. Lots more.

Chapter 3

YOUNG GUNS

She looked like the crossing guard at the epicenter of trend. The woman, a petite blonde on the sunny side of fifty, was dressed in black Chanel, very proper, very official. She would have looked right at home at a lunch at Lasserre, with its opening roof and eternal springtime of flowers, or at any number of soirees in the rue de Grenelle or the avenue Foch, or even the Elysée Palace. She could have been the wife of a cabinet minister, or even a minister herself, but the time was the mid-seventies and female ministers were rare. Yet here at this Andy Warhol party, in the midst of Yves Saint Laurent and his two muses, Loulou de La Falaise and Betty Catroux, and his lover/business partner, Pierre Bergé, and young models like Jerry Hall and old models like Bettina, the last lover of Aly Khan, and quasi-artists like Thadée Klossowski, the son of the real artist Balthus, among numerous other species of flashy Warholiana, she didn't really fit.

Maybe she was the real estate agent, speculated the young American who was studying interior design at the Ecole du Louvre and was dazzled by the altogether different and dizzying celebrity perspective of Paris from the Warhol periphery. He had been brought to the fête by Baron Léon Lambert, the Belgian banking tycoon and Rothschild grandson, one of the rare financiers in the Warhol entourage. The American, who had studied comp lit at Yale, was fascinated to see these trendsetters and stars of Paris fashion.

The American, call him "Lee," was even more fascinated that the venue for that evening's fête, Warhol's new Paris apartment on the rue du Cherche-Midi, which probably has more fancy women's shoe stores than any other street in the world, had been the old apartment of the author Violet Trefusis, the lesbian lover of Vita Sackville-West, of Bloomsbury fame. Notoriety ran in Violet's family. Her own mother, Alice Keppel, was the "official" mistress of King Edward VII, aka "Dirty Bertie," the most lascivious of all English monarchs. Edward VII kept a *garçonnière* apartment in Paris on the avenue de l'Opéra, which was the main drag of deluxe commercial sex, *maisons closes,* et cetera; its reputation was such that one British writer described the street as "the clitoris of Paris." With Violet's antecedent the mistress of one English king, her descendant, great-niece Camilla Parker-Bowles, eventually became the mistress of Charles, Prince of Wales.

With all the power-mistress talk circulating around the trendy Warhol fête, it was only fitting that the proper little lady outlier was eventually identified for the visiting American, who had speculated that she was perhaps the agent for the prestige property, as an agent of a very different sort—none other than Madame Claude herself. Lee had never heard of Madame Claude. Thinking she had to be some sort of celebrity, as everyone else here was, he first had guessed that she might have been the author Françoise Sagan, who was also tiny and blond and famous enough to be here. Sagan was far more bohemian, though it turned out that she was Claude's closest women friend. In any event, Lee was adrift in this sea of fame, and Madame Claude was the only one who paid any attention to him whatsoever when he sat down beside her to observe the swirling Warhol circus.

"She broke the ice by telling me that I looked like a Swiss schoolboy," Lee recalled. "Which I had been, so that got me right away. We spoke in French, and we spoke about everything, Sartre, Camus, the Vatican, Degas, Proust. I still had no idea who she was, but she seemed way too culturally knowledgeable to be a real estate broker. And she wasn't trying to sell me anything, not that I looked like I could afford an apartment in the sixth. I had just come back from trekking in the Himalayas. I was as lost as if I had wandered off into a glacier. What she did do was bear down on me and ask me what I wanted to do with my life. She saw me with the baron, and she could tell I was drifting, a kept man. Maybe I was feeling guilty. She didn't say anything, but I could just tell she *knew,* she knew everything."

Lee went on, still mesmerized by the encounter with the anonymous woman. "She sensed I didn't belong in this glamorous fashion crowd. I wasn't an Yves Saint Laurent type, maybe Brooks Brothers, with a Hermès scarf. Again, it was a party, but it was more like life counseling than party chatter. We talked about the décor, the furniture, the wallpaper, the art. She had the most amazing eye, but she told me that mine was good, and that I should really take seriously becoming a decorator. She meant it. She made me feel so special, that I had a place in the world, my own place. And she kept telling me the key thing in life was to seize the opportunity when it came my way, because those golden opportunities were very few and far between."

Lee never found out she was Madame Claude until Baron Lambert told him whom he had been talking to after they left the party. "The most powerful woman in Paris," the baron told him, then described what she did. Lee was blown away by the revelation. The woman hadn't talked at all about sex. But, as he reflected back on the conversation, she had talked about feminine power, although it didn't seem like that at the moment.

She had been holding forth on King Edward. She never called him "Dirty Bertie"; she was rather formal. She had great respect for Alice Keppel, who, in retrospect, was like a Madame Claude girl of her time. Tall, fair, and regal, Alice, Claude had recounted, was the daughter of a British admiral, grew up in a Scottish castle, and married the son of an earl. But that son had no money, so he became his wife's "manager," identifying unhappily married rich, titled men and arranging for Alice to meet, charm, and ultimately be kept by them, most lavishly by the king of England, whose wife, Queen Alexandra, Alice ultimately befriended. The key point was that Alice and her husband, George, who carried on his own affairs, had, in those Victorian times, not only a beyond-modern open marriage but a blissful one that lasted fifty-six years; they died two months apart in the lavish Italian villa outside Florence that her "wages of sin" had paid for.

Madame Claude had also talked about antiques from the king's favorite *maison close,* Le Chabanais, behind the Palais Royal, where Bertie had his own private bedroom, decorated with the Windsor coat of arms. Le Chabanais, like Le One-Two-Two (its name appealed to its heavily English clientele), had a panoply of theme rooms. The brothel was the informal, nocturnal arm (if that is the apt appendage) of the Jockey Club, one of the most exclusive of all Paris male social organizations, whose members had financed it as their after-polo retreat.

The auction of the décor of Le Chabanais following its being shuttered under the Richard Law in 1946 was a major event for Paris connoisseurs, Madame Claude had recalled, without any obvious reference to her own profession. The sale had been conducted by Maurice Rheims, a Rothschild in-law and France's greatest art expert and auctioneer, as well as a connoisseur of women and a client of Madame Claude's.

One of Rheims's pièces de résistance was King Edward's famous huge copper tub, expanded to fit a girth (and that of his *cocotte* of choice) achieved by his gargantuan consumption of five multicourse meals a day. The tub, decorated with a half swan, half woman, was sold for a fortune to Salvador Dalí. Rheims also got top dollar for the king's "ménage à trois" silk brocade love chair. Again Madame Claude was talking décor and investment, not prurience. She never mentioned the founder of Le Chabanais, a former Irish barmaid known as Madame Kelly, who was something of the Madame Claude of the Belle Epoque. This same Madame Kelly was the inspiration for *Queen Kelly,* the ill-fated Joe Kennedy–produced film vehicle for his mistress Gloria Swanson.

In fact, the woman later revealed as Madame Claude never talked about herself in any way. "It was all about me," recalls the American, who gives Claude credit for inspiring him on to his career as one of the world's top decorators. "She made me feel like I had a destiny. *'Engagez la vie!'* was what she urged me. While we were talking, which was at least an hour, a lot of people came by, wanting to talk to her. But she made it clear that she was otherwise engaged—with me, of all people. I later got to know Pamela Harriman, and Madame Claude had that same quality of making a man feel unique. Of course, Pamela had a special way of clapping her hands behind her back to signal her assistant to rescue her and say she had a call. Madame Claude was equally focused, equally charming, but more sincere. I never saw her again. But she stayed with me, this woman who had known every key man on earth, paying such attention to me. She was absolutely delightful. When she died, I went to St. Patrick's and lit a candle for her."

Notwithstanding the decorator's profound appreciation of Madame Claude, he was adamant that his glowing opinion not be for attribution. "Most of my clients are women. Madame Claude was their wildest nightmare," he said, alluding to the fear that one night with a Claudette could be the death knell of a marriage. "Talk about threatening. These women despise the very notion of her." Accordingly, very few American husbands would ever own up on the record to having used Madame Claude's services. And most American men, even if conjugally untethered, saw the patronage of Claude as not something to boast about.

On the other hand, most European, Asian, and African men considered the possession of Madame Claude's unlisted number as one of the world's ultimate status symbols and a session with one of her "creations," as she called them, on the same level of conspicuous consumption as a meal at a three-star Michelin temple, front-row courtside seats at the NBA finals, or an invitation to Bohemian Grove or Davos. Claude, to most foreigners, was something to brag about, a genuine, unforgettable "experience."

Then again, outside of America, prostitution is either legal, tolerated, or viewed with far less scorn than it is in the United States, where any direct exchange of sex for money is reduced to the lowest common denominator. Madame Claude herself had as much contempt for the *p* word as any of the Park Avenue trophy wives who were threatened by her, often because they had sometimes worked for her themselves. What Madame Claude was selling was not sex per se, but fantasy, and sometimes, in her most fruitful matchmaking efforts, a lease on fantasy that would last a lifetime.

Typical of these foreign full-disclosure types is Arthur Sarkissian, one of Hollywood's most sophisticated and successful producers, who created the blockbuster *Rush Hour* comedy franchise. "It was 1967. I was an eighteen-year-old virgin in an English boarding school in Somerset that had one hundred and ten boys and seven girls. I knew nothing about sex. Madame Claude came to my rescue." Sarkissian was going home to Beirut to visit his family, which had relocated there from Tehran, where his father was a major industrialist. His London-based uncle Eddie, "the richest one in our family," had told him to stop in Paris on his way home and have Madame Claude "take care" of his virginity.

"I flew to Paris and checked in to the Château Frontenac, on the avenue François Premier and called Madame Claude," Sarkissian said. "I spoke good French and dropped the name of my uncle, who had already called. I got the warmest welcome. She asked me if I preferred blondes or brunettes, as if nothing else mattered. I said brunettes, for some reason. Then she asked me how old I was. I told her eighteen. She began laughing. 'You're my youngest client,' she said. She asked me if I had the fee, one thousand francs, which was two hundred dollars then. I told her I did. 'Be ready at seven,' she told me. 'And be good.'

"I was too nervous to take a nap. I took two showers. At precisely seven, there was a knock on the door. I opened it and was blown away. She was a cross between Isabelle Adjani and Jacqueline Bisset. Her name was Alexandra. We spoke French. She was wearing a full-length mink coat, even though it was June. She had green eyes and black hair and was around twenty-seven or twenty-eight, a grown-up compared to me. We went to dinner at Fouquet's, on the Champs-Elysées, which was where all the movie people went, like Spago or Elaine's. We saw Alain Delon. He and Alexandra smiled at each other. I didn't ask.

"I had no idea what I was doing there. I felt like Dustin Hoffman with Mrs. Robinson in *The Graduate*. I have no recollection of what we talked about, but Alexandra was charming and took a real interest in me and my English school and what I wanted to do with my life, about which I had no clue at the time. After Fouquet's, we strolled the Champs and went to a café for coffee, which made me even more nervous. She could see that, and took charge, leading me back to the hotel.

"When we got back to the room, I awkwardly asked her when she wanted the one thousand francs. She just laughed and took her clothes off, saying she had never been with a young virgin guy before and how exciting this was for her. She left at five in the morning. A few hours later, she called and thanked me for a wonderful time and wanted to say good-bye. That did it. I decided to delay my trip. I stayed four more days, and saw her every night. I blew all the money I had, which was supposed to be for gifts for my family, which was a big tradition. I had to call Uncle Eddie. He bailed me out.

"The first time I ever met Madame Claude in person was in 1972. When I called her after those five years, she immediately remembered me. 'My little client,' she greeted me. In that time, I had changed completely. I grew up. I'm not sure how much my time with Alexandra had to do with it, but it certainly gave me a confidence I never had before. I had finished university in London and was starting my own men's boutique on Jermyn Street. I was a swinging bachelor, with plenty of money of my own. I was really ready for Madame Claude, in a different way.

"London was still 'swinging,' though not as much as in the sixties, when the Beatles and the Rolling Stones ruled the world. Now the Arabs, with their oil, were ruling, if not the world, certainly London and Paris, which was where they loved to go. They had driven prices crazy, including those of Madame Claude, which had jumped from one thousand francs a night to two thousand francs [four hundred dollars] an hour. London, all of Europe, used to be a deal. No more. My background and ability to speak both Farsi and Arabic left me in a great position to cater to this booming market.

"Aside from the Arabs, all the royal families of the Gulf, like the Al Maktoums, I had a lot of celebrity clients, Richard Burton, Rod Stewart, Telly Savalas, Lawrence Graff, the diamond king, who all wanted to dress hipper than Savile Row. I sold Italian-made custom suits for one thousand dollars, which would be like eight thousand to ten thousand dollars today. I was to London what Bijan became to Beverly Hills. He stole the idea from me. The store was called Vincci. I got the idea from the world's most beautiful lighter, the Vinci, by Flaminaire. I added an extra *c* so they wouldn't sue. Everybody smoked then, Davidoff cigars. Everybody went to Tramp and Annabel's.

Everybody used call girls. It was before AIDS. Life was so easy, nothing to worry about.

"Whatever, I was making so much money that I lived in a fabulous house in Rutland Gate, and I had three cars, a Ferrari Daytona, a Lamborghini Miura, and a Mini Cooper I bought from Elton John. My friends were rich, and we started going to Paris on weekends, each driving our Ferraris, putting them on the Hovercraft so we could tool around Paris and date Madame Claude girls, taking them to the best restaurants, like Pré Catelan, and stay in suites at the Plaza Athénée, drinking Dom Pérignon. This was all part of the Madame Claude lifestyle. Her 'little client' became one of her big clients, though obviously not like the Shah, who would fly planeloads of her girls to the palace in Tehran.

"I was such a good client that Madame Claude actually had dinner with me at Fouquet's. It was like an honor. We talked in French. She was so elegant. She knew everything about wine, food, art, clothes. I could see where the girls got it from. I fell hard for one of her girls, Stéphanie, who I got hooked on. She looked exactly like Candice Bergen, but was French. As classy as anybody could be. One of the only other times I saw Madame Claude in person was one day on the rue Saint-Honoré. She was coming out of one of the big houses, Lanvin or Cardin, someplace like that, with the most beautiful girl that she was 'creating.' 'You don't like to change girls,' she teased me. I felt a little guilty, because Stéphanie had given me her private number. I wasn't sure whether she was giving Madame Claude a continuing cut.

"Eventually I was back on the phone to Claude, because Stéphanie disappeared, totally disappeared. That was the problem with falling for her girls. You were always paranoid about who else they were seeing. You could never believe them, the way you could with a regular girl. But no regular girl was like these. Years later, when I was getting into films, I was having dinner at Pré Catelan with Carole Bouquet and I ran into Stéphanie. She was wearing a twelve-karat diamond ring. She was married. Obviously big. Most of Claude's girls did. That was their goal, and Claude's, too. It was like they 'graduated.' I gave her my number. She never called. I moved to L.A. in 1976. I think Claude came the next year. When I saw her at Ma Maison, I was so surprised. I guess if she could be somewhere not Paris, it had to be there."

One of Madame Claude's key constituencies was show business, whether from Hollywood or the rue de Ponthieu. Hollywood was built on beautiful women, on-screen and off, so it was only natural that stars and moguls would want to experience the best femininity that money could buy. While Arthur Sarkissian was an outsider to this glittering world, wanting to get in, David Niven, Jr., was a consummate Hollywood insider who knew Madame Claude and was not afraid to say so. In many ways her "romance bureau" was a variant of "the love that dares not speak its name," the quote from the Lord Alfred Douglas poem that was cited in Oscar Wilde's trial for gross indecency.

"I had a horse and named it after her," said Niven, the son of the actor and the successful producer of the *That's Entertainment* anthology series. "Jimmy Goldsmith and Gordon White dared me to do it, so I did. I named another horse Far Golf, which sounded like 'fuck off' when the race announcer called it out." Goldsmith and White were two English lords and con-glomerateurs/corporate raiders who were part of yet another of Madame Claude's key and often intersecting constituencies. What they all had in common were huge amounts of money and an obsession with beauty as part of their vision of la dolce vita. "I would have lunch with Claude at Fouquet's with Jimmy and Gordon. They just loved her. She was a great aid in helping them close their big takeover deals with these wide-eyed innocent gents from the provinces who had never gotten laid outside their marriages."

In Los Angeles, when Claude was in her long exile from Paris, Niven used to lunch with her—and occasionally Orson Welles—at Ma Maison, Hollywood's ultrasnobbish French canteen of the seventies and early eighties. One day at the restaurant, he introduced her to his friends Joan Collins and Evie Bricusse, the ex–horror film actress wife of *Goldfinger* songwriter Leslie Bricusse. Sharing an interest in French antiques, Claude invited the two beauties to see her collection at her Beverly Hills home.

They went along, and, according to Collins's memoir *Second Act,* after a cursory tour of her Louis XIV desks, highboys, and assorted bibelots, Claude, noticing the Bulgari and Bucellatti jewelry the women were flaunting (de rigueur at Ma Maison), suggested that they might want to earn some extra pin money. How? they queried. By seeing some of Claude's L.A. clients who didn't insist on her typical amorous offerings of goddesses in their "first flush of youth," as Collins described it. These men, Claude said, enjoyed sampling someone "more seasoned." Titillated by the suggestion, the women nonetheless never took it seriously and went off into the sun, "giggling like hysterical schoolgirls."

Niven told a slightly different, harsher story, describing how Claude pitched Collins, in career purdah before her *Dynasty* resurrection, not because of the allure of her "seasoned" age but because of her residual fame. Men would pay big money to sleep with a star, even a faded one. Fame has one of the longest half-lives of any aphrodisiac. Toying with the notion, Joan pressed the supermadam: "What about my friend?" "Absolutely not," Madame Claude, never one to mince words, replied, dismissing the notion. Bricusse may have been an English starlet, but she had never become celebrated enough to be negotiable. Claude, as brutal as any modeling agent, often said that women should not be allowed to have sex after forty. She was always strictly business and as realpolitik as Metternich.

"But I never used her," Niven averred. "I didn't *have to.* I was a young puppy then. I was involved with Natalie Wood, who was the biggest star in the world after Elizabeth Taylor. I was a hot agent at William Morris's Madrid office, representing Ava Gardner and Orson Welles, who stiffed us on commissions, by the way. I didn't need hookers. I had stars and starlets. Although sometimes there may have been an overlap," Niven conceded. His "I don't have to pay for it" take on Madame Claude is typical of the American macho view of prostitution, that it represents a decadent European, Caligulan indulgence that somehow diminishes the rugged self-reliant masculinity of the American Marlboro Man ideal. The Hollywood alternative of the casting couch has proven to be a very false economy (c.f. Cosby, Ailes, Weinstein, et al.) in today's feminist times.

"Everybody paid for it in those days. That was the only way to get it. Even Porfirio Rubirosa, the greatest playboy in the world. I certainly did," counters Taki Theodoracopulos, the Greek shipping heir and longtime columnist for the London *Spectator*. "I first heard of Madame Claude around 1959, when I was twenty-three and living in Paris. She was already a legend by then. *Le tout Paris* was talking about her. She was it. This was pre-Pill. Girls didn't give it away back then. Going to hookers was totally acceptable. But she took hookers to an altogether different level. At that point, she was famous for picking up failed models and actresses and giving them a new life. When I say 'failed,' I don't mean failures. These were stunning girls, who for whatever reason—the beauty business is cruel—had just missed the cut. Madame Claude was a second chance. You met the right men, and you certainly got a lot more money than models were being paid in those days. That was before the time when [eighties supermodel] Linda Evangelista said she wouldn't get out of bed for less than ten thousand dollars. These girls would get into bed for two hundred dollars, though Claude always gave them the option of saying no if they didn't like the client."

Theodoracopulos recounted his inaugural visit to Madame Claude's apartment *de rendezvous* at 18, rue de Marignan. He came as a guest of his tennis mates and older friends: Rubirosa, the legendary Dominican polo star and playboy, who had married both of the world's richest heiresses, Doris Duke and Barbara Hutton, and Philippe Washer, the Belgian tennis champion and himself the heir to one of Europe's major pharmaceutical fortunes, Solvay International Chemical Group. Even in her early days, "normal" men weren't on Claude's client roster. You almost had to be superrich, even though her prices had not yet hit the Arab-driven stratosphere they would a decade hence. It was a sort of club.

That day, Theodoracopulos met a French actress he had seen in several New Wave films, which he found thrilling. Rubirosa, who had putatively had everyone, chose a much bigger, more buxom type, which was his taste when lust, rather than social ambition, was his objective. Washer chose a classic French blonde, "*très pudique.*" Then the three men all retired to separate bedrooms for an hour and reunited afterward for postcoital drinks. It was like a château dinner party, the gentlemen going for cigars and cognac in one room, and the ladies sipping tea in another. "I had a small account at the Banque Rothschild, which had an office right below the apartment," Theodoracopulos recalled. "I found myself going there all the time, making withdrawals and going upstairs. It was a magic fantasy, a dream house."

As compelling as he found the women, Theodoracopulos, having been initiated into this club of bon vivants, was equally fascinated by Madame Claude herself. "She had a small tattoo on her wrist," he recalled. "She told stories about surviving the camp that were thrilling. As a Jew herself, she had a special hatred for the Jews who collaborated with the Nazis in running the camps—the *Kapos* and *Soderkommandos.*" Just as Claude was a strict constructionist in terms of her girls' etiquette and manners, she could be just as tough on her clients. "She scolded me for being *trop bavard,* which meant that I talked too much and shouldn't be such a chatterbox."

But when it came to Madame Claude, Theodoracopulos couldn't stop talking. He even credits her with winning him the respect of his hard-to-please father, one of the Greek shipping tycoons, perhaps not on a par with Onassis and Niarchos but a tycoon nonetheless. Theodoracopulos *père*, annoyed by his son's profligate ways and days in Paris, finally came up with an assignment worthy of his son's elegant idleness. "He called me one day and said, 'I have five Indonesian generals who run the national oil company. I want to charter them ships,'" Theodoracopulos recalled. "He said, 'I need to fix them up.'

"At first I was at a total loss. None of the society girls I knew would deign to date an Indonesian general. God forbid! Then I had a brainstorm. I went to Madame Claude and told her my dilemma. No problem, she said. She came up with five society girls I *didn't* know. I set up a dinner at a restaurant called Moustache on the Left Bank. The girls were splendid. The generals were bowled over by the elegance and class. Plus, they all *got laid*! Which I paid for out of my allowance. But it was well worth it. My father got his deal and leased the tankers at great profit. He decided I wasn't so bad after all.

"In 1965, I got married to a lovely French girl, a countess, the daughter of the duc de Caraman. She was what a lot of the Claude girls aspired to be, although there were plenty of girls of titled families who aspired to be Claude girls. My wife had been disinherited, so there was no honeymoon château. Instead, we moved into Rubi[rosa]'s house in the parc de Saint-Cloud, just outside Paris. He had been the best man at my wedding," Theodoracopulos recalled with nostalgia. "Neither he nor I did much in those days. We left the house each morning, worked the polo ponies, had lunch, and then more often than not visited Madame Claude's. Rubi inisited these visits made for a happy married life. The contrast was invigorating. It was like stepping into a sauna after a cold shower." Rubirosa turned out to be wrong in this case about the conjugal stimulation of a Madame Claude habit. The countess divorced Theodoracopulos after a year.

"Over the years, I have obviously met a lot of Claude girls," Theodoracopulos said, "although I personally never met one who hit it big the way the legend said they all did. Every time you'd come into Castel or Annabel's or Le Club in New York with a really pretty girl, the tongues would all start wagging, 'Oh, she's a *Claude girl.*' It was the prefect catty revenge for all sorts of jilted lovers and dumped wives to say things like that. But none of my girls whom they said that about were Claude girls. At least not that I knew."

When Madame Claude addressed the postschoolboy Arthur Sarkissian as "my little client" she actually had one who was even younger. This young player was only fourteen, although he didn't realize at the time that he was playing with fire. The boy, who will be called "Antoine," was a scion of the preeminent dynasty in French advertising. The family name was originally Bleustein. They had come to Paris from Russia and made their living selling furniture in Montmartre. Young Marcel Bleustein came up with the idea, a brainstorm in France, to use newspaper ads to sell that furniture.

Marcel was as precocious in business as Antoine would be in sex. He dropped out of school at twelve and, after some odd jobs, took a tramp steamer to New York to see the "modern" world. Although he didn't speak a word of English, the advertising that Marcel saw all over the city and its newspapers and airwaves didn't not get lost in translation. In 1926, at nineteen, he returned to Paris and began selling musical ads on radio, featuring Edith Piaf and Maurice Chevalier singing for the first time on the air. Eventually, he became the radio king of France and soon branched out into cinema with a chain of theaters. He named his umbrella company Publicis.

During the war, the Nazis destroyed all of Marcel Bleustein's radio stations. He fought back, escaping to England with Charles de Gaulle and becoming a reconnaissance pilot. Like so many French Jews, traumatized by anti-Semitism, he adopted a French surname and became Marcel Bleustein-Blanchet. And after the war, he transformed the Champs-Elysées into Madison Avenue by converting an old hotel at the top of the grand avenue that had served as Allied headquarters into the flagship of Publicis, which quickly became the biggest agency in Europe. In 1958, Marcel further Americanized the street by opening the twenty-four-hour Le Drugstore on the first floor of Publicis, both shocking and intriguing the traditionally xenophobic, ever-snobbish French. Le Drugstore became little Antoine's clubhouse, where he held court for his young pals over gastronomically sacrilegious Yankee feasts of burgers, fries, and milk shakes.

However, a far bigger sacrilege was Antoine's dreadful academic performance in his high school, where his indolence and sloth were threatening to blot his family's stellar escutcheon. Antoine's alma mater was Lycée Janson-de-Sailly, one of the two most prestigious high schools in Paris. (The other is the Lycée Louis-le-Grand, next to the Sorbonne.) Located in the sixteenth arrondissement, the Lycée Janson was the future alma mater of Carla Bruni. It is testament to the sexism of the French system that Bruni is the most famous *jansonienne,* as the graduates of the school are known, while *jansoniens* include Prime Ministers Valéry Giscard d'Estaing and Lionel Jospin, as well as Minister of Culture Frédéric Mitterrand, art auctioneer Maurice Rheims, anthropologist Claude Lévi-Strauss, and American director Preston Sturges, whose mother had remarried a rich Paris stockbroker who raised her son there in splendor.

Antoine was in no danger of joining this list of distinguished alumni. He was small but handsome and sporty, although basically a wastrel with no future other than what his family would give him. But because that family was one of the highest-achieving clans in France, anything less than making it on your own was considered a disgrace. Antoine was on the road to oblivion. And then, adding insult to indolence, he met and fell in love with Madame Claude's top hooker/booker, a wild and crazy omnisexual girl in her mid-twenties named Catherine Virgitti. A sleek tomboyish blond Venus who dressed in leather from head to toe, Virgitti liked to cruise on her Yamaha motorcycle around the boulevards of Paris, scouting for talent on behalf of Madame Claude. One prime recruiting spot was the Lycée Janson, where Catherine hoped to recruit Lolita types from rich families. The age of consent in France was a shockingly low fifteen. Suffice is to say that all the hormonal *jansoniens* like Antoine were entranced by this mystery biker, the sexy serpent in their adolescent Eden.

Because there was no real drinking age in France, Antoine and his wealthy confreres were also allowed to hang out and run huge champagne tabs at the leading Paris nightclubs. This was another reason for Antoine's atrocious grades. There was no way he would ever be admitted to France's most leading university-level institutions, its Grandes Ecoles, specifically Sciences Po, for future politicians, or the Ecole Normale Supérieure, for future scholars. The best Antoine could hope for was more likely Alcooliques Anonymes.

Then one night at Castel, Antoine saw Catherine Virgitti across the dance floor, literally the devil in the flesh, in a throng of Claudettes. Recognizing her from the playground and fortified with Krug, he asked her to dance. Normally, such impudence would have gotten the teen rejected and laughed out of the chic boîte. But Catherine was different. Under Claude's mandate to know everything about everyone, she quickly assessed Antoine's lineage. It was a family both she and Madame Claude knew quite well. Antoine's bona fides having been vetted, Catherine began dancing with him. And then she took him, in her night transport, a Maserati, home to her avenue George V apartment and to bed. It was the highlight of Antoine's young life. And she didn't even charge him.

Learning that her new conquest was in danger of becoming the black sheep in a family of sacred cows, Catherine developed a longer-range plan. She started a weekly affair with him on the condition that there would be sex only if his grades improved. It was motivation of the highest order. Antoine fell hopelessly in love with this older siren. How could he not? Catherine was a real sportswoman. In addition to the Yamaha, she rode horses, shot guns, went hunting, played tennis. She had a sideline customizing old Volkswagen Beetles, adorning them with Rolls-Royce "Winged Victory" hood ornaments. Yet Catherine was also proud of being a great cook, in the grandmotherly French tradition. She was born in Toulon and had grown up in Saint-Tropez, now home of the Bardot cult of sun and sex, and she was Bardotesque in many ways. Her family was originally from Corsica, which had endeared her to Claude, whose life among the gangsters had made her a born-again Corsican. Both women could shift from deep loyalty to vicious vendetta in a blink.

Catherine's father was a dentist—hence her perfect white teeth. Because Saint-Tropez had become a town for the beautiful rich, her father had developed a lucrative practice and his daughter had developed expensive tastes. As she put it, she loved perfume, but she also loved women, which was a scandal in her bourgeois world. She had her first lesbian romance at seventeen with a "Lorelei" she met and seduced on the beach, behind the rocks. Catherine had wanted to become a doctor, but she quickly gave it up, traveling around the "rich places" of Europe—Paris, Geneva, Athens—and going as far as Tehran, seducing both the daughters and sons of rich arms dealers and shipping magnates.

Catherine thus had a lot of practice in dealing with jeunesse dorée like Antoine. Back in Paris, at age twenty, she met a manicurist who changed her life by giving her the "magic number" of Madame Claude, who took to her instantly and installed her as her chief factotum. Heiress apparent would have been appropriate, but Claude was young herself and not thinking of legacy this early in her career, although the ever-calculating Catherine, as it turned out, would have her own succession plans.

Catherine's motivational program worked so well that Antoine's grades went from Fs to As, so good that his family decided to send him off to boarding school at Ecole des Roches (literally, School of Rock), an elite English-style all-male "college" where entrance to the Grandes Ecoles was fairly assured, the same way Eton or Harrow guaranteed admission to Oxford or Cambridge. For Antoine, it was a booby prize. For all his efforts and his transformation, he was exiled into a celibate grove of academe. He was desperate not to go and deeply depressed. Now it was time for Catherine to submit her invoice. Through Claude, she made a rendezvous with Antoine's father and revealed to him the sexy secret of his son's success.

The father might have been furious, but this was France. Instead, Antoine's *père* was thrilled and put Catherine on a large retainer for the next two years, assuring she would visit Antoine at Ecole des Roches and keep his spirits up, along with his grades. Under Catherine's continuing tutelage, Antoine made it into a Grande Ecole and a grand career in Paris business. His story was transmuted into a 1975 novel, *L'Amant de Poche* ("The Pocket Lover") by Voldemar Lestienne, editor of the newspaper *France-Soir,* and, in 1978, into a film with the same title. Catherine, never one to be tied down, moved on to more conquests and even greater fortune, while Antoine became one of Claude's most loyal clients. He knew that she had changed his life, and for the better.

For a young man in Paris in the sixties like Antoine, it was a singular achievement simply to have Madame Claude's number, to have the money and stature to have access to her unique fantasyland of distaff charms. Of course, aside from movie, music, and soccer stars, who had earned big fame and big money at an early age, the "achievement" of most of these young men was genetic good fortune. Such was France, where the Establishment, which began with the old monarchy, only seemed to get increasingly established, at least until the student rebellions of 1968 initiated upheavals in society that a decade later would drive Madame Claude out of the country.

Among these privileged young men, there was yet a higher honor, perhaps the highest in the annals of male sexual privilege. That was to be selected by Madame Claude as an *essayeur,* or tester, one of an elite corps of particularly attractive, rich, and courtly Frenchmen in their early twenties who would take out aspiring Claudettes and rate them, preparing exhaustive reviews of their sexual, social, and intellectual allure that would determine which girls would make the cut. It seemed at first blush like the Michelin restaurant-rating system, where anonymous *inspecteurs* would fan out across France to judge and rank the country's best restaurants.

The Claude selection process was also, and more appropriately, very much like the application process for the Rhodes Scholarships, where candidates would be taken to dinners and other events by former Rhodes scholars. The "old boys" then wrote reports on the suitability of the candidates, most of whom had already hit the pinnacle of the Ivy League, to advance to this highest rung of academic elitism at Oxford, which would then be a passport back into the power elite that dominated American politics and business.

France had a series of highly selective public schools and universities whose mostly male graduates had a similar stranglehold on the jobs that ruled the country. Madame Claude gave the women of France their own form of competition, whereby their grand prize would be to marry these men. It was as sexist as anything on earth. But France was still a game of thrones, and who would ever argue that Marie Antoinette was not the real power behind Louis XVI. That her excesses provoked the French Revolution is another story that Madame Claude, too, would have, in time, to deal with.

As with the Rhodes Scholarships, Madame Claude had a gradated system of these life-changing judgments. At the very top, the "finals," as it were, were a group of fortyish plutocrats, considered among the greatest ladies' men in this country of ladies' men. Below them were the junior testers, a dashing corps of rising twentysomething playboys who would carry on the French tradition of *fraternité, egalité* notwithstanding. Among the senior *essayeurs,* the list was headed by Baron Elie de Rothschild, who could be considered the quintessential Madame Claude client. One of the heirs to Europe's greatest banking fortune and the owner of its greatest vintage wine, Château Lafite, the Savile Row–dressed, craggily aquiline, mustachioed baron, who was born in 1917 and was in his virile forties in the 1960s, had a special lust for life occasioned by his arrest and imprisonment during World War II by the Nazis in Colditz Castle, the Alcatraz of Germany. Although he was forced to wear the yellow star, his being a French officer (and a Rothschild) spared him from going to Dachau for extermination.

While in prison, de Rothschild arranged a mail-order marriage with his childhood sweetheart, Liliane Fould-Springer, the heiress to a rival banking fortune, the Crédit Mobilier. Liliane, who had the greatest of all collections of Marie Antoinette memorabilia, had everything except looks, which drove the baron into the octopuslike embrace of supermistress and future American ambassador to France Pamela Harriman, and later, and more lastingly, into the warm hospitality of Madame Claude.

The second of the supertesters was Frédéric Chandon, the Conete de Briailles, and president of Möet & Chandon, the champagne colossus. Chandon, born in 1927, hunted wild boar at his country estate and collected antique Rollses. He rode a souped-up

Honda motorcycle to work at his office near the Arc de Triomphe
and to his all-night tasting dinners at Régine's and Castel, the
twin towers of Paris nightlife. "I have to be elegant, entertain
beautiful women, and eat well," he once told an American reporter while promoting his Napa winery, the first such French
outpost in California. "You can't be a champagne merchant and
drink water." Chandon, like de Rothschild and so many other
French aristocrats, had a seemingly open marriage and/or a su-
premely tolerant spouse. Chandon's wife, a painter, and he maintained separate apartments in a twelve-room penthouse complex
overlooking Notre Dame.

Not an aristocrat like these two chief *essayeurs* but no less a
player was Jacques Quoirez, the brother of Françoise Sagan, the
globally bestselling young author, who ranked up there with Madame Claude and Coco Chanel as one of the few truly rich self-
made women in France. Jacques was accused of riding the
coattails of his eight-years-younger baby sister, who in 1954, at
eighteen, published *Bonjour Tristesse,* a then-scandalous novel
about the life and loves of an amoral teenage girl, which was set
on the Riviera among the future Madame Claude crowd. The
book, which sold millions all over the world, was number one
on the bestseller lists in Paris, New York, and London, and became a film starring Jean Seberg as Sagan's alter ego and David
Niven as her philandering father. The precociously brilliant Sagan had taken her nom de plume from one of her favorite Proust
characters, the Princesse de Sagan, because she liked the sound
of the name.

Francoise Quoirez, known in girlhood as "Kiki," had grown
up in an *haut-bourgeois* country home in the picturesque southwest
province of Lot, which was also the home of future French president Georges Pompidou, and in a grand Paris Haussmann flat
on the boulevard Malesherbes, where her best school friend was
the daughter of Jackie Kennedy's idol, André Malraux. She became overnight the richest wild child in France, smart like de

Beauvoir, cute like Seberg and Bardot, and rich like the Rothschilds. She was world-famous, and a major phenomenon, a precocious literary celebrity and a party animal who promptly bought her own Jaguar XK-120 and an estate in Deauville, where she gave booze and drug parties that continued for days, long before most people were taking drugs. With her seemingly endless royalties, she was treated like French royalty, and *frère* Jacques, who himself loved a wild ride, went along on his sister's. Sagan was crazier about her big brother than about any of the countless men who were now pursuing her.

"I loved him," said Françoise Sagan's only son, author-photographer Denis Westhoff, of his uncle Jacques. Unlike tiny Françoise, whom Jacques called *"petit oiseau,"* or little bird, Jacques was a big man, like their father, who was also figuratively a big engineer turned industrialist who drove Bugattis and gambled in Deauville with the Rothschilds. Father and son fought like "two roosters," Westhoff said, so much so that, right after World War II, when Jacques was eighteen, he fled to Manchester, England, to work in a factory as a day laborer. He also had two children with an English girl, but she left Jacques without marrying him. When Françoise sold her book and became a superstar, Jacques returned to France.

"They were the best friends in the world. She took him everywhere," Westhoff said. Hanging out with the rich and famous soon paid off for Jacques. He met a doctor named De Barges, who had created a wonder drug for upper-respiratory illnesses. Jacques became his partner, created a pharmaceutical company to market the drug, and was extremely successful, making as much money as his sister. "They both bought fast, fancy cars, Mom an Aston Martin, Jacques a Lamborghini," said Westhoff.

"They were so extravagant," he continued. "No wonder they lost all their money in the end. They loved dogs, and when the dogs wouldn't fit into their sports cars, Jacques went to Italy and had Lamborghini make him a stretch model for the dogs, like an SUV before they ever existed. He also bought a huge house on the rue de Seine (one of the most exclusive streets on the Left Bank). They had parties every night. They flew to Africa for weekend safaris, things like that." He was a huge man, stylish but huge, big bushy hair, like a bear in a Cardin suit. He was very witty, much funnier than my mom, who was serious. But his main thing was that he loved beautiful women, really, really beautiful women. That's how he met Madame Claude and became her tester. He loved her, and my mom did, too. She was a key part of the world they were in."

For all his playboy activities, Jacques Quoirez eventually met another woman, not necessarily through Madame Claude, and married her. They had a daughter, who became best friends with her English half sister, who had come to live in France with Jacques when he got rich. His daughters became even richer, when, one night at Castel, they met the Taittinger brothers, heirs to the champagne fortune that was the rival of Frédéric Chandon's. The double Taittinger-Quoirez unions took place on the same day in 1970 at the Taittinger château in Reims. Notwithstanding his own profligacies, which would bankrupt him before his death, in 1989, at age sixty-two, Jacques's daughters were set for life. Françoise Sagan was even more wasteful with her finances than her brother was with his. To protect her, she was eventually put under the financial guardianship of none other than Madame Claude's chief tester, Baron Elie de Rothschild, who became Sagan's chief banker. *Comme le monde était petit.* And Madame Claude was at the dead center of this privileged universe, simply because she had the one thing that all these men wanted.

When Sagan married her editor, Guy Schoeller, in 1958, she was twenty-two, he forty-two. Because of the family friendship, Madame Claude put Schoeller on her tasting panel. Sagan, who was anything if not open-minded about matters of pleasure, applauded the move, although when Sagan divorced Schoeller two years later, Madame Claude dropped him, as well. Although Madame Claude was close to many of the famous playboys of her time, all of whom were regular clients, men like Rubirosa, Aly Khan, Claude Terrail, Gianni Agnelli—in short, a near list of Pamela Harriman's conquests (or conquerors, depending on one's perspective)—none of them was as obsessed with female perfection as her Big Three, who remained Claude's supreme arbiters.

Below the Big Three was the position that all the young men of the Paris social world were dying to achieve. One who did was a twenty-one-year-old, six-foot-five blond Adonis from a distinguished French colonial family, today a well-known sportsman-about-town, still fit and rakish in his early seventies. He had grown up on the family estate in Morocco, where the family's fortune was made in minerals and livestock. "I came to Paris in 1961, when I was seventeen, for university," he said. "By the time I was nineteen, I was bored with school and mostly interested in hanging out at Régine's," the Montparnasse nightclub.

If sixties Paris had two queens of the night, one was Madame Claude and the other was Régine Zylberberg, a Polish Jewish émigrée who used to sell brassieres in the street markets under the arcades of the rue de Rivoli, then worked her way up the nightclub scene from coat-check girl to DJ to hostess to social arbiter. The two women were diametric opposites and claimed never to have even met each other. Claude thought Régine was coarse and classless. Régine thought that Claude was, well, a madam. *Res ipsa loquitor.* Nonetheless, the Paris of the beautiful people couldn't have lived without either. And where the junior testers were concerned, Régine's nightclub was ground zero for their discovery and recruitment.

"My only goal in life when I was nineteen was to be allowed to sit in Régine's front room," the tester, call him "Daniel," recalled. "That's where all the stars, the models, the best girls would be. That's where Onassis and Niarchos and the tycoons were. Maybe their sons could sit there. But not me. I did have some rich school friends, and that's how I got into the club at all, but never the front room. I dreamed of having my own seat, my own whiskey bottle with my name on it, where the waiters would mark off usage and send me a bill. I dreamed of being part of this special club within a club that was the front room.

"My family was fine, but we weren't the de Bourbons or the La Rochefoucaulds. We didn't go back to Charlemagne. Régine may have been from the street, but she knew every bloodline as if she was the president of the Jockey Club. What a snob! The only thing I had going for me was my looks. I *looked* like I came from where I did, only maybe more, because of my size. She liked big blond guys, and that was me. My friends told me that Régine was looking at me. That was good and bad, they said. The good was that I might get seated in the front room. The bad was that I would have to fuck her for it.

"I thought they were just teasing me about having to sing for my supper, as they said. But when one night she invited me for supper after the club closed, I knew they weren't joking. Of course I agreed. I would have done anything. She was much older, but really, how bad could it be? The supper part was great. Régine was famous for her spaghetti dinners. Sartre and de Beauvoir loved them. So did Malraux and Vadim. Everybody wanted to go for three A.M. spaghetti upstairs at Régine's. But that night I think she put something in my champagne, Spanish fly maybe. I could see where this was heading, and now I felt really drunk, way drunker than just the alcohol. I was big and could handle a lot. But not this.

"Régine pulled me into her bedroom and took her panties off. She got on the bed, otherwise fully dressed, and got into a doggy position. She wanted it that way. I was glad to be drugged. I did what I had to do. The next night, I had my own whiskey bottle and was seated in the front room. I got what I wanted. I felt like

a king. She always smiled at me, welcomed me, but she never asked me to do it again. Once was enough for her. Thank God.

"One night a few weeks later, I met Jacques Quoirez in the front room. He often came in, always with the most beautiful women, but he never spoke to me. Tonight was different. He was all alone. He had been checking me out. He sat down with me and asked me straight out, 'How would you like to meet and fuck beautiful girls?' What could I say? Of course I did. That's why I was sitting where I was. 'This is even better,' he said. Then he arranged for me to meet Madame Claude.

"We met in her apartment right below the Eiffel Tower. I know she had her brothel on the rue de Marignan, but that was like an office. This was where she was living. It was very tasteful, but I wasn't paying attention to the décor. There were just the two of us there. There were no drinks, no coffee, no small talk. All business. She was testing me to be a tester. She said what she wanted were 'intelligence reports.' I thought she meant how smart the girls were. That, too, she said, with one of the few laughs of the meeting. She gave me the name of one girl, her address and phone number, and handed me an envelope, which had what was probably equivalent to one thousand dollars today. My job, she said, was to use the money to take the girl to dinner, dancing, then to a discreet three-star hotel, not the Ritz, but a *hôtel de rendezvous.*

"She made a list of the things I was to look for. The way she holds her fork, chews her food, smokes her cigarettes, how she dances, what she talks about, to things about describing her blow jobs, how her pussy looked, was it shaved, did it smell, how big were her vaginal lips, doctor stuff, if she'll do anal sex or make love if she's having her period. She said something about sex being hotter when a girl was menstruating. It was a lot of work. I had never been so observant. And I wasn't getting paid for what I was doing, not in cash. 'Do you want to do it or not?' she asked impatiently, as if she was doing me a huge favor. 'Of course,' I

said, and thanked her for the amazing opportunity. Then she smiled.

"I remember going to pick up the girl. She was beautiful, as promised, a very refined French girl. I brought flowers. She seemed happy to see me, relieved that I wasn't some scary old man. I was amazed that she was doing this. If I just saw her, I would have thought no way would I ever be able to have casual sex with this girl. Not in those days. I would have had to marry her. We went to a nice restaurant, Lapérouse, which went back to Louis the Fourteenth and which I could have never afforded to go to as a student. It was the place where Hugo and de Maupassant set stories. It got three Michelin stars then and was supposedly the most romantic place in the city, an old house on the Seine, where every party dined in its own room.

"The legend was that you could have sex in the rooms during dinner. We didn't. We were by far the youngest couple there, or at least I was the youngest guy. I think the duke and duchess of Windsor were there that night. If they only knew what I was up to. Then we went to Régine, who gave me a big smile and a big welcome. She probably knew what was up. And then we went to this little hotel in the fifteenth, where nobody on earth would ever see us. I took the room for three hours. And it was great. It wasn't all anxious, like a wedding night. I thought she'd be like a virgin, but I was way more nervous than she was. I got the feeling that this wasn't her first time at this. She had the most expensive lingerie for a girl who worked in a travel agency, which is what she did. She said she loved to travel. I'm sure she got her wish. I took her home at five A.M., just as dawn was breaking. It was very romantic. Too bad I never got to see her again.

"I never saw any of them again. One night only. I called Madame Claude the next day and set up a time that afternoon to give her my report. I pushed to get an appointment. She asked me what was my hurry. I said I didn't want to forget anything. 'Then she must not have been any good,' Claude said. 'You never

forget the great ones.' I went back to the Champ-de-Mars and spent no more than forty-five minutes telling her what happened. She pushed me for more details, like what exactly was she wearing, what perfume, what kind of shoes. How was her makeup? Was she wearing jewelry? Stuff guys never notice. 'You better learn,' she told me. I was focused more on the sex, what her body looked like, how she moved and kissed. But Claude also wanted all the *Vogue* stuff, which was not what I knew. She thanked me and saw me to the door. I thought I had failed my test, that she might not use me again.

"Two weeks later, she called me again and asked me to come over. She had a new envelope of cash, a new girl. I had passed the test. For the next two years, from 1963 to 1965, I must have tested seventy or eighty girls for her. I never met another young tester. I have no idea how many juniors she had or who they were. I never knew how many other guys tested a girl before Claude gave her the green light. I never saw another girl at Madame Claude's place. She had these Chinese walls. She was more proper and guarded than any aristocrat. Maybe she tried harder to be like them, or at least like she thought they would be, saying nothing. It was beyond discreet.

"I knew not to ask questions, only to give her information. Every time she gave me an envelope, there was never money to pay the girl. Madame Claude always took care of paying them. It may have been some legal rule, connected to *proxénétisme*, where she didn't want to be seen having girls bring her a cut of their earnings. Or maybe she was just sparing the guys the awkwardness of paying for this big romantic evening, which would take the romance out of it. Money spoils the mood. Claude wanted her clients to be happy. Again, I knew better than to ask.

"I can't remember all the details of those nights. I was so exhausted paying attention to everything that it all became a blur. To tell the truth, I remember their pussies more than their faces. I did start reading *Vogue* and *Elle,* to figure out all the fashion stuff. One thing I will say was that the country girls, the ones from the poor families in the provinces, the less sophisticated ones, at least before Claude got them all sophisticated, were a lot hotter than the *haut-bourgeois* girls from Paris who had gone to good schools and came from good families, and were the classic Claude girls. The Paris girls were, in general, nowhere as good at sex. They were too busy being chic. My craziest experience was one day when I went to pick up a Claude girl. The door opened, and it was one of my *cousins*! Neither of us could believe it. We didn't know each other that well, but we were definitely cousins. After the shock of it all, we had a drink and a big laugh.

"By 1965, it was all over. Claude stopped calling me. I never ran into her in public, anywhere. I never saw her again. It had been the most intimate thing I ever did, but we didn't become friends afterward. She became more and more famous, but for me she just vanished. Régine never spoke of it. It was like a dream. I did see a few of the girls I had tested, more than a few. They married well. Some were countesses; some were the wives of the very rich; some were stars or had big jobs in fashion. A lot more than I would have ever guessed became kinds of stars. I saw them, but I never betrayed them by recognition. If we ever met, it was something unspoken, erased from memory, a stain that was removed."

Chapter 4

THE SEXUAL OLYMPICS

I am the last person I thought would ever work for Madame Claude. If you had asked me, I would have said that is ridiculous. But it did happen, in a crazy way, and it did change my life," said the woman, now in her late sixties. She is a world-class art dealer, who, like all ex-Claudettes, required anonymity. Tawny, sleek, and chic, she looks like a fashion person who follows the duchess of Windsor's adage that a woman can never be too rich or too thin. She would look equally at home on Madison Avenue, avenue Montaigne, Bond Street, or the Ginza, all venues where she is likely to be found, depending on when the art auctions are held. Today she is the platonic ideal of the worldly woman a Madame Claude girl could grow up to be, wealthy, cultured, agelessly beautiful, endlessly sophisticated, global. But, unlike the stereotype of Claudettes either being downwardly mobile nobility or upwardly mobile *haut-bourgeois* girls next door, this woman, call her "Véronique," was neither of the above.

Véronique was born in Calais, the port city in northern France on the English Channel where the ferries from Dover would dock. "Calais was the most British city in France," Véronique said. "I spoke English like the queen, wore miniskirts, and was obsessed with the Beatles. I had every album." Véronique's father was, like so many other businessmen in Calais, in the shipping trade. She was middle-class and grew up in a small house with two brothers. "Nobody molested me," she said, "No dirty uncles, no drugs, no poverty, none of the things you think about with being . . . you know." Like all Madame Claude girls, and like Madame Claude herself, she will not use the *p* word.

In some ways, given the success it led to, working for Madame Claude was arguably a point of pride, but Véronique was nonetheless ambivalent about embracing this part of her past. Unusually for a Claudette, Véronique had never been married, which was the holy grail of the Claude experience, notwithstanding that Claude was the matchmaker who could never be revealed. Véronique's life was that rare triumph without benefit of clergy. "If I were married, I'd *never* be talking about this at all." While many of Claude's male clients will brag of their exploits, albeit usually without allowing their braggadocio to be attributed, ex-Claudettes are another matter. Perhaps because of her single status, with no family to "disgrace," Véronique is indeed one of the rare Claudettes willing to reminisce about her adventures in the world of love for money.

"When I was a teenager in the sixties, everyone in Calais was mad for English clothes, the Carnaby Street look," she recalled. "I was dying to live in England, anywhere in England, just to be part of that world. It was so different from France, so exciting, so modern. And just a ferry ride away." The dandy George "Beau" Brummel, the ultimate English clotheshorse, was perhaps Calais's most famous decedent, expiring in a madhouse for paupers (his downfall was gambling) there in 1840. "I said anywhere, so I got Manchester," Véronique said with a laugh. After high school, her father found her a job in a Midlands clothing store, part of a low-budget, teen-oriented chain owned by one of his shipping clients, who also was a major hosiery manufacturer.

"I hated Manchester. There was a Who song called 'Teenage Wasteland.' This was it. I was expecting London, or 'A Hard Day's Night.' This place had all the bad stuff of England, the fog, the cold, the gray, the gloomy industrial feeling, but none of the cool stuff. So I just worked hard, and I moved up fast, from sales-girl to knitwear buyer. I guess my big break was becoming the leg model for their stockings line. My legs were my best feature. They went on and on. I was tall, at least for France, five feet six. It wasn't like a model in magazines. I was mostly a fitting model. I think I made a few of the catalogs. I wasn't Jean Shrimpton, but I wanted to think I was. That was my fantasy. But I was too short to do anything more than this.

"The company was a family business. There were five brothers, all Orthodox Jews who had come originally from Poland. They were all married to nice Jewish girls. They all chased after me. I slept with three of them. I was Catholic, but Calais, being a port city, was what you would call liberated in the sixties. I wasn't a virgin. But my bosses weren't like Paul McCartney or Gerry Marsden or Dave Clark. If only. They were the real England, hard workers, money, serious, but not close to sexy. Brian, the oldest brother, the big boss, was the playboy of the family. He would take me up to London on buying trips for the teen shops. The excuse was that I was a buyer.

"We'd stay at the Dorchester in London. In Manchester, he'd keep kosher, but on business trips he'd scrap the yarmulke and wear his best Savile Row suits and order foie gras and lobster at places like Mirabelle and the Savoy Grill. We went gambling at Les Ambassadeurs. I felt all grown-up, and he'd buy me nice clothes, not the stuff from their shops. We'd see some of the older British movie stars, Dirk Bogarde, John Gielgud, Laurence Harvey. They were known in Calais, because we were almost English. We saw Charlie Chaplin at the Savoy Hotel. And Vivien Leigh, right before she died of tuberculosis. *Gone With the Wind.* Brian was thrilled. He was that generation. I would have loved to see Marianne Faithfull. Though not where we went.

"The place I wanted to go was the Bag O'Nails in Soho. That was Paul McCartney's favorite, a lot of the rock stars. Brian

wouldn't be caught dead there." How the times had changed. The
Bag O' Nails, before becoming a rock pub, was formerly the Pin-
stripe Club, where Minister of War John Profumo was first introduced to Christine Keeler, in the prostitution affair that
brought down the British government in 1963 and echoed the
rise of the "scandal-proof" Madame Claude across the Channel.
That was slightly before Véronique's time, even though Véronique
was now beginning to tread down similar thoroughfares.

"Brian started taking me to Paris on buying trips, but I think
they were just a big excuse, because fancy Paris fashion wasn't
what he was selling to the shopgirls of England. He bought me
a dress from Givenchy, which I could never wear in Manchester
or Calais, for that matter. I wasn't complaining, but I felt like
his dress-up doll, that he was just playing with me, as a kind
of prop for him. We'd stay at the George V and go to all these
fancy restaurants like Tour d'Argent. He also took me once to
Castel, which was the hangout of the Madame Claude girls, but
I had no idea at the time. Brian never danced. He just liked showing off, going to the 'in' places, being away from his wife. But
he soon got tired of me, too, and he stopped taking me on these
trips.

"Soon Brian started using me in a different way—as his procurer. It started on one of his business trips to Paris—by himself. He said he was alone in his room at the George V and he was
reading *Lui* magazine, which was the French version of *Playboy.*
That's where he first read about Madame Claude. Brian came
back and gave me this assignment, to get him an introduction to
Madame Claude. Brian, like his brothers, was a sex maniac. He
wanted to sleep with everything he could. Money was no object.
I was a little insulted at first. What was wrong with *me*? But I
think I was mostly relieved that I didn't have to sleep with him
anymore, that I had 'graduated.' With a sex maniac, you can't
be possessive.

"The best part of it was that Brian sent me to Paris to open an office there. He got me a small apartment on the Left Bank, on the rue des Saints-Pères. I would have still preferred London at the time, but Paris was fun, too, a lot better than when I was growing up right after the war, when there were shortages of everything. Business was great and Brian could afford it. We had started branching out from hosiery to manufacturing sportswear, and the French kids loved the British look. Brian's main obsession was to get to Madame Claude, which wasn't that easy, because she was so big by the late sixties and the hall porters simply didn't have her number anymore. She didn't need hall porters. She had heads of state, ministers of finance. Hall porters, no. Maybe when she was starting out.

"I could afford nice clothes now, and could afford to go out. Paris is a small town, at least among the chic people, and once you start connecting, you meet everyone fast. I mean, there were only two nightclubs, Castel and Jimmy'z, which was the name for Régine's. How small a world is that? The way I first got to Madame Claude—as a client—was through one of the models we hired for a catalog advertisement. She was a beautiful Swedish girl name Gunilla, who worked for Paris Planning, the agency that was the correspondent agency for Ford in New York. Somehow Gunilla and I became friendly enough for me to ask her if she knew Madame Claude. She didn't. She had a successful boyfriend, so she said she wasn't interested. But she did have one friend from Stockholm, a girl named Helene, who did work for Madame Claude, and she gave me Helene's number directly.

"Helene was very suspicious when I called. She refused to admit anything, and she certainly wasn't about to give me Madame Claude's number. I had to get Gunilla to call her and tell her I was okay and that our company was legitimate and paid her well. Finally I did speak to Helene, and she gave me the hardest-to-get number in Paris. So I called Madame Claude, and the first thing she said was, "*Allô, oui.*" That was her famous greeting, but there was nothing friendly or welcoming about it. It was like,

Why are you bothering me? What do you want? I told her what I wanted, and she asked me more questions about Brian than any police inspector. Who was he, who was his wife, where did he live, what was his background. It was all in French, and she was suspicious as to why a French girl was working for a British company. Finally, she said she had 'to do some research' and that I should call her back in a week.

"When I called again, it turned out that Brian had checked out. She asked me what kind of girl he liked. I told her he was spoiled by being in the fashion business, and that he only wanted very tall models. I had come to the right place, she assured me. I then called Brian with the good news, but then he made my life difficult by insisting that I meet whoever the girl was that Claude was going to introduce him to. He was coming to Paris in a few weeks, and Brian didn't like surprises.

"So I called Gunilla's friend and asked if we could meet. We did, at the Drugstore on the Champs-Elysées. I was so impressed. She was six feet tall, too tall to model, she said, but not too tall for Madame Claude. You could never be too tall for Claude. Helene was this giant fantasy creature, elegant and overwhelming. I had never been so intimidated by a woman. I can't imagine Elizabeth Taylor, who was the greatest beauty of that time but so different, or Julie Christie, who was the hot girl of the era, being that overwhelming. She was most like Veruschka, the giant Russian countess turned model. Out of this world. There was no question Brian would be thrilled. I might even get a raise for this.

" 'I just had big parents,' Helene said. She was modest and sweet. We ordered *croque-monsieurs* and American milk shakes and got to know each other a bit. Then Helene hit me with a shocking suggestion. 'Why don't *you* come to work for Claude?' she asked me candidly. I'm sure I turned red and laughed at her. *Me?* I might be able to have sex, cold sex, with Brian. But become a . . . *prostitute?* I could not even say the word, not out of any false modesty, but for fear of insulting Helene. France might have been full of streetwalkers—it's legal here—but when it came to public attitudes, being a prostitute was just as shameful in France as it was in the States. Sure, I had read about La Belle Otero and the *grandes horizontales,* but that was ancient history, like Marie Antoinette. Nice girls, and I still saw myself as a nice girl, despite my thing with my bosses, didn't do that.

" 'It's not so bad,' " Helene said, always in her modest way. 'Claude is actually nice. You meet the top people in the world. You travel everywhere, first-class, the greatest places. And she never makes you . . . er, *go* . . . with anyone you don't like. If I see your guy, and I don't like him, I can leave.' And then Helene blushed herself, embarrassed to be bragging. 'And you can't believe how much money you can make.'

"It was now the early seventies, and the Arabs seemed to be ruling the world. They were everywhere you turned. They owned London, and they seemed to be buying up Paris, as well. You could make three hundred dollars an hour with guys like Brian. But that wasn't what interested Helene. It was the six-hundred-dollar nights, the two-thousand-dollar weekends, the gifts of diamonds. I did a quick calculation and figured out Helene could be making well over one hundred and fifty thousand dollars a year, even if you took away Madame Claude's thirty percent commission. I was making sixteen thousand dollars a year and thought I was on my way up.

" '*Bupkes!*' I exclaimed under my breath. 'What's that?' Helene asked curiously. I tried to explain that it was Yiddish for small change. 'Are you Jewish?' she asked. 'No, my boss, your date.' I told her how in the garment business, everyone spoke a little Yiddish no matter where they came from. *Bupkes, oy vey, schmatte, chutzpah,* that was the language of the Sentier, or garment district, where we had our branch office. '*Bupkes,*' she said to herself, like playing with a new toy. Somehow, the word didn't fit her.

"But it had to be too good to be true. There had to be a catch. Well, one catch was that it was against the law. I knew prostitution was legal in France, but anybody making that much money had to be committing a crime. I doubted even actresses like Jeanne Moreau were making that kind of money. It seemed like a fortune. Mostly, it just seemed crazy. Plus, I was deathly afraid of Arabs. I'd seen them at the Ritz, the George V, in their robes and worry beads. I couldn't sleep with them for all the money on earth. There's always a catch, and for me the Arabs were the catch. I thanked Helene for meeting with me, told her how great a guy Brian was, went back to my little office and called Brian and told him that I had found him the girl of a lifetime.

"Just as I thought, Brian loved Helene. He saw her the next four times he came to Paris. I don't know how much he spent on her, but I knew it was more than he ever spent on me. I tried not to be jealous. But then Brian decided that even Helene was not enough for his endless needs. He asked me to contact Madame Claude and find him someone new to try. What could be wrong with Helene? I asked him, genuinely curious. Nothing was wrong, he said. She was perfect. But just think *who else* Madame Claude must have. That did it. That was when I decided to take Helene up on her suggestion to meet the woman herself.

" 'You're so short' was the first thing Madame Claude said to me, maybe just to take me off guard. Although I was a good head taller than she, I felt like a midget. 'I'm tall for a French girl.' I tried to make excuses for myself. 'The men don't care what country you're from,' she said, cutting me off. We were meeting at what must have been her private apartment. I knew she had a kind of brothel, near the Champs, because that's where Brian had his first hour with Helene. But there were no signs of any girls here, just an incessantly ringing phone, which Claude left me every five minutes or less to answer. I felt like leaving, but I couldn't, not after having gone this far.

" 'How's your figure?' she asked, putting me on the spot once again. This time, I took charge. We were sitting down on an expensive antique sofa. She hadn't even offered me tea. I thought I was dead. So I played what I thought was my best hand. I didn't wait for her to challenge me to take my clothes of. If I had hesitated a second, she would have assumed I had something to hide. I stood up, right in front of her, and stripped.

"I was ready for this, and had worn my most expensive lingerie, a beautiful bra and panties and garter belt Brian had bought me at Cadolle, this famous lingerie shop near the Ritz, for a small fortune, when he was still interested in having sex with me. 'You have good legs,' she said, which was high praise. I told her I had been a leg model. 'Your breasts will do,' she allowed once I was completely naked. 'You're fine.' 'Not too short?' I asked her directly. 'We'll see' was all she could say. I had no idea how tough she was. She made me leap at the challenge, like bait. 'Get dressed,' she told me. It was chilly in the room. 'The worst thing a girl can do is give a man a cold.'

"Once I had put my clothes back on, Claude became kinder and less intimidating. She offered me tea and *macarons,* from Ladurée, the top place, of course. It was so frustrating, trying to talk, when she kept leaving to answer the phone. There was another phone on the table beside us, but she never picked it up. She was too discreet to speak in front of me, a stranger. She didn't apologize. Between rings, she asked me about my background. She seemed disappointed in my not having gone to college but seemed to think I was up-to-date on current events. Going between London and Paris, and having that affair with my rich boss, had given me a certain sophistication that made up for my lack of a degree.

"What seemed to interest her most was Helene's having told

her I spoke Yiddish. I explained that I had picked up only a few words on the job. 'You *seem* Jewish,' she told me. Was that supposed to be a compliment? I had no idea. 'Do you have a lot of Jewish clients?' I asked her. 'Many,' she said. 'But most of them don't want Jewish girls,' she added. 'My Arabs, though. A lot of them want Jewish girls.' 'I won't see Arabs,' I said, my worst fear flashing before me. 'That's your problem. Not mine,' she said. 'It's a big problem.' I said. 'I just can't. I know that.'

" 'Can you afford to be such a racist?' she asked me. I just held my ground. That was the line I would not cross. I didn't want to see Africans, either, no matter how many diamonds they had in their mines. Maybe I was a racist. The French were liberal, but when it came to intimate matters, we had the right to choose. This wasn't some café or hotel.

"Claude wouldn't relent. 'Would you see Aristotle Onassis? Stavros Niarchos?' She reeled off the names of several more Greek tycoons whose pictures were always in *Paris Match,* on the social pages. I said I would. 'You're thinking of Saudis,' she said to me, with her first smile of the day. An *aha* smile. She had solved the mystery of my prejudice. She wouldn't sell me into bondage to some sheikh, she assured me. 'You're too skinny for them. They like much lusher women.' What she was talking about was her huge contingent of rich Lebanese and Persian businessmen and bankers. 'They're just as civilized as your boss,' she told me. 'Maybe more. You won't know the difference. For some reason, they like the idea of Jewish girls. Maybe because it was forbidden to them growing up, maybe because you are the enemy. . . .' 'But I'm not Jewish.' I felt I had to remind her. 'You're Jewish enough,' she insisted.

"The phone kept ringing. She needed to send me away. 'We'll want to do your nose,' she said in closing. Another shock. My nose? I liked my nose. 'My surgeon is the best in France,' she assured me. 'You have a peasant nose. He can make you . . . *raffinée.*' She could see my discomfort. 'Be glad that's all I want to do. Some girls need much, much more. Do you think all those models you see started out perfect?' She rose to show me to the door. 'I'm not sure . . .' I said, all hesitation. 'Nor am I,' she parried, putting me back on the defensive and making me feel even more insecure. 'Before we do anything, I have to get you tested.'

"Tested? I thought she wanted me to get blood tests, to see if I had some disease—worse than the cold I would catch for sitting naked in her flat—that I would pass on to her gentlemen. She laughed at my confusion. These weren't blood tests at all. These were sexual versions of the Olympic trials. She would have favored clients of hers take me out, spend the evening, and then rate me to her on how I did, both in bed and out. How were my manners? How did I dress? Did my breath smell sweet? And how good was I at sex? Again, I wanted to quit before I began. I don't think even airline pilots, who have the lives of thousands of people in their hands, went through a more rigorous vetting, which is the word now. I always hated being judged. I didn't like school because of the grades. I didn't like facing the stigma of failure. But, somehow, the higher the hurdle Claude set for me, the more I wanted to jump it. I guess she was a good motivator. Maybe it was the money.

" 'What if I don't like him?' I remember asking Claude when she informed me of my first date. 'You'll like him. Everybody likes him. He's one of the most attractive young men in Paris,' she said, with a great whiff of intolerance at my anxiety, making clear that it was *she* who was doing me the favor. The man, Yann, did call me up. He was so sure of himself, cocky, as if he knew he was going to 'score' with me. Which was the case.

"He told me we would be going to dinner at Maxim's, and on Friday night. That was black-tie night, the dressiest night of any restaurant in Paris, a throwback to the fin de siècle. It was the one night of the week where there was also an orchestra, and dancing. God, was I nervous. I needed a fancy dress, really fancy, which I lacked. And I had no idea how to waltz, or do whatever cheek-to-cheek dances they did at the fin de siècle. My parents never sent me to dancing school in Calais. I knew how to twist. From Chubby Checker. Dancers didn't touch anymore.

"I spent what seemed like a month's salary on an evening dress at a sale at Yves Saint Laurent. I was planning to wear it once, then bring it back and say it didn't fit. Helene had told me the name of a salesgirl to ask for who gave discounts to Claude girls. They apparently did enough volume purchases to make it worth Saint Laurent's while. I got the discount, but it was still a fortune, and I'll never forget the looks that the salesgirl gave me. Maybe I was imagining it, feeling guilty. I felt so naughty. It was like being back in Calais in confession. I even thought about going to a dancing school to take a couple of lessons after work. But when I went by the studio, on the rue La Fayette, all the pupils were little kids, who hated every second of it. I decided that I would just drink a lot of champagne and take my chances.

"The guy, Yann, was handsome, to be sure, but he was a real arrogant prick. He was tall, looked a little like Alain Delon, but not as pretty, more masculine, with great clothes, way better than mine. He drove a Porsche convertible, with the top down. It was winter, and it ruined my hairdo. But I tried to pretend I was having a gay time. He was very young, early twenties, younger than me, but you could tell he was a rich boy, a *fils de papa*, who had been everywhere, had every privilege, was a catch. I felt like he was a gigolo and that I was an old lady who was hiring him.

"Only once at dinner did I feel like a whore. We were slow dancing, which I could handle, no waltzes or rhumbas, thank God. There was this crazy Hungarian violinist circling around us playing 'Fascination.' And Yann said that in the old days, which meant before the war, Maxim's was a place where *women* were seen, but never *ladies*. I could have taken that as an insult, but then again, when I looked over in one corner and saw Paloma

Picasso, and in another saw Countess Jacqueline de Ribes, and then he pointed out Babe Paley, whom I didn't know, but whose husband, Yann said, was the television king of New York, I figured I was in good company. Although Yann did mention in passing that Babe Paley's husband was a Madame Claude client, we didn't discuss Madame Claude on our date. Otherwise, it might not have seemed like the 'date' we were pretending it to be.

"The night before this date, another panic had erupted when I got my period. I called Claude, who seemed annoyed by all my problems, which to her were not problems. Her problems were when the client wasn't happy. 'Of course you must go,' she insisted. 'He was in the army. He fought in Algeria. He's not afraid of blood. He's a man.' After Maxim's, Yann raced through Paris like Stirling Moss. He liked showing off. We went through the Etoile five times, almost getting killed each one. It was like foreplay for him. My hair was ruined. I was freezing. I'd have done anything to get out of that car.

"We went to a little lovers' hotel off the place des Ternes. It was a real letdown after Maxim's. The Ritz would have been a better follow-up. 'Nobody fucks at the Ritz,' Yann said. There was nothing kinky about the lovers' hotel, no ceiling mirrors or sex toys or anything like that. It just rented rooms by the hour, which the Ritz did not. It was discreet. I can't remember the sex. All I remember is that I was trying to be cute, play hard to get, and Yann accidentally tore the dress trying to pull it off. I was going to have it cleaned and try to return it, but now it was too late. Now I was in debt. All I could think about was paying for the dress.

"I think Yann was a little turned on by me, but he had a job to do, a checklist to complete, like a sanitation inspector of restaurants. Were there insects? How cold was the refrigerator? Was there old food behind the stove? Did the toilets flush? I do remember that Yann was *big,* things were messy, and the bedroom looked like a bloody crime scene. I made sure Yann left a big tip for the poor maid. We ended up laughing a lot. Sex can be absurd, and the odd thing here was the absence of passion and the tension that came with it. We had a fun time, and then we fucked. I was used to it, from Brian, so there was no loss of innocence. When I kissed Yann good morning as the sun was rising, it wasn't that 'I could have danced all night' feeling.

"Did I 'pass' the test? Who knew? All I know was that Claude gave me an envelope with six hundred dollars and arranged another test for me a week later. This one was with another of her 'junior playboys,' a dashing young hipster called Félix, whose picture I had often seen in the party pages of the magazines, in Saint-Tropez, Saint Moritz, Mykonos, Deauville, all the beautiful places where the beautiful people went. His family owned one of France's largest chains of grocery stores. Another heir. Yann represented the Establishment. He would grow up to be a banker, join Le Racing or Le Jockey, and marry someone his fancy family set him up with. I know Claude was selling these Cinderella stories. Her girls were thinking they could be the next Grace Kelly and marry their own Prince Rainier. They forgot that Grace Kelly was from a very rich Irish family in Philadelphia; plus, she was probably the biggest movie star in the world, after Marilyn Monroe.

"Every one of the dates could be that knight in shining armor who would sweep the girl off to his castle. From what I could see at the time, it was less the castle than the *hôtel de rendezvous,* and the only sweeping was by the maid after the mess we made. My new tester, Félix, seemed much more the Beatles generation, a less stuffy, longhaired guy who listened to rock and probably used marijuana, if not harder stuff. He looked and dressed like one of the Bee Gees. He had an apartment in New York and divided his time between the two cities, hanging out. He said he was thinking of becoming a film producer, which was a favorite nonoccupation of the idle rich.

"Félix wasn't going to test me at Maxim's. Instead, he invited me for sushi, which was a new thing then that I hadn't tried, at this tiny but extremely expensive Japanese restaurant on the rue Sainte-Anne. This was an area behind the Palais Royal that was both Japan town and boys town. I remember being shocked when he said, 'If you won't eat sushi, you won't eat pussy.' I showed him how game I was by eating every raw thing the chefs placed before me. I had grown up in oyster country, and it wasn't that different. I thought he was getting me primed for a ménage à trois, maybe with one of the exquisite geishalike waitresses who poured us sake, but his comment was only a passing observation.

"After dinner, we walked down the street, lined with gay hustlers, some outrageous in leather, boots, and chains, to Le Sept, a gay club for famous people, both gay and straight. The owner, a nightlife impresario named Fabrice, was a former hairdresser from Calais. Félix introduced us, as if we'd have something in common, like losers from nowhere who had made it in the big city. Fabrice was way ahead of me. He quickly left me and memories of Calais to welcome Mick Jagger. Wow! Mick Jagger and I in the same place. I felt totally out of it, at the mercy of Félix. I was like his accessory.

"But I knew I mustn't look uncomfortable. One of the hallmarks of a Claude girl was her adaptability. She had to seem right at home anywhere, whether in a château or a dungeon. Maxim's or Le Sept. I knew I was being tested. Félix said hello to Rudolf Nureyev, and to Kenzo, the designer of the hot line Jungle Jap. Because I was in the rag trade, I might have been able to have an intelligent chat with Kenzo, but he wasn't there to talk business. Cocaine was being passed around. I certainly could have used something to dull my anxiety, make me feel confident, as if I belonged. Again, I knew better. Félix partook, but I refused. There were a lot of drugs. Le Sept was like a pharmacy, cocaine,

Valium, Quaaludes, poppers. I had never done any. Orthodox Jews may have loved medicines, but they never did drugs. Nor did I.

"Claude was hard-line against drugs. She believed that drugs were what would turn an elegant courtesan into a desperate whore. I knew Félix had to enjoy his position as a tester, and he would inform on me in a second in order to keep it. I stuck with champagne, and then we went downstairs to this sweaty mirrored disco with all the beautiful people grooving on themselves to the Temptations and Marvin Gaye. There were no partners. Everybody was just dancing with everybody else or nobody but themselves. I almost wanted to ask Félix to get me out of there and escape to Maxim's.

"We danced until four in the morning. Félix had picked up this handsome Italian male model, who had come with a stunning Ford female model—I think from Holland. I thought they were a couple, until by night's end Félix and the Italian were a couple, and the Dutch model had disappeared. That was the way of clubs like that. I thought Félix would just send me home, but no such luck. Off we went, into the crack of dawn, with the Italian, to a really grotty gay lovers' hotel in the neighborhood. Gay couples were lined up at the check-in desk. I was the only woman. The boys, mostly gorgeous, gave me the funniest stares and smiles. Félix, the grocery heir who could have sprung for a suite at the nearby Ritz, got a bigger kick out of this kinky slumming.

"The best part of the evening was my relief that the sheets and the room were spotlessly clean, which was the opposite of what the lobby promised. I had had serial sex with Brian and his brothers, but I had never done a threesome before, much less one with two pretty men who might be gay, or bi. By morning's light, when we squeezed into Félix's XKE to go home, I still wasn't sure. Let me just say that Félix's gusto at the sushi bar was a preview of his oral skill in the bedroom, both with me and with his new friend. He was a taster as much as a tester. He dropped the Italian off first, kissing him deeply on the lips. I sensed a major connection had been made. The fact that he would probably never want to see me again did not leave me depressed, as if it had been a bad date, with my expectations dashed. I had no expectations, not those kind.

"After my first two test dates, Madame Claude made no comment whatsoever as to whether Yann or Félix had liked me, or if not, why. Nor did she ask me how I liked them. I didn't ask her how I did. She was like the Sphinx, impossible to read, and I didn't want to seem too eager. Hard-to-get worked with men, and it may have worked with her. The fact that I was still being paid and tested meant I was still alive in this crazy game of love.

"When she told me that my next test was Baron de Rothschild, I was totally blown away. This meant that I had 'arrived.' I later learned he was one of her senior testers, one of the great ladies' men of France and the world. In France and in England, the Rothschilds were like gods, the richest family in Europe. I didn't think they even *talked* to ordinary people, much less *slept* with them. That she even knew Baron de Rothschild was proof that Madame was real, that all these stories about her famous clients were true. Otherwise, she might have been just another madam sending girls to Arabs and expense-account execs.

"Then again, I thought maybe it was a huge con job. Maybe she was just saying it was the baron. That could have been part of the test. Maybe it was just some guy saying he was the baron. There were a lot of guys like that in Paris. Just go into any bar off the Champ-Elysées, and you will meet more 'royalty' than you'll find in the *Almanach de Gotha*. Yet both Yann and Felix had been 'real,' so maybe it was true. If so, this was definitely the call-girl version of Cinderella.

"I began believing it for real when Claude gave me the address on the rue Masseran, in the seventh, behind the Bon

Marché department store. I walked by it a week in advance, just to case it. It was a palace, a genuine palace, one of those *hôtels particuliers* in this area near the Hôtel des Invalides that had triggered the French Revolution and got the royals guillotined. Was this a joke? Why would he have me come to his home? The only person I could speak to about this was Helene.

"If anybody was a Rothschild type, it would have been her, but she had never met him, she said. She had only had one tester, a young playboy type, and that was that. But she told me not to worry. She had been in a number of these *hôtels particuliers*. The wives were never there. They were always traveling. The rich people had country houses, beach houses, ski houses. If I were being sent, the coast was clear. It was normal. If you had a house like that, Helene said, why go to some little hotel? She speculated the wife, whoever she was, was probably at the Château Lafite, down in Bordeaux. I hadn't realized until then that Elie de Rothschild was the Rothschild who owned Lafite, which was the best wine in the world, which I had never tasted. Even Brian said it was too expensive. I was doubly intimidated.

"Before my date, I decided that I would be wise to do some homework, no matter how nervous it was bound to make me feel. So I went to a library and looked at some old copies of *Paris Match* and *Point de Vue*. What a mistake. To begin with, Elie de Rothschild, then in his late fifties, looked incredibly handsome, in a way that combined David Niven's elegance and Sean Connery's masculinity. He had been a war hero, and he looked it. He had an eye patch, from a recent accident playing polo. Then there was his wife, who looked like she could have been his sister, plain and elegant. She was as rich as he was, from another famous Jewish banking family. They had been in love since childhood. She was herself a great art collector and had one of the best collections in Europe. Her close friend, according to the press, was Greta Garbo. She lived on a different planet from me. Still, she was his age, and while you could call her a queen, you couldn't call her sexy. Like the queen of England, Elizabeth.

"Although the French papers were too afraid to print a negative word about the sacred Rothschilds, I somehow learned from the English papers—I read both; the English ones were much better—that the baron had had a famously 'secret' affair with Winston Churchill's daughter-in-law, Pamela Harriman, who became Bill Clinton's ambassador to France and died at seventy-six, after suffering a cerebral hemmorhage in the Ritz Hotel's swimming pool. On paper, she seemed like the model Madame Claude girl. She came from a poor but noble family and had had high-profile affairs with a lot of other famous men from all over who, I would get to know, were Claude clients—Aly Khan, Jock Whitney, Gianni Agnelli, William Paley, Frank Sinatra, the Broadway producer Leland Hayward. Averell Harriman apparently was too cheap, or too old, to use Claude girls; yet when I saw her picture, a busty redhead, Pamela Harriman didn't seem like a Claude girl at all, not on the surface.

"Claude hated busty. She made big-breasted girls who were otherwise thin get breast-reduction surgery. Pamela H. had a round face, which didn't have the angular, Nefertiti look that Claude defined as aristocratic; plus, she was a redhead. Claude thought all redheads were Irish maids. She had the strongest opinions. I surely wasn't the baron's type. Then I thought about the wives of these other famous clients, and none of them looked like Pamela Harriman, either. I took Mia Farrow, for example, who was more like me, but tinier and with less shape. She was like Twiggy. So Pamela Harriman had to have something else. I think she was just a status symbol. What man wouldn't want to have Churchill's daughter-in-law, and she turned it into a chain letter from there. That made me feel a little better.

"But no less nervous. On the appointed day, I showed up at the rue Masseran. There were liveried butlers and uniformed maids, and so much help that I felt like I was on a state visit. The men servants all wore white gloves. I would have thought one of the many staff would have told on me to the absent baroness. But I guess nobody informs on a Rothschild, including myself. All I can say is that he was one of the greatest gentlemen I have met in my lifetime. He served me the best food, and, of course, the best wine I had ever tasted, and showed me the finest art I had ever seen, from Rembrandt to Picasso, and gave me some hints how to look at it. In fact, my tour of his art collection inspired me to eventually get into that business.

"The evening was beyond perfect. Except for one thing. I assumed that the "arrangements" had been made with Madame Claude, as was the case on my other tests, and that she would take care of me when I saw her. I was called by Madame Claude later that week. She said to come over. That seemed like great news. She wouldn't have me face-to-face if she wanted to tell me I had failed her tests, that the men hated me.

"I also assumed she would give me my *petit cadeau*. Instead, all she did was tell me that she had made my appointment with her plastic surgeon, Dr. Elbaz, to start the process of getting my nose job. That was her way of saying that I had run her gauntlet and would now have the honor of joining her stable of women. That was supposed to be an honor, the top rung of any ladder a young woman might reach. It was kind of like a fake prize. You pass the test of having to make love in every contortion with strange men, and your big reward is getting to go under the knife.

"It got worse. Claude next informed me that I, not she, would be paying for it. Helene, who was perfect and had needed nothing, had not told me about this. I was taken aback. I couldn't afford it, I started to say, but Claude cut me off. She would advance the surgery fee. I would pay her back out of future earnings. That, I soon found out, would be the case with clothes as well, anything couture that I would need for balls and events even fancier than Maxim's. 'You'll make it back,' she assured me, at which point I mentioned the baron's having not paid me. 'Don't be a *whore!*' " Claude barked. 'Or you can leave right now.' I guess the moral of the story was that nobody charges a Rothschild, not even Madame Claude."

Véronique did get the plastic surgery and went on to work for a little over three years for Madame Claude. That was the typical tour of duty, though some Claudettes blew out after a month or two, and others stayed on the rolls for a decade or more, dropping in and out between romances and divorces. The goal, at least as stated by Claude herself, was to marry her girls off, ostensibly into a union that provided even more money and security for the swan than Claude could herself. Véronique never married. As she put it, "I didn't have to." She made a small fortune with Claude, serving the market that Claude foresaw for her rich Westernized Lebanese and Persian industrialists and politicians, none of whom ever wore a tribal robe in her presence. She didn't have to flavor her bilingual dialogue (the Lebanese preferred French, the Persians English) with Yiddishisms.

What Madame Claude perceived as "Jewish" (given her much-debated biography, it may have taken one to know one), her clients embraced as witty, urbane, and immensely verbal, the quintessence of Paris (or London) sophistication. Claude under-lined this by having Véronique subscribe to every trendy jour-nal in Paris, London and, New York, *Point de Vue, Tatler, The Spectator, W, Vanity Fair,* the gossip columns of the assorted tab-loids, so Véronique could successfully name-drop on two conti-nents. She became a virtual Pan Am commuter, shuttling between New York and Paris almost every week for different dates. Despite Claude's reputation for bold-faced names, the only celebrity Véronique ever serviced was the French pop star Claude François, who wrote "My Way" and who died by being electro-cuted in his bathtub at age thirty-nine.

In a short time, ironically, Véronique developed a Jewish

clientele in Manhattan, specifically in two areas, real estate moguls and, especially, garment moguls, in whose argot she had
achieved her fluency with her job in Manchester. However, Véronique had no desire to go home again, neither to Calais nor to
Manchester. Inspired by her first encounter with world-class
connoisseurship on that superficially unremunerative evening
with Elie de Rothschild, she started spending her time, and her
income, at the museums and art galleries of the cities where
Claude's assignations took her. She caught the eye of a famous
art dealer, an ostensibly happily married family man with whom
she began an affair. He had no idea of her secret life with Madame Claude, even though the sex he enjoyed was the art of a
prodigy. Claude had a significant clientele in the art world, both
at Sotheby's and Christie's and among the top gallerists.

Claude had missed the art boat for Véronique. She saw her as
a rag doll, not a gallery girl. Véronique's first romance didn't
work out, but several other genuinely passionate art-driven affairs later, she hit pay dirt. After a stint as mistress, she became
partner in a very important gallery. She became a working girl
again, but for the first time, Madame Claude included, she was
doing something that she loved. Véronique rode the wave of contemporary art to a fortune of her own, exceeded by only a few
of the gilded unions brokered by Madame Claude. As with many
of her successes, Claude was prouder of Véronique than Véronique of Claude. Once Véronique left, they never spoke again,
though Claude often spoke *of* her, albeit never by name, when, in
her retirement, Claude would reminisce about some of her most
successful alumnae.

Chapter 5

HEADMISTRESS

$\mathcal{H}$ow rich was Madame Claude? In a word, very. Just do the math. Taking Véronique's quotes of six hundred dollars a night from the early seventies, which was midway in Claude's "first empire," between 1957 and 1977, a Claudette who worked 250 days a year, the equivalent of a normal workweek, would earn $150,000 annually, tax-free. And that was someone Claude might call a lazy girl, who did only overnights, without a few three-hundred-dollar quickie nooners thrown in, nor the far more remunerative foreign trips, which could yield $7,500 or more a week. Out of this Claude would take her 30 percent commission, or fifty thousand dollars per girl annually. On the average, she always had thirty girls on her rolls, to meet the surging global demand.

That adds up to a gross annual revenue of $1,500,000, tax free. And French taxes were high, if not confiscatory. Claude's overhead was low, just rent and telephone. There was all that surgery and dentistry and diction lessons that Claude always fronted, but she invariably got it back Those were self-improvement costs that the girls rightfully had to bear. There have been no stories about girls who took the surgery and ran. Once the effort began, the would-be swans stayed with the program. Unlike in so many other countries, there were no police bribes and payoffs. Not in France, where Claude may have been *getting* payoffs from the Elysée Palace and the quai d'Orsay that were more than she was making from her girls.

The bottom line, and Madame Claude was purely bottom line, was that she was a multimillionairess, up there with Coco Chanel as the richest self-made woman in the country. Not bad for someone from the wrong side of the tracks in Angers. Claude loved being rich. That was her self-identity. Money symbolized power, and power quickly went to Claude's head. She went nearly twenty years keeping her mouth zipped tightly shut. But when Jacques Quoirez convinced her that she was so powerful, so important, and so untouchable that she could write a memoir, a notion seconded by his sister, lit-queen Françoise Sagan, Claude was hubristic enough to jump at the bait.

A memoir at fifty-two? Why not? She could write even more memoirs. And she did. After all, Sagan was only eighteen when she hit the jackpot with *Bonjour Tristesse.* Claude was convinced by her best friends, Jacques and Françoise, that it was her duty, as the greatest expert on sex in the world, to rise to the occasion in this most literate and literary of countries, where a book was a power and an honor unto itself. Her memoir would be the last word on sex, the Book of Love.

In *Allô, Oui,* the result of Jacques's inspiration, there is a jarring shift of tone from the chapter where Madame Claude, just opening her service, waits by the phone in an anxiety state to the next, when she describes how she got her girls and how she transformed them. This is hubris speaking. There is a leap from diffidence to arrogance, the utter and unalloyed self-confidence of someone who not only dominates her profession but holds an impregnable monopoly over it.

If France was regarded throughout the world as the capital of *l'amour toujours,* Madame Claude was the biggest brand name in the world of *l'amour luxe.* She was rich and famous and had a genuine mystique. Everyone in the world, or at least those in the luxe world who knew her brand, wanted to read what she had to say. Of course she was writing in 1975, at the height of her power, with the overweening pride that came directly before her fall, and her flight from France. It is fascinating nonetheless to witness the confidence Madame Claude had in herself and in her elite corps.

The tone is set by the book's prefatory quote from La Rochefoucauld. *"En amour, il ne faut pas craindre d'être dupe."* "In love, don't be afraid of being tricked." Claude was trumpeting the triumph of her grand illusion. Don't question it. Just lie back and enjoy it. Assuming, naturally, that you could afford it. Claude became aware of her global hegemony through her magic telephone, which was ringing off the hook with requests from all over the world, particularly from the big business centers of New York, London, Milan, Tokyo, São Paolo. Surely these places had luxury madams who catered to their carriage trade. But that trade was calling Paris, and not just when it was going to France for a visit. The rise of jet travel in the sixties allowed the rapid export of deluxe sex. Claude was doing a huge "male-order" business. Plus, it was duty-free.

In 1971, Xaviera Hollander, the Manhattan-based Dutch call girl/madam, wrote the world's number-one bestseller, *The Happy Hooker.* Claude, who had never been to New York at that point, had assumed that Gotham had her glamorous counterpart, perhaps many of them. But the "high-class" business Hollander described was one of fifty-dollar quickies on Castro Convertible sofas in shag-carpeted apartments that were forever being vacated following vice raids. If this was the best that New York could offer, it was evident that Madame Claude had the luxury niche all to herself.

As the mistress of her domain, Claude took as her role model the head monitor of the fancy convent that may in itself have been a figment of her imagination. If she seemed "harsh," as she put it, it was because the head monitor at the Vistandines had also been harsh. Call it tough love. Claude professed a fondness for all her charges, all of whom were special, though some more special than others. Her job, her duty to them, was to "correct their weaknesses." She admitted that she did become "attached" to the "most gifted" and pushed these teacher's pets harder because of her great expectations for them.

She regarded her operation not as an out-call brothel, but as an academy, the Miss Porter's of sex, if she knew what Miss Porter's was. There was no girls' school in France, anywhere for that matter, that was as selective and as exclusive as hers. Madame Claude was able to turn snobbery into an erogenous zone. In doing so, she developed an elaborate business philosophy that, as a sop to France's Catholic shame, was partly an apologia for what she was doing but mostly a bold advertisement for herself.

"I do not recruit," she often declared. She didn't have to. She had so many applicants from so many countries that she described her erotic finishing school as a "tower of Babel." And she described the process by which she "finished" the candidates she selected as "ennobling" these women. She took girls who were already aristocrats of nature and refined them into aristocrats of nurture, not to mention the long-term goal of getting them listed in the *Social Register* or *Burke's Peerage*. She outlined the "3Bs" that any of her candidates had to have an A in before she would take them on: Beauty, Brains, Bed.

Those became Madame Claude's famous "Three Conditions," the sinful converse of the Ten Commandments. A girl had to have them just to get in Claude's door, but she had to bring them all to the pinnacle of potential if she were going to succeed as a woman by Claude's strict terms. Excellence in only one *B* was a failure, Claude wrote. Two out of three "wasn't bad," she conceded, guaranteeing the girl would probably make serious money with her and possibly, but not surely, marry well. But a trifecta, superiority in all three *B*s, guaranteed, Claude noted ironically, that the girl was ready to leave her for the big time. "I was never

wrong," Claude said. Unlike the alumnae of girls' schools, however, Claude's summa cum laude graduates never came back to
a reunion.

If beauty was in the eye of the beholder, the eyes of Madame
Claude were sharper than any others. If a girl were *too* beautiful, Claude wouldn't take her, because the goddess would be too
self-absorbed to "practice her art with the required rigor," as
Claude put it, with a pomposity worthy of the court of the Sun
King. She also turned down girls she judged to be nymphoma-
niacs, on one hand, or too proper, on the other, as well as girls
who came to her out of sheer curiosity.

The Claudian application process was one of self-selection.
Girls she considered "ugly" or "unattractive" would rarely darken
her door. Most women who sold their bodies, Claude said, did
so because they couldn't *give* them away. She derided such women
as "stupid." Then again, these were prostitutes and her swans
were not, and *vive la différence*. And sometimes, out of a combination of perversity and generosity, Claude would choose an ugly
duckling and turn her into a swan just because she knew how to
do it. "I loved giving an ugly girl the chance to redo her life,"
she wrote, describing how a "redone nose, straight white teeth,
a loss of five kilos, and a sophisticated hairdresser" could work
miracles.

Claude told the story of one such beneficiary, a German girl
whose only assets were her height and her brains. At first, Claude
thought she was a transvestite, and a hideous one at that. Claude
cataloged her defects (she loved to take such inventories) too
skinny, big nose, jutting jaw, acned skin, frizzy hair, teeth so
crooked that she couldn't smile, and breasts so small that they
underscored the candidate's "ambiguity." Above all, she had a
gloomy demeanor. "How can you be cheerful when you look like
that?" Claude asked. Cruelty thy name used to be Fernande Grudet, who may have beheld a reflection of her former self.

Claude went to work and paid for months of expensive

surgery, dentistry, and dermatology. Claude had proudly created a bionic woman, her own Frankenstein creature, yet a
perfect beauty and not a freak. The girl had acquired so much
debt, it seemed that she would be forever indentured to Claude
to pay it off. However, one of the first clients to whom Claude
unveiled her creation was a Los Angeles real estate magnate,
who decided on the spot that she was the greatest "natural
beauty" he had ever seen. Because even in the mid-sixties Los
Angeles was on the cutting edge, as it were, of the cosmetic-
surgery revolution, such man-made, as opposed to God-given,
beauty may have been in the eyes of the Bel Air beholder. Wanting to rescue her from bondage to Claude, he paid Claude a
lavish "finder's fee," which more than covered all the makeover
work Claude had invested in, brought the girl to L.A., married
her, and transformed her socially the way Claude had physically. Today, she is one of the mainstays of L.A. society, a pillar
of the arts and philanthropy. If and when the name Madame
Claude comes up at parties, as Madame Claude's legend in L.A.
is as great as it is in Paris, there is not the slightest glimmer of
recognition, much less remorse, from Lady Frankenstein. Madame Claude? What's that? A new French maid service for the
Angeleno elite?

Most girls, alas, were beyond miracles, especially the small
girls. Like herself, though Claude would never compare herself
to her charges, even if she knew she was remaking them in the
image she would have loved for herself. The self-loathing was
always an undercurrent, but never expressed. The key thing
was size. Bigger was better in every way. That was the bottom
line. Professional models were tall for a reason. Rich men, Claude
insisted, preferred the tallest girls, just as they preferred the
biggest houses and the longest yachts. Furthermore, the larger
girls were tougher, better able to handle the physical demands
of Claude's job of jobs, and not so much the sexual workouts,

but the endless travel, the skiing, the swimming, the tennis, all
the games they had to play to keep their men happy, the all-night
parties, the daybreak power breakfasts. Being a trophy was hard
work. It could take its toll. Big girls didn't cry.

Beauty, Claude could lecture on. Brains were something you
either had or you didn't, and she gave the impression that most
of her applicants came to her door on rue de Marignan straight
from their philosophy classes at the Sorbonne. When they did
not, she took pride in her pedagogy and ability to acculturate.
She often shared a story of one of her great clients, an industrial
tycoon who was an amoral capitalist six days a week but never
on Sunday, when he spent his mornings at Mass praying for for-
giveness.

His church was Saint-Eustache, the Gothic masterpiece looming over Les Halles, where Louis XIV had taken Communion
and Mozart had buried his mother and Molière had been married. The tycoon, like most of Claude's tycoons, was a terrible
snob. He had to be in the right company, when he fucked as well
as when he prayed. One Sunday, he was shocked out of his sin
when, in the cathedral's Chapel of the Virgin, he saw two German Claude girls with whom he had enjoyed a particularly lascivious ménage à trois now equally enjoying a celestial Bach
cantata. Claude girls could go high as well as low. That agility
was part of Claude's program for creating the total woman.

Back to the 3Bs. As for the bed, that was something high-class
courtesans simply did not discuss. It was infra dig. Claude took
Coco Chanel's dictum "Elegance is refusal" and put it in a sexual context, calling her brand of love "controlled eroticism." Hers
was the art of the tease. The essence, the reassurance, the war-
ranty of the Claude client experience was the guarantee of sub-
mission. Refusal was not an option. However, the elaborate
euphemism of the cash exchange and the near-Kabuki level of
the sexual aspect of a Claude encounter created the impression

that a Claude girl was unbelievably hard to get. And the only way to get her was to be part of the world's power elite. The real turn-on was the exclusivity, not the lubricity.

All Claude would say about what happened in her bedrooms was that there was "not a series of degrading acts," but, rather, a process of education, where the Claudette became a "professor of desire" and the tycoon, who was in control of his world, if not *the* world, became the pupil and got his own sentimental education in the art of love. At the same time, the girl could never let the man feel that he was not the prime mover. She had to *appear* submissive yet *be* dominant, all in the goal of convincing the man that he was a great lover, going places with the girl that he would never go with his wife. Claude admitted that men were "disarmingly naïve" when it came to making love. "Faking it," when it came to the girl's pleasure, was not only perfectly legitimate; such Method acting was de rigueur. The Madame Claude academy of *l'amour* was in this way less Miss Porter's than Stella Adler.

Madame Claude believed that her grand illusions were the key to the job. Academy it might be called, but a job it was, or perhaps an internship, a *stage* on the way up to the big payday of a royal marriage. The pay was great and the girl should be more than grateful for it. The last thing she should ever expect was an *orgasm*. "The women's empire," she wrote, "is like the Roman Empire: seek pleasure and you will be defeated." If the rising women's liberation movement had even been aware of Madame Claude, it would have come after her far harder than the French tax authorities ever did.

Nobody could match Claude in her objectification of women, notwithstanding the enormous income she enabled them to earn and the connections that would make so many of their lives the stuff of fairy tales. Looks and sex were too high a price for "modern" women to pay, too much a Faustian bargain for enlightened and liberated women. Claude, who would be the devil in their eyes, laughed in their faces. You want to give up the world for an orgasm you can probably never have. That was her attitude. She quoted statistics. Sixty percent of all women cannot have orgasms, and 90 percent cannot have orgasms "like a man. The marvelous apple of Eve," she wrote, "has become the panacea of all the ills of our sex."

Claude didn't see herself as the serpent in the Garden of Eden. She saw herself as a girl's best friend, a wise voice of reality in a world gone amok. "After too much time forbidding everything, now everything is promised, and women, as always, will be the victims of it." Women have all the power over men, who may be stronger and richer and favored by the legal system, because, "once in a while, they have the need to love us. When a strong woman feels the same way about a man, she becomes like a weak and vulnerable man." Claude wasn't calling for women to storm the barricades in the battle of the sexes. Woman had already won. They should just shut up and not declare their victory. Where pleasure was concerned, Claude was telling them to fake it. A woman's pleasure is different, Claude declared, and if anybody knew about pleasure, it was this woman who said that women over forty shouldn't have sex at all. "If they have to let out more cries than they are actually experiencing, my God, what's the big deal?"

Again, it must be remembered that Madame Claude, writing in the seventies, was not perceived as the anti–Gloria Steinem, France's answer to Anita Bryant. France was a royalist patriarchy, a superelitist man's world that Claude was catering to, but it wasn't that different from the elitist microcosm of Harvard University during that same period. A 2017 study in *The Harvard Crimson,* entitled "Feminist Hysteria: A History of Sexual Violence at Harvard," describes the Harvard of the sixties and seventies as a kind of harem where privileged young Harvard men were allowed to have their often unwanted way, without reprisal, with equally privileged, albeit unequally treated, young

Radcliffe women. "Everything was done to facilitate the acquisition of husbands and wives," noted a Radcliffe freshman who left the supposed Eden of Cambridge after being raped by a Harvard senior football hero in his sports car, with no action taken either by the university or the local police. From Harvard to Hollywood, sexual harassment, which was just in the process of being named, was rampant. By contrast, Madame Claude's girls were not getting raped; they were getting rich.

Money may have been enough for Madame Claude, who never married, other than for two immigration scams. Money was necessary, but by no means sufficient, not enough for the students in an academy that was a cross between a school for scandal and a school for wives, pace Molière and Sheridan. Entering this academy, the girls' three most popular motivations, according to Claude, were all cash-related. The first was agrarian, to be able to move back to the country and buy a farm. The second was urban, to open a fancy lingerie shop. And the third was economic, to invest in the stock market, under the tutelage of their hoped-for banker and broker clients. By the time Claude had trained them, their goals became far more elevated.

Claude liked to crow that marriage, specifically the institution's unimaginative, regimented, and predictable sex, if there was any at all, was what brought men to her. On the other hand, it was to this very same institution that Claude was preparing her charges to go on to once they completed their work at the institution that was hers. This was Claude's sexual paradox, a variant of Harvard sociologist Daniel Bell's *The Cultural Contradictions of Capitalism.* Call the Claude version, if you will, "The Concupiscent Contradictions of Conjugality."

Claude didn't regard marriage as surrender or defeat. To her, it was sweet victory, long-term payback for men's exploitation of women. This grand bargain of love for money was seen by Claude as the prime form of revenge. "Every woman hurt in love by a man is ready to avenge herself on the next one by taking his money," she wrote. No one ever called Claude sentimental or starry-eyed. Getting that money was winning the battle of the sexes, she assured her girls.

Once the battle was won, the vows of matrimony did not have to be a prison of misery. After a while, the husband would stop bothering his wife for sex; he would have returned to Madame Claude for his next mistress, as the chain of fools went on and on. Meanwhile, the wife, once vested, could begin to "exert talents, until then unused" to take control of her husband's business empire. The empress could become the emperor, getting to savor all the "guy stuff" of big business that women of the time were excluded from by a very low glass ceiling. Claude didn't rule out the nonmarital road to success; her own creation, the unmarried art dealer Véronique, was someone she bragged about as having beat the system, just as Claude had herself. But in the seventies, the *entrepreneuse*, whether in France or elsewhere, was a rara avis.

Every once in a while, a Claude girl would have a "conversion." The Damascus moment for one of her swans, who had taken a recent interest in yoga and spirituality, came when she went on a Claude-suggested cultural vacation to see the Greek temples in Sicily. She decided it would be a classical gas to spend a few days in a nudist colony not far from the Valley of the Temples in Agrigento. The place was a sort of naked Club Med, which itself was a beloved French institution. The Claudette loved flaunting her perfect body, but, until then, such exhibitions were for the costly delectation of Claude's millionaires.

This time, however, her *corpore sanum* caught the eye of a naked hippie whose body was as perfect as the girl's. Upon her return to Paris, she announced to Claude that she had found true love and was renouncing all her materialist desires to move to New York and marry her destitute Adonis. She had enough of the high life. Now she was ready to take the vow of poverty. However, when she got to New York, she found out that her

inamorata was actually the son of a Greek tycoon who had gone
to the colony to see if anyone could love him for his pure self
and nothing else. The girl immediately left him, feeling that she
had been duped and betrayed. She never got over it, refusing to
retake her Claudian vows of wealth and comfort. She married a
noncelebrity Greek chef in Astoria, Queens, almost as if to prove
her point. At least she ate well.

Madame Claude was all about the money. Her girls' basic
training was to achieve the goal of marrying a millionaire. Not
a title, which was nice, but impecunious titles were ubiquitous
in postwar Europe. Claude had to teach her girls how to separate the glitter from the gold, and to go for the latter. She also
had to teach them how to become comfortable around great
wealth and the pomp and ceremony attendant thereto. This was
no easy task for many of these stunning but initially unsophisticated wannabe farm girls. The myth of Claude was that her girls
were the regally lovely, secretly oversexed daughters of royalty.
(Think Lady Di, ahead of her actual time.) The reality was that
only a few came from top families, either in terms of lineage or
assets. Claude's challenge, and one she rose to admirably, was
creating this grand illusion out of a usually mundane reality.

Where did her girls actually come from, then? Madame
Claude was as big an advocate of ethnic profiling as Donald
Trump. Today she would be attacked for being as politically in-
correct as one could be. In her time, she was as politically *correct* as one could be, given her connections at the top of the French
political system. This was a system that looked the other way
for two decades as far as enforcing any laws against her were
concerned. Because snobbery and prejudice were ingrained in
the character of the French colonialist upper classes that she
served, Claude reveled in being as ruthless in her stereotyping
as the Nazis who had allegedly held her prisoner at Ravensbruck.
And for all that despised imprisonment, her favorite ethnicity

by far was that of her former enemies and captors. Over half of her girls were German.

Why Germans? Let me count the ways was Claude's frequent explanation. "The teeth, the breasts, the height, the health," she went on and on, in her favored catalog mode, sounding as if she were echoing the Führer's description of the "master race." And it wasn't only looks. They were organized, precise, showed up on time, and were always ready to go at the call of duty. Claude often cited as a prime example of why she liked Germans a Hamburg mannequin who always had three separate suitcases, Vuitton of course, fully packed and ready for a different kind of assignation, or assignment. There was one bag for, say, the sea in Sardinia, one for a weekend at the château in Bordeaux, and one for a business affair in New York or Milan. The Germans, as Claude extolled them, worked like the peasant farmer's daughters who had won the genetic lottery that they usually embodied, having come to Paris mostly to become models. The one catch was the "peasant" bit. That didn't fit the Claude fantasy that these were blue-blooded descendants of the Red Baron or von Hindenburg.

But that was where Claude came in, challenging these girls to discover their inner aristocrat, to learn to love those Bach cantatas. And what girl didn't have fun dressing up and pretending to be a baroness? Claude did her part, once the medical and dental procedures were done (less necessary with the Germans than with any others) by hiring a whole retinue of Henry Higginses to Pygmalionize the girls. There were diction teachers (voice and accent were vital), dance teachers, tennis teachers, horseback-riding teachers, ski instructors, and many more. If a girl had some natural talent, like playing the piano, Claude would send them for music lessons to make them even better. For example, she had one client, a highly successful businessman but frustrated classical pianist, who liked playing Chopin in the nude to whomever Claude dispatched to him. When one girl turned out to be a classical pianist who joined him for a duet, he told Claude it had been the happiest night of his life. In many ways, Madame Claude was the precursor of the modern "tiger mom" who wants to program her offspring for the Ivy League, as driven as the evergreen New York social climber who wants her kids to have all the contacts and advantages that she never had. "If it were up to me, I would have had nothing but Germans," Claude said.

"The true background didn't really matter," said a Paris resident and Danish count who married two of Claude's German girls and saw many others. One of the wives died young; the other left him for an Arab oil sheikh. "A lot of French aristocrats married these girls. They were beautiful. They had good manners. They didn't talk too much." But what about their lack of pedigree? What did you say about the girl you were taking home to your countess mother, to your snoopy aunts? Wasn't the girl's family the first thing they would ask about? "Not really," the count said. "A lot of us, me included, were lazy boys, bums, if you wish, playboys on our family's money. We might not have been the first sons, the protectors of the line. Our mothers would be delighted to be marrying us off. They didn't ask that many questions. It was the looks. That was what mattered. The Claude girls looked like aristocrats, at least what regular people who went to movies thought aristocrats were supposed to look like. Actually, lots better. You should see my female cousins."

After the Germans, the remainder of the Claude roster was a United Nations of pulchritude. She had her usual strong opinions about every ethnicity. Because she had a lot of English and American clients, she wanted as many English and American girls as she could find. Aside from models, who would come to her through Ford and other agencies, Americans were in short supply. Getting them was even harder because, aside from Nevada, prostitution was illegal in the United States. The 1910 Mann Act, which felonized the transport of women across state lines for "immoral purposes," reduced, in the public mind, all forms of prostitution, high or low, into the catchall, reverse-racist epithet of "white slavery." Despite such celebrity madams as New York's Polly Adler, who in 1953 wrote the bestselling book about her Manhattan brothel, *A House Is Not a Home,* by the 1960s the attitude of most Americans toward prostitution, however euphemized, was "nice girls don't." And in post-Eisenhower America, every female seemed to want to be thought of as a "nice girl."

In England, on the other hand, the nation-shaking sex scandals of the sixties and seventies had given the oldest profession a new mystique. Now it was seen as the fastest ticket up and out of the slough of despond that was the unshakable English class system. First it was the Profumo scandal, where two poor country girls, Christine Keeler and Mandy Rice-Davies, became strippers, then hookers, slept their way to the top of that class system, and then toppled the Conservative government of Prime Minister Harold Macmillan in 1964. Then in 1973, the very kinky commercial dalliances of two top ministers, Lords Lambton and Jellicoe, helped unseat the government of Prime Minister Edward Heath.

Lambton's mistress and dominatrix, Norma Levy, worked for the "Mayfair Madam" Jean Horn, who, before the Lambton affair, had been Madame Claude's occasional correspondent procuress in Britain. (Lord Lambton, the earl of Durham, was also a Claude regular in Paris.) When on occasion one of the two cross-Channel madams' clients would call on short notice in the other's city, suitable last-minute arrangements would be made. In general, though, Claude, control freak that she was, preferred not to entrust her clients to the arms of a stranger. The fact she was scandal-proof, while Jean Horn was not, only underscored this point of concern.

In any event, the fame of these illicit romances sent many ambitious English girls, many quite posh, scurrying across the Channel, seeking to enroll in the Claude academy of the fine but secret arts. In general, Claude didn't care for them. While they tended to have lovely English rose complexions, and, if the right class, then the right accent, their diet of Wimpy burgers and pork pies did not make for the right figure. Furthermore, Claude did not take to what she called their "whimsical" personalities, which sounded like something from *Mary Poppins*. Many of them came across to her as "bored," with a uniquely British sense of ironic humor that did not play well outside of the Sceptered Isle. They were fun only if the man drew them out, which was not the duty of Claude clients, who expected to be played to, not to play.

Even more bored were the Scandinavians. Even if they resembled Greta Garbo, which would have endeared them to Claude, they often had Garbo's "I want to be alone" aloofness, which was anathema to the good show a Claude girl had to put on. Claude may have wanted "controlled eroticism," but not *that* controlled. She lumped all the Swedes, the Danes, and the Norwegians together in one white, snowy blur, unable to tell one from another, not that she wanted to. She could get the same Aryan looks, plus alacrity, from the Germans, and be done with it.

Then there were the Italians, of whom Claude had very few. Claude complained that inside of every Italian call girl was a "mama" waiting to get out. Her Italian girls would fall madly in love on the first date, even if the date lasted just an hour, and start planning the wedding and the family. Of course, the clients could feel this and run for the hills. Claude was all for marriage, but in due course. She wanted to keep her girls for at least two or three years, to earn out her investment in them and then get an appreciable return. If that made them sound like chattels, so be it. Claude didn't get to the top by altruism. Even fairy godmothers had expenses to meet.

One might have expected a supersnob profiler like Madame

Claude to have been unreconstructedly racist, as well. Because she was market-driven, as they might say at Harvard Business School, she was only partially racist. She grudgingly conceded that *many men* had "exotic" tastes, which ran to "Eurasians" and, to a lesser extent, to *"les métisses de Noirs."* She couldn't seem to bring herself to say "Asians" or "blacks." To her, if her clients were going to walk on the wild side, they would go only so far. Gentlemen preferred mixed. Granting that *"les Asiatiques"* had grace, soft skin, and mysterious smiles, she then decimated them by saying they were terrible in bed, way too passive to please a normal man. Embracing the stereotype, she went on to say that such passivity was a trap, arguing that these women were nothing but eastern Trojan horses, calculating masters posing as meek slaves.

Where blacks were concerned, Madame Claude took a "go back to Africa" approach more worthy of George Wallace than Charles de Gaulle. She had found a few *superbe Noirs,* part-black runway models whose feline grace and gazelle bodies left most white girls looking stiff and mannered. She had admitted the models into her charmed circle, usually at the insistence of her German clients. But it had been a waste of her time, because they didn't stay long enough for them to "earn out." Instead, they had followed "tribal traditions," going home to the Dark Continent to marry local men and live in primitive villages, eating manioc but surely dreaming of the caviar at Maxim's that they had given up.

Lastly, Madame Claude set her viperish sights on the French, whom she obviously held to an even higher standard than any other nationality. Accordingly, she took them hard to task. To begin with, she exploded the myth that, just as nobody could cook like the French, nobody could fuck like them, either. All they really had was a mystique, that French women were the world's best lovers. Men, specifically non-Frenchmen, were buying a myth, and to Claude, the customer was always right, even if he were dead wrong. The reality was that *les françaises* made terrible call girls. They were undisciplined, flighty, and lazy, wanting something for nothing—in short, enfants terribles. But just as Italian restaurants in Paris kept expensive French vintages on their wine lists, Madame Claude put up with the annoyances of French girls just because they were what a lot of horny men came to Paris for.

Madame Claude had a specific French "type" in mind, the insouciant spoiled blond rich bitch from avenue Foch, the wide boulevard with a huge park as its median that by the seventies invasion of the oil sheikhs was known as the "Suez Canal," with rich Arabs on one side and rich French Jews on the other. The Foch wives that Claude was intent on producing were neither Muslim nor Jewish, but, rather, proper upper-crust French convent girls like the self she would have liked to be. Foch was primus inter pares among the thoroughfares of the sixteenth arrondissement, but avenues Victor-Hugo, Kléber, d'Iéna, and Marceau would do as well. This was Paris's answer to Manhattan's Upper East Side, where status ruled and snobbery reigned, as the wives of the sixteenth, like the call girls of Madame Claude, narcissistically devoted themselves to their own perfection, in beauty, mind, and spirit. *Groomed* is the word for them.

The model for these supertrophies was the French actress Mireille Darc, star of the original *The Tall Blond Man with One Black Shoe*. Born Mireille Algorz in 1938 in Toulon, the tough port town near Marseille, Darc, like most Foch types, came from nothing like the bourgeois comforts and stratifications of the sixteenth. Mireille Darc was not a Claudette. However, she looked the part, and therefore, in the popular mind, deserved the part. She was very tall for France, five nine, and a sleek, tanned, and tawny blonde, which was the preferred look for Madame Claude. She had come to Paris in the early sixties, was embraced by Jean-Luc Godard, who cast her in *Weekend*, and then was embraced by France's number-one pretty-boy heartthrob, Alain Delon, its answer to Warren Beatty. They starred together in a host of films, like the gangster epic *Borsalino*. They were a couple for fifteen years.

Hollywood mogul Robert Evans has said that he had been introduced to Madame Claude by his friend Delon, whom Evans tried to help become a star in Hollywood, an effort that did not translate into American box-office success for Delon. That Delon knew Claude is no surprise. Most famous men in Paris, especially movie stars and directors, were in her orbit. His romantic partner, Darc, may have known Claude, as well. But there is no evidence that Mireille Darc, prestardom, was a working Claudette, just a lot of typecasting and wishful thinking. Proof and Claude seemed mutually exclusive. That's why she was the Teflon Madam when it came to scandal.

One of Paris's favorite games—and it remains so even now—was to speculate as to which famous actresses worked for Madame Claude before they were discovered. Almost all of France's most famous stars have been nominated as candidates for inclusion in the School of Claude. None has been more frequently speculated about than Catherine Deneuve, the star of *Belle de Jour,* the seminal Buñuel film about a bored housewife who moonlights for a madam. Director Roger Vadim, who was one of Claude's most loyal patrons, wrote in his autobiography *Bardot, Deneuve, Fonda,* that he took Deneuve to spend time with Claude for the sake of authenticity.

Jane Fonda wrote in her own autobiography that Vadim forced her to participate in ménages à trois with Claude girls. That may have helped with her own authenticity when she played a fancy New York call girl in *Klute* and won an Oscar for it. But these acting lessons didn't mean that either Deneuve or Fonda ever worked for Madame Claude, as much as their looks and hauteur might have qualified them for the job. In later years, even after Claude fled to Los Angeles and when she came back to France to decades of scandal and spotlight that she had avoided in her sixties-seventies prime, the typecasting would continue. Oddly enough, the one French actress who was considered the country's major sex symbol, Brigitte Bardot, was never, ever mentioned as a possible Claude girl. Her being off the gossip radar in this regard underscores Claude's insistence that she wasn't selling sex. She was selling class.

The Platonic ideal of the Claude girl, in the French mind, was someone whom that same mind would have never thought could or would *be* a Claude girl. Yet Madame Claude herself, once she began talking for public consumption, nominated this same woman as her model for what her ideal Claude girl should aspire to be. This woman was Claire Chazal, who retired in 2015 after twenty-four years as the top female news anchor in France, on its top channel, TF1. She might be compared to Diane Sawyer or Katie Couric, with an erotic spark no American anchor has ever struck.

Patrician, tall, blond, sleek, supergroomed, articulate, and altogether perfect, Claire Chazal had all the "right stuff" Madame Claude was looking for. But like most Madame Claude girls, Claire Chazal was made, not born. Although she looked like the quintessential aristocrat, she, like Claude, was a provincial girl from the Auvergne, in the sticksy southwest, whose parents were middle-class schoolteachers. However, when Claire was five, her parents moved to Paris and settled—where else—in the sixteenth.

Not only did Chazal pick up the style of the neighborhood but she was also physically just right; her childhood ambition was to be a ballet dancer. Instead, she became a print journalist until the eighties, when her telegenicity catapulted her in front of the cameras. She became known as La Reine de l'Info, and given that Madame Claude was a news junkie who never turned off her television set as she was fielding assignation calls night and day, she was unable to keep her eyes off Claire Chazal. Thus, whenever the question arises in France, who was the typical Claude

girl, the answers, depending on the age of the responder, are invariably Mireille Darc and Claire Chazal.

Given the fame and power—and the mystery—of Madame
Claude, it is surprising that no efforts were made by journalists
of the period to pierce her veil. Perhaps this reluctance on the
part of the press had something to do with the French notion
that reporting on the sex lives of its leaders and icons was an invasion of privacy. Perhaps the press was simply terrified of the
Elysée Palace, which protected its Madame de la République.

In America, press respect for its leaders was why the priapic
presidency of John F. Kennedy was only dissected decades after
the event. While the English tabloid press found its lifeblood in the
sex scandals of the powerful—viz Profumo and Lambton—the
unstated French policy, like the American one, was hands-off.
The French loved sex; they just didn't want to spoil the fun
behind closed doors by writing about it. America was just plain
ashamed. Until 1987 and the escapades of presidential candidate Gary Hart with model Donna Rice on the yacht *Monkey
Business,* American journalism took a "see no evil," hands-over-
eyes approach to political matters amorous.

An exception to this journalistic politesse where Madame
Claude was concerned came in 1974, when two young academics, Elizabeth Antébi and Anne de Boismilon, decided they would
go undercover as call girls and report firsthand on what really
went on in the Claude harem. They were an unlikely pair of aspiring call girls, even in light of Claude's desire to recruit brainy
types. They were both historians in their late twenties. They
looked like what they were: serious academics. Neither of the two
petite, then still-schoolgirlish brunettes could be said to resemble Mireille Darc. De Boismilon taught geography at a religious
Catholic school in Neuilly, Sainte-Croix de Neuilly. Antébi had
just finished her Ph.D. on the work of Baron Edmund de Rothschild in creating a Jewish homeland in Palestine and had done
some magazine writing on subjects ranging from health food to

Buckminster Fuller to Satan cults, which conceivably triggered her desire to explore the Claude underworld.

Unlikely investigators as they may have been, Antébi and de Boismilon plunged into their new guise as intrepid "undercover girl reporters." Today, a teacher in the Lycée Français in Düsseldorf, Germany, Antébi described her adventure as one motivated by wanting to expose Claude's connections to the French power elite. Antébi had unearthed evidence of Claude's early connections to the Corsican Mafia and the vast political influence of the little island of little Napoléon. There were ties to the Sanguinetti brothers, Cairo-born Corsicans, one a top admiral in the French navy, the other a leading politician and architect of Charles de Gaulle's return to power in 1958 (he had been out since 1946), just as Madame Claude began her own rise to power, aided and abetted, and artfully ignored, by the Gaullist government. The two sleuths seemed much more interested in the politics than the sex.

"Curt Jurgens started it all for us," Antébi recalled. She had met the German star on a plane to Berlin. The six-four, Aryan-handsome Jurgens was Hollywood's go-to Hitlerian. He had become a household face as the quintessential Nazi U-boat commander opposite Robert Mitchum's American submarine adversary in 1957's *The Enemy Below* and the quintessential Nazi general in 1962's *The Longest Day*. Jurgens would later be the quintessential Bond neo-Nazi villain in 1977's *The Spy Who Loved Me*. Jurgens was equally famous to French audiences as Brigitte Bardot's sugar daddy in the first mainstream naked sex film, 1956's *And God Created Woman*.

Roger Vadim, who had directed *And God Created Woman,* and Darryl Zanuck, the epic Hollywood studio head who had produced *The Longest Day,* were avid Madame Claude clients and had brought Jurgens into the fold. Now Jurgens agreed to do his best to get Antébi and de Boismilon an inside track. In later years, Jurgens gained some notoriety for having claimed, throughout the world press, that he had had a near-death heart attack, during which he went to Hell. Because Antébi had written about Satan for *Elle,* maybe this mutual interest led Jurgens to help pry open an otherwise-closed door.

Where Jurgens directed Antébi and de Boismilon was to a restaurant in the distant twentieth arrondissement, near the Père Lachaise Cemetery, where Chopin, Rossini, Balzac, Proust, and Oscar Wilde were interred, not to mention more recent arrivals Edith Piaf and Jim Morrison. The restaurant was a place where Madame Claude aspirants went to be "discovered." It was called La Tentation de Saint-Antoine, after surreal paintings by both Bosch and Dalí, and an 1874 novel by Flaubert about the temptations of food and flesh.

The three works of art were inspired by Saint Anthony, the fourth-century Christian evangelist who lived ascetically in the Sinai desert. Although it may seem counterintuitive, Saint Anthony became the patron saint of pork butchers and charcuterie makers, perhaps because in many paintings of him, there is always a little pig at his feet. Another theory is that in medieval times pig fat was used as a rub to cure skin diseases; Saint Anthony is also considered the patron saint of dermatology. In any event, the restaurant became acclaimed as a sort of hog heaven. What most visiting gourmets did not know was that it was a hog heaven of another sort—for what feminists would decry as male sexist pigs.

"We went out to the end of the world to the restaurant, between lunch and dinner," Antébi recalled. "We found a waiter, and we told him Curt Jurgens had sent us. Then the waiter introduced us to the maître d'. They looked us up and down, asked us a lot of questions. I guess we passed the test, because the next day I got a call from this woman who asked us to come over to meet her at the apartment on avenue George V. It was near to where Madame Claude had her place on rue de Marignan." Her name was Catherine Virgitti, the Claudette who seduced the Publicis heir and eventually got on his father's payroll as the boy's *maitresse*. She was Claude's recruiter. As Claude's right-hand woman, she was, as Antébi and de Boismilon called her, Claude's "dauphine," or heiress apparent. They didn't know that Virgitti was too impatient to enjoy waiting for any polite inheritance.

Antébi and de Boismilon nervously went to their interview with Virgitti. Antébi recounted being received by Virgitti who was lounging in a vast bed on black satin sheets, wearing sexy silk pajamas. She was blond, bronze, and slinky, very Mireille Darcian. She had almond eyes, a pert nose, perfect, gleaming white teeth, showgirl legs. When she got out of bed, she described to the "applicants" how she liked to make her recruiting rounds on her Yamaha motorcycle. She sounded equally at home in lesbian bars as at the Ritz bar, as well as at fancy boutiques and hair and nail salons and famous Left Bank cafés like the Flore and the Deux Magots, and at prestigious high schools like Lycée Janson-de-Sailly, all the places she searched for talent.

If Virgitti would want a girl for herself, Claude would most likely want that girl for her men. The two women's tastes and needs were congruent, and Claude trusted Virgitti. According to Antébi, Virgitti's first question to her and de Boismilon was, "Are you two working together?" which implied that she thought they were a team of lesbians. It turned out to be wishful thinking. Virgitti was officially bisexual when she saw Claude's clients, but said to be homosexual when she was off the meter. But the fact that she liked the two undercover girls was a good sign for them.

Virgitti described to the girls how she first met Claude. It was in 1966. Her manicurist had made the connection. She went to the rue de Marignan. The elevator was out of order. She climbed the stairs. She rang the bell. A little blond maid answered the door. She asked for Madame Claude. "That's me," Claude said. Virgitti could be as harsh and nasty a judge as Claude. That's why they ultimately got along so well. Virgitti noticed four tall girls chatting with one another in the hallway of the apartment. Claude had eyes only for Virgitti. She needed only a few minutes to size up a girl. She saw, as Antébi and de Boismilon described it, that Virgitti was a wild and crazy country girl with "a desire for power, a taste for money and revenge." Claude decided, on the spot, to take her on.

Antébi and de Boismilon were not so lucky. Virgitti, despite her initial encouragement, refused to see them again. They worried she might be on to them, that she realized she had told them too much. But then she called them back and invited them to meet her at a chic nightclub on the avenue Victor Hugo called L'Aventure, owned by the one-named pop star Dany, the self-made daughter of a Perpignan cobbler. She was a beautiful version of Régine. *Le tout Paris* speculated Dany was a former Claude girl, just as it did with most beautiful stars.

There the two square brain girls met Virgitti, who was wearing skintight black leather pants and a backless blouse. She was with two towering African models that they were convinced were Claude girls cosseting an out-of-town fat cat. Another likely Claude big blonde joined the party and all the women danced wildly and suggestively together. It reminded the writers of both a cockfight and a battle of praying mantises. Already bored, Virgitti kept dancing, but she turned her focus away, concentrating on a new conquest, a beautiful tall Chinese girl by herself at the bar. The scene made them think what an insane idea their trying to be Claude girls was.

They weren't dead yet. Virgitti enjoyed their minds, and she kept talking to them, revealing to them her supposedly "secret" life with Claude. Antébi believed Virgitti kept up the dialogue because she fancied de Boismilon and was willing to spin her web to get this unlikely conquest. Whatever, she told them how she had won Claude over, how she had gotten Claude to let her guard down for someone in whom she saw an idealized reflection of the carnal, confident self she would have liked to be. There was a sexual charge, a flirtation that Virgitti would have acted on if Claude had given her the chance. Virgitti was amoral. She would have romanced anyone, male or female, to get ahead. However, Claude kept it familial rather than romantic. Virgitti became her virtual adopted daughter and putative successor. She loved living vicariously through Virgitti, walking with her down the Champs-Elysées in some provocative outfit, watching all the male pedestrians stop dead in their tracks and stare. Fernande Grudet never got stares like that. They felt good, even if they were by association, because despite whatever else she felt, Claude believed that she controlled Virgitti, like she controlled all her girls, as their master puppeteer.

According to Virgitti, if she was Claude's new surrogate child, she was still a child who caused her lots of distress, as children can do. Virgitti was profligate with her windfall earnings from all her Claude dates. She opened an account downstairs on rue de Marignan at the Banque Rothschild, "Claude's bank," as they called it, because of her ties to the family. Virgitti was quick to throw her money away, on loans to wayward girlfriends, big parties with foie gras and champagne, gambling junkets to Deauville and Monte Carlo.

She didn't neglect men. As Antébi and de Boismilon wrote, "Girls excited her; men kept her." Virgitti fell for a seventeen-year-old Belgian virgin, a runaway hippie from a commune who had became a porn actress. Virgitti introduced her to a rich businessman obsessed with young virgins. A big entertainment lawyer had set her up in the George V apartment; a big film producer had offered to make her a star. She took the money but rejected both. Virgitti would give her body to an older man but never her heart. As with Antoine, the Publicis golden child, Virgitti had lots of gratis affairs with teenage men, but nothing stuck.

To her wide-eyed interlocutors, Virgitti quietly chafed against Claude. Her image of Claude was a Carmelite mother superior who worshipped money instead of God. Her image of herself was as the ultimate party animal, a contemporary Liane de Pougy, the Folies Bergère dancer who became a cocaine-addicted lesbian courtesan to some of the richest women of the fin de siècle. She predicted that she and Claude were doomed to clash.

Virgitti did introduce her new friends to Claude as potential candidates. They went up to meet her at the rue de Marignan apartment. She rejected them out of hand, on the spot. Antébi noted that she had been living with her boyfriend and had confessed this to Claude. She was also tiny, but she didn't believe that was why Claude said no. The grounds for Claude's passing on her and her writing partner were, in Antébi's opinion, not that they weren't Darc-like enough but something much deeper; she quoted Claude as saying, "You love men too much."

The would-be collaborators refused to give up. If they couldn't join Claude, they would beat her at their own game, the game of money. They would get an advance from a publisher to bribe her girls to talk to them. At this point, Virgitti, plotting to stab Claude in the back and steal her business, found the writers around a dozen girls to talk to—for a fee. For a Claude girl, there was no such thing as free love or free information. Antébi and de Boismilon also hired a well-connected journalist friend to be their own tester. That writer, an occasional Claude client, was able to hire some of the girls and report to the authors what went on behind closed doors.

Most of the Claudettes the two women spoke to had been discovered by Virgitti and were more loyal to her than to Claude. Consequently, their comments about her all tended to be negative. Still stung by the rejection over forty years later, Antébi had nothing good to say about the woman she had investigated, harping on her icy obsession with money, her own mini, mousy appearance, her rank exploitation of her Cinderellas, the students this headmistress was supposed to love.

"She was so, so vulgar," Antébi said again and again. "She

dreamed of fucking famous men, to be with a rich man. But she could never do it. No man would want her. So she *hated* men. She had hated them since she was a little girl, in her father's bar. She saw there what men did to women, how all they wanted to do was *rape them*." How, then, could Claude, so undesirable, become the professor of desire? "She studied it; she studied the ways of rich men; she studied this the way you'd study English until you were perfect," Antébi explained.

"When she found out that we were doing a book, she went crazy with rage," Antébi recalled. "She threatened us. 'I'll burn you with sugar,' she said." Sugar can be weaponized by being mixed with scalding water. It sticks to the skin and can destroy a face, a Claudette's biggest asset, and leave no fingerprints. It's a Corsican vendetta-tool method. Corsicans were poor. They found bargain ways to kill. Sugar was cheaper than a gun or a knife. "We were terrified. Just terrified," Antébi said. "We even went to the police. They tried to seem sympathetic, but they worked for her. They did nothing."

Complicating matters was the fact that Antébi and de Boismilon, who out of fear had taken the pen name Anne Florentin, were able to sell their book project to Stock, the famous house that had published the works of Voltaire and Rousseau and, later, Capt. Alfred Dreyfus. The catch to that good news was that Stock was the new publisher of Françoise Sagan, the bestselling writer in France and the best friend of Madame Claude.

Word quickly got to Sagan and her brother, Jacques Quoirez, about the Antébi/Florentin project. They were not pleased, and pressure began to mount on the women's agent to find another publisher. Stock, which had stood by Dreyfus at the darkest moments of his affair, for a while held firm to the literary traditions of France, where the writer was royalty unto himself. Eventually, though, the pressure from Sagan was too great. Antébi and de Boismilon were able to take their book to another house, Julliard, which had discovered Sagan in the early fifties but which she had just left. In what was becoming a game of the presses, Jacques Quoirez then came up with the idea of doing *Allô, Oui*. This would be the *real* Madame Claude, in her own voice. The other book was hearsay. It wouldn't stand a chance.

Antébi's loathing for Quoirez matched that she felt for Claude. She called him "a pimp. He looked like a clochard, a bum, dressed in bad clothes, with a half beard. He was ugly. They were both ugly, so ugly." Still, she acknowledged Quoirez's all-pervasive influence, noting that he had made himself one of the top advisers to the state-run television system. Antébi derided Quoirez, and the whole Claude system. "These men, the clients, they didn't want to fuck. They wanted to *brag*. They wanted to say, 'I fucked the same girl as Johnny Hallyday, the same girl as Mick Jagger. And the Arabs, the ones who made her fortune—they were so brutal. Their idea of sex was to put the women in the hospital."

Antébi and de Boismilon's book came out in 1974. It was entitled *Les Filles de Madame Claude: Un Empire qui ne tient qu'à un fil*, or "Madame Claude's Girls: An Empire Hanging by a Thread." The book was small, five by eight inches, and short, 182 pages. The cover featured a slender, innocent-looking blonde on a red couch in a noninnocent red peekaboo lounge outfit and gold high-heeled slippers that matched her hair. Inside the book, there are staccato paragraph-long sketches of the "witnesses," the Claude girls to whom Virgitti introduced the authors. These Claudettes were clearly far more rushed with the authors than with their clients. Their time was money, and what author could pay like a tycoon? Hence the brevity.

Les Filles was never translated into English or any other language. It did not become the phenomenon the authors, like all authors, hoped for. Today, it is a collector's item. Claude's *Allô, Oui,* because it came from the horse's mouth, or that of Jacques Quoirez, was hoped to become the French answer to Xaviera Hollander's *The Happy Hooker*. However, unlike Hollander, who was a tireless exhibitionist and naughty self-promoter, Madame

Claude was a haughty, arrogant concealer and secret keeper. She refused to go on television, and gave only a handful of cryptic press interviews.

Despite her brief stint on the sidewalks of Paris, Claude kept sex, certainly Hollander's brand of (porno)graphic verbiage, out of her memoir; Hollander, who was quick to sleep with her clients, wrote a book that reeked of sex. Hollander didn't have that many famous names to drop. (She later said that she had taken care of director Jean-Luc Godard for Claude when he came to New York.) Claude, true to her fashion and to her black book, was way above name-dropping. In the end, *Allô, Oui* came across as less *The Happy Hooker* than *The Unhappy Madam*. It, too, is a collector's item.

The reading public, it seemed, was hungry for either hot sex or famous names. Neither *Allô, Oui* nor *Les Filles de Madame Claude* provided either. Each of the girls briefly profiled in *Les Filles* represented a type. Geneviève (all names were made up) was the bourgeoise who got a giant emerald from a client. Sophie was the top-model daughter of a truck driver and turned her first trick at fifteen, then married a rock star at eighteen. Vanina was a hippie who liked old men, became a heroin addict in Ibiza, then went to Kathmandu and found God. Ursula was the "specialist" who had studied the ways of Oriental pleasure in Bangkok and gave men release with oily naked body rubs and a special trick called the *"coup de pomme,"* which involved inserting lubricated apple cores in a man's derriere. But that was it, a few sentences and they were offstage. If Claude was a big tease, so were these authors.

Without further detail, the girls seemed like archetypes, not real people. The impression was that they were pretty, perverse, spoiled, and, in general, hardly worth the money Madame Claude charged for them. The authors recounted an ugly tale about how Claude interviewed her girls. She insisted that they sit on a bidet in front of her and wash themselves. If they didn't scrub hard enough, they were out. If they gave themselves an orgasm, they were also out. Claude felt if they were having too good a time, they weren't doing their jobs. Cleanliness was essential, but pleasure was the devil's workshop. The only pleasure that mattered was that of the customer.

And who might the customers be? There followed a coy guessing-game chapter as to the identity of some of Claude's famous clients, because that was the question most readers wanted answers to. Here again the big tease came into play. The easy guesses were Anthony Quinn (an Irish Mexican who played a Greek), Steve McQueen (a blond motorcycle-riding star who liked car chases in San Francisco), and Adnan Khashoggi (an Arab arms dealer with a giant yacht and a plane set up as a boudoir). There were thinly veiled sketches of director Billy Wilder and producer Sam Spiegel.

Repulsion seemed to be the impression Antébi and de Boismilon wanted to convey. Alas, it was cutting off their noses to spite their faces. The book quickly disappeared in the wake of *Allô, Oui,* which then disappeared in its own wake. Readers wanted a fantasy, not a critique. The authors of *Les Filles* couldn't help themselves. They were serious academics, protofeminists. They reflected with some bitterness that one by-product of the feminist revolution was that women like Madame Claude now had one more "man's career" open to them: *pimp.* Was that progress worth the fight?

The authors were no fans of their chosen subject, who had not only rejected them but threatened their lives. With sugar! Their book concluded in near-satiric materialistic awe at how rich Claude was: ten million dollars in Swiss banks, one hundred pairs of expensive shoes in her closet, six mink coats, the best hairdresser at Carita, the best decorator in the Marais, her custom Alfa Romeo. The book then described in corporate bigger-is-better jargon how vast her empire was: five hundred girls, at least fifty first-class long-distance airline tickets a month from the top travel agency at the place Vendôme to every glamorous corner of the globe, the first harem in the new age of the petrodollar. What *Les Filles* could not conceal was its condescension to the emptiness of Madame Claude's existence—how she lived with nothing but her phone, how she ate alone, watched television alone, and went to bed alone. Its most telling comment was that her role model was not Coco Chanel, but Napoléon Bonaparte. She always had a thing for Corsicans.

Chapter 6

CRIME WITHOUT PUNISHMENT

The primal fear of most madams, wherever they may be found, is law enforcement. It is the old story of the oldest profession, the irresistible objects of the bordello meeting the immovable police force. The force invariably wins. However, Madame Claude's sex objects were so irresistible that, for once in the last century, the force was moved.

"She was protected, completely protected," admitted Claude Cancès, the former Paris chief of police. "She knew what we needed to know. She worked for the police, and she also worked for the secret service. My boss would go to see her every week to get a full report from her. But she was so important, I was never allowed to meet her myself, and I was high up in the brigade. She knew everything, and she only dealt at the top." Cancès, a slender, stylish man of eighty, is much more the Technicolor boulevardier of Louis Jourdan than the black-and-white Inspector Maigret of Jean Gabin. Cancès grew up in Provence, served as an army officer during the Algerian War, then went to Paris to join the police in 1963, as Madame Claude was becoming an institution.

A former saxophone player, Cancès was assigned to Pigalle, which was Paris's nightclub district, a neon fantasyland of jazz clubs, strip clubs, transvestite cabarets, sex shows, and thousands of prostitutes, both in the bars and on the streets. He was a

member of the Brigade Mondaine, or Vice Squad, and its sub-
group the Galanterie, whose origins in medieval knighthood had
everything to do with the protection of "damsels in distress."
The stated mission of the Galanterie was to uncover and then dis-
mantle luxury prostitution rings, which were light-years from
the standard Pigalle beat of harpy hookers fleecing hicks from
the sticks. Madame Claude fit Cancès's mission, but she had gov-
ernmental immunity. She was serving a far higher cause. She
wasn't dealing in sex; she was dealing in intelligence.

The Brigade Mondaine, technically the "worldly brigade," was
more and bigger than its name. It was more a truth squad than
a vice squad. Despite their lip service to *liberté,* the French authorities were dedicated to the notion that *connaissance est le pou-
voir.* ("Knowledge is power"). Here, though, the operative word is
more *reconnaissance* than plain old *connaissance.* Where Madame
Claude was concerned, the Brigade Mondaine was more like
the Russian KGB or the East German Stasi, a spy bureau. If you
were rich and important in France, Big Brother was watching
you night and day, at work and at play. *Le boudoir, c'est le vrai pou-
voir.* Madame Claude had the power of sex, and the French government would allow her to get rich and be free as the quid pro
quo for her inside information.

The Brigade Mondaine had its roots in the seventeenth century
in the court of Louis XIV, when Prime Minister Colbert created the post that was the precursor of Paris's chief of police. In
this police department was the Office of Moral Discipline, staffed
by an unsavory cadre of informants known as *les mouches,* "the
flies." Despite its pristine-sounding name, the purpose of this office wasn't to suppress debauchery in general or prostitution in
particular. Rather, it was an intelligence agency that *used* prostitutes and brothel keepers to amass compromising information
about their clients, who might be enemies of the state.

The French Revolution saw an even greater proliferation of
prostitution, which coincided with the postrevolutionary era of

tolerance. This was also an era of sanitation. All prostitutes had to be registered and tested for disease. This was carried out under the Office of Moral Discipline. When it came to administrative discipline, the police had none. Corruption was rampant, and the police got rich framing innocent women as whores and shaking them down for bribes not to ruin their reputations. The office, which had become a sex gestapo, was finally shuttered in 1881 and replaced in 1901 by the Brigade Mondaine, which would last until 1975. The end of the brigade was the beginning of Madame Claude's reversal of fortune and legal nightmare, which would consume the second half of what had seemed, for a while, to be a charmed life.

The brigade had three chief targets: prostitutes, gays, and drug dealers. Until 1946, by far the biggest task was regulating Paris's over 250 legal brothels and the prodigious information flow that came from them. At the best of the brothels, the clientele included the heads of state, ministers, and top politicians of the Entente Cordiale between France and Britain and their vast colonial empires, from Dirty Bertie, the Prince of Wales, on down. After the Great War, these same bordellos were the away-from-home bedrooms of the League of Nations; and during World War II, the playgrounds of the Third Reich and Vichy. What better way for the crafty French to find out the ambitions and strategies of both friends and enemies.

Now that *maisons closes* were closed, there were the smelly *maqueraux,* the pimps, to worry about. Pimps had never been a problem in the century of the brothel. The madams who controlled operations ran tight ships. Le Chabanais, for example, had 230 girls, 60 of whom lived on the premises at any one time. Everyone got along, including the ambassadors of rival countries, who frolicked in the nude together at wild international orgies. Everything happened behind closed doors. Nothing got out of hand. The only leaks were to the Paris police, and no one knew the better, until, for them, it was too late.

Now that the girls had hit the streets, things got wild, and the pimps came out in force. Many were Corsicans. Then again, so were many of the police and politicians, so it was an entente cordiale of its own. The only prostitution rings, Claude Cancès said, that his Galanterie would go after were the troublemakers, the rough ones, where the girls were maimed or killed, and which usually were dealing in narcotics as well. Madame Claude was left alone, to kiss and tell. And so were her chief rivals, old-school madams like Madame Billy, a former cashier at Le Chabanais, and Madame Hélène, the ex-manager of Le One-Two-Two. The great houses were all owned by men, financed by the anonymous fiscal elite, and managed by women.

These women, like Billy and Hélène, and a handful of others, fewer than ten, ran brothels on a smaller scale than the legends, but with similar amenities and ambience—bars, dining rooms, piano players, billiard parlors, wine *caves*. They were like men's clubs plus sex. And the old madams cosseted the clients, listened to their woes, cheered them up. Not so Madame Claude, who ran several minibrothels in the eighth and sixteenth arrondissements but was really fixated on the telephone. The flats were loss leaders, bait for newcomers, and they became less and less important to her as her fame grew.

Claude was not warm and cuddly like Billy, in time her only rival. She was twenty years younger, a different generation, the first high-tech madam of the modern age. Billy didn't send her girls out on calls. The phone, to her, was an alien device. She didn't trust it. She didn't believe in blind dates like this. Let the buyer see for himself, face-to-face. Madame Billy was no Pygmalion wannabe. She took her girls as she found them. They were old-fashioned whores, and Billy didn't fear the word. She embraced it, and so did her old-fashioned clients, who, alas, began dying off, while Claude's men were twisting the night away at Castel.

What both madams had in common was the immunity from

the Paris police, and, in the acquisition of this invisible protective shield, all roads and all ferries seemed to lead to Corsica. Corsica was to crime in France what Sicily was in Italy, though Corsicans in France seem to have been more respectable, more part of the visible power structure than their Sicilian counterparts. No French connection could have been more instrumental in the transformation of Fernande Grudet into Madame Claude than Maurice Papon, Claude Cancès's "big boss," the prefect of police in Paris.

Papon *was* the law in Paris from 1958 to 1967, the first decade of the Claude juggernaut. *"L'état, c'est moi"* could never have fit anyone better. This was the man who officially met with Claude every week for her surveillance report, and who reputedly met with her unofficially for the delectation of her swans. There was, of course, never a charge. Papon had strong ties to Corsica as France's chief administrator there after the war. He had even stronger ties to de Gaulle as one of the architects of the de Gaulle reascendancy, with his landslide election as president in 1958.

In a scandal that did not break until 1981, when Madame Claude was safely in exile in Beverly Hills, Papon was dramatically exposed to have been the most heinous and deadly of all Nazi collaborators in Vichy France, having sent nearly two thousand French Jews to their deaths at Auschwitz. There may have gone Fernande Grudet, who would wear her concentration camp tattoo as a badge of courage and loyalty among ostensible fellow heroes of the Resistance, as Maurice Papon long pretended to be, fooling both France and the whole world.

Maurice Papon might best be described, in the words of Donald Trump, as one "bad hombre." But he didn't look like one. Tall, smooth, rakish and dapper Papon was a central-casting politician, Fernande Grudet's beau ideal of an important man of affairs, an elite civil servant, and the template of the Madame

Claude client-to-be. Fernande wasn't alone. The whole country bought Maurice's act. Papon had the lineage for credibility. His father was an industrialist and the mayor of Gretz, a Paris suburb. He went to high school with future President Georges Pompidou at the Lycée Louis-le-Grand, on the Left Bank, next to the Sorbonne. Louis-le-Grand was considered one of the two most prestigious secondary schools in Paris, up there with the Lycée Janson-de-Sailly, where Catherine Virgitti scouted for teen Claudettes as well as for future power clients. Papon went on to university at Sciences Po, which was the French West Point of politics.

Papon was rising to the top of French politics when World War II broke out. He fought the Germans in Libya and Syria until the 1940 fall of France, when, like most rising politicians, he did not follow de Gaulle to London, but stayed in France and joined the Vichy government, where he continued his rapid rise. He soon became prefect of Gironde, the region that contained the key port of Bordeaux, in charge of the Service for Jewish Questions. Until he was exposed decades later for being the SS point man in Bordeaux and architect of the mass shipments of French Jews to the concentration camps, Papon had created the heroic image of himself as one of "Hitler's *unwilling* executioners." He claimed to have done the best he could under nightmarish circumstances, such as deporting the Jews to the camps in posh *wagons-lits,* or sleeping cars, rather than freight train boxcars.

People assumed that Papon protected many other Jews from deportation, particularly "French-born" Jews, as opposed to immigrant Jews from Germany and other countries who had come to France seeking shelter from the Nazis. His was a kind of "Sophie's Choice" dilemma, but given that the French were highly nationalistic and xenophobic, Papon's intercession on behalf of the French Jews and his ultimate association with the Resistance when it was clear that the Nazis were losing the war were "spun" to turn him, in the turmoil of liberation, into a war hero. In 1948, he was awarded France's highest medal, the Légion d'honneur, for "general wartime service." When the truth finally did come out, it turned out that Papon had been as ruthless with French Jews as German ones, stealing their art, their properties, and their companies.

Madame Claude's chief protector sat atop the Paris gendarmerie in his massive and foreboding police headquarters on Ile de la Cité, next to Sainte-Chapelle and across from Notre Dame. Papon was a secret Satan in the midst of all the Gothic angels, as destructive a force as the apocalyptic demons in the Angers tapestries that had riveted Fernande Grudet as a child. His greatest atrocity, among many, as prefect of police, was the 1961 Paris massacre, in the midst of a wave of national protests against the Algerian War by the mostly North African Muslim supporters of Algerian independence. Papon rounded up and arrested eleven thousand of these people, mostly based on their "dark" appearance. Some historians have estimated that two hundred Algerians were executed by the police, with over a hundred bodies found floating in the Seine. The de Gaulle government admitted to only two police-related deaths, claiming they were a matter of self-defense.

Papon didn't limit his atrocities to Jews and Muslims. He also conducted a reign of terror against trade unionists and any other enemies of the right-wing de Gaulle regime. That included the OAS, or Secret Army Organization, composed of leading French military men even to the right of de Gaulle in opposing Algerian independence. Because many of these generals were her clients, Madame Claude was instrumental to Papon in being one step ahead of his enemies. Just as France had no idea how bad Papon was, these generals and other enemies of de Gaulle had no idea that Madame Claude was a Gaullist spy and secret weapon. Claude also had a big clientele of high-level Moroccans in the royal entourage of King Hassan II, a Gaullist ally.

When Hassan's chief adversary, Mehdi Ben Barka, was exiled by the king in 1963, he became a Paris-based "traveling salesman of the revolution," meeting with Castro, Che Guevara, and Malcolm X. Handsome, brilliant, and cultured, the first Moroccan to get a degree in mathematics from one of the French Grandes Ecoles, Ben Barka was also thought to be a Claude habitué. When he was arrested by Papon's police in 1963 and subsequently disappeared, a wide net of suspicion was thrown, which included not only the French authorities but also the CIA and the Israeli Mossad, which was said to have lured Ben Barka to Paris and into a police trap. Madame Claude may have been part of the allure, as she was so often an essential Paris pit stop for visiting politicians, just as she was for President Kennedy.

The mounting public scandal forced President de Gaulle to protest, perhaps too much, that his government had had nothing to do with Ben Barka's vanishing act. Two police officers were put on trial for the kidnapping, and in 1967, Maurice Papon himself was pressured by de Gaulle to step down, to stifle the continuing public outcry. As ever, the French elite took care of its own. Papon failed upward, quite literally, as he was named president of the colossal aircraft company Sud Aviation, which was building the Concorde. Papon simultaneously stayed active in public life; he was elected to the Chamber of Deputies and became the treasurer of the UDR, the Gaullist party, and a member of the cabinet of Giscard d'Estaing, before his wartime atrocities finally came to light. If Papon were the Devil, Madame Claude was the Devil's disciple, the purveyor of death and the purveyor of sex. But no one, except a few high-ranking members of the Galanterie, like Claude Cancès, knew of this unholy alliance, and no one at the time had any idea how unholy Papon's part of it had been.

By the time Maurice Papon went from the police to the Concorde, Madame Claude had become a made woman. Madame Billy had been vanquished. She had become an artifact of a glorious but vanished past, like the ancient restaurant L'Ami Louis, where nostalgists could pay one hundred dollars for a roast chicken the way Maurice Chevalier or Charles Boyer would have liked it. Madame Claude was the new girl in town, the nouvelle vague of prostitution. She was the out-of-bed counterpart to the radical change represented by Brigitte Bardot in the bed.

Nevertheless, Claude treasured her ties to the Old Guard, like Papon and de Gaulle. Ever mindful of the Corsican power behind the Elysée Palace and the workings of the government, she hired as her lawyer a Corsican *avocat* who was the counsel to the most important godfathers of the Marseille Mafia, Paul Carbone, born in Corsica, and François Spirito, who inspired the gangster film *Borsalino,* starring the French idols Delon and Belmondo. Carbone and Spirito made their name and fortune in Egypt, where they became the Conrad Hilton of bordellos up and down the Nile Delta and befriended the playboy sex addict King Farouk. They then relocated to Marseille, took over the major brothels there, and became Nazi collaborators, in order to pioneer the Indochinese opium trade and transform those poppies into heroin, laying the cornerstone of the international empire that was the French Connection. In 1966, the mob mouthpiece incorporated as a limited liability company Claude's new deluxe apartment bordello on the rue de Boulainvilliers, in the sixteenth, to be disguised as a hotel, the "Résidence de la Muette," named after the hunting lodge of French King Henri IV. Despite her delusions of royalty, to say that Madame Claude was "mobbed-up" and "lawyered-up" would have been an understatement.

So confident was Madame Claude at this point in her life that she took her first real boyfriend since she and her gangster lover had broken up after trying to live temptation-free in Provence in the mid fifties. Although Claude frequently asserted that women over forty should not have sex (if she had included men, she would have had no business), all indications were that this was a romantic love affair, albeit a one-sided one. The man's name was René (Claude accorded only first names to her lovers). He ran a printing company, was eight years older than she, and was tall and slim, with hypnotic blue eyes behind his accountant's wire-rim glasses.

If René had been a real accountant, he would have worked for the underworld, because he had that gangland aura, a Corsican je ne sais quoi that had been a fatal attraction to Fernande Grudet, and remained so to Madame Claude. On the other hand, if René had been an accountant, the several small companies that he had started and then let drift into bankruptcy would not have had to have been bailed out by Claude. Still, she liked him, and liked being the dominant partner. To keep him under her wing, she made him the manager of her new Résidence de la Muette, but she got vituperatively jealous whenever she thought he was noticing her girls with lust in his heart. It was a thankless job, destined for disaster. René was also her driver and houseboy, forced to chauffeur her to her hairdressing, shopping, lawyer, and police appointments and wait outside while she did her business. By 1971, René had left her for a twenty-year-old blond secretary from Greece, petite like Claude but passive rather than dominant. It was said that Claude had the girl's apartment destroyed no less than three times. René disappeared. He was replaced as manager of the Résidence de la Muette by three women from Senegal, who kept the place in perfect order.

If Madame Claude was protected by Charles de Gaulle, she was no less protected by the man who succeeded him in 1969, Georges Pompidou. Pompidou, who was from the same part of France as Françoise Sagan and Jacques Quoirez, was an old-school, meritocratic right-wing politician who had worked his way up in the system in the same manner as his high school classmate Maurice Papon. Pompidou, the son of a Spanish professor, was an even better student than Papon.

While Papon went on to Sciences Po, the more intellectual

Pompidou proceeded to the Ecole Normale Supérieure, the French Harvard, where he was first in his class and took a special prize in Greek. He went to Marseille, where he became a classics professor. A self-styled dandy, chain-smoker, and bon vivant, Pompidou was no one-note bookworm. He enjoyed bouillabaisse at the best restaurants and enjoyed the brothels of Carbone and Spirito. He then met his wife, a law student. She was a tall, blond, well-groomed, classy doctor's daughter totally in the Madame Claude mold. Her name was also Claude; these "two Claudes" would cause Pompidou major headaches at the outset of his presidency.

During the war, Pompidou was no Resistance hero, but he didn't take Papon's path of Nazi collaboration, either. Instead, he went to Paris and taught in one of the lesser high schools. There was a French joke about Pompidou's "Resistance" being his refusal to sit below the second balcony of the Comédie Française to avoid mixing with German officers. When de Gaulle returned to France in triumph and made his famous victory march down the Champs-Elysées, Pompidou, in awe of the spectacle, contacted an old friend on de Gaulle's staff and used his school ties to get a job.

Pompidou proved indispensable. He became the general's top aide in writing his memoirs. But then a seemingly even bigger opportunity arose in 1954 to join the resurgent Banque Rothschild, where he quickly rose to second in command, under Baron Guy de Rothschild. Even as one of the Nazis' prime targets of ultragreed, the Rothschilds somehow managed to keep their fortune, the greatest in Europe at the time. Madame Claude couldn't have been prouder of any client than this family, hence the elevation of Guy's cousin Baron Elie to her triumvirate of supertesters.

In 1962, after being de Gaulle's behind-the-scenes genius for Algerian independence, Pompidou, at fifty, was appointed prime minister. He was criticized as someone who had never held elective office. He was the "Rothschild puppet," the Left wailed, saying that the RF over the doors of the Elysée Palace stood not for République Française but for Rothschild Frères. He was also criticized as a bloodless "technocrat," a number-crunching automaton that was less than a man, and way less than the soulful Frenchman the electorate expected after the charismatic de Gaulle. Pompidou gave a full-blooded retort. "There are three ways to ruin," he replied. "Women. Gambling. And being a technocrat. Women are agreeable, and gambling quick. But being a technocrat is the surest path to destruction."

Eventually, France began to like Pompidou. He became known as "Pompom." He became the force behind his friend Maurice Papon's Concorde, not just for the prestige but also for the thousands of jobs it would create. And when France's biggest upheaval since the war ended came with the student riots and workers revolt in May 1968, Pompidou took charge, while de Gaulle fled to a French army base in West Germany to marshal military support in case the riots became the next French Revolution. They did not, but the French saw de Gaulle as old and out of touch. De Gaulle got the message and resigned in 1969. "Pompom" was elected president by a landslide. For Madame Claude, it was a case of Pompom, Papon, what did it matter? They were all the same, cut from the same right-wing Establishment power elite cloth. They needed her and would take care of her.

The Establishment, however, was soon to be rocked. The first gong of what was considered the death knell of the old order as represented by Pompom and Papon was sounded in 1967, before the first riots, by an essay that became a book, *Le Défi Américain,* ("The American Challenge"), by Jean-Jacques Servan-Schreiber. The book, which was translated into fifteen languages and sold nearly as well as those of Françoise Sagan, basically said that France was finished, left in the dust by American technology, culture, and energy. Just look at the Boeing and Douglas jet planes at Orly Airport. Look at the McDonald's on the Champs-Elysées. Listen to Elvis, Dylan, Motown, not to mention the Beatles and Stones, then listen to Johnny Hallyday. Look at the Corvette, then look at the Renault. Look at IBM, then look at France's main computer company, Bull. The name said it all. It didn't compute. Something was happening, and Servan-Schreiber, a scion of a Jewish publishing dynasty who trained as a fighter pilot in Alabama for the Free French Air Force during World War II and became a friend of JFK, was a total Yanko-phile who knew exactly what it was.

Until now, all the world had seemed to bow down to France because of the inarguably superior French way of life, *le savoir-vivre*. There was a German expression that all Europe quoted and believed: "*Leben wie Gott in Frankreich*" ("Live like God in France"). France was the most beautiful country, with a glorious history, had the greatest art and literature, the best food, and, by far, the best sex. So what that it had lost a few big wars. Make love, not war. Wasn't that what the American hippies were chanting? Nobody could top the French at love. Just ask Madame Claude, if you knew how to find her. Until now, the French view of America was that of World War I prime minister Georges Clem-enceau: "America was the only country that had gone from bar-barism to decadence without passing through civilization." Now that arrogance was about to be shaken.

It was clear from the riots at the Sorbonne led by "Danny the Red" Cohn-Bendit and echoed across the Atlantic by the riots at Columbia led by Mark Rudd. The message was the same on both sides of the Atlantic. The Establishment was no good. Call it French Indochina, or call it Vietnam, it was the same exploited country. "Ho Ho Ho Chi Minh, the NLF [Vietcong] is gonna win!" was the chant. It was the sixties. Women were liberated by the Pill. Sex was easy. Only a warmongering colonialist cap-italist sexist pig would go to someone like Madame Claude. Such was the idea, but at the time Madame Claude was a secret of the power elite that the students were rioting against. Only a few of the children of the Gaullist Establishment at the top Lycées and the Grandes Ecoles had any idea who she was, and they kept it well among themselves.

The state secret of Madame Claude popped out of the hat during the Markovic affair of 1968, France's much more sordid version of England's 1963 Profumo scandal, both of which involved call girls and statesmen. In October 1968, in the Paris suburb of Yvelines, not far from Georges and Claude Pompidou's weekend house, a body was found in a garbage dump, rolled up inside an old mattress. It was a very fancy body, toned and muscular, dressed in a Pierre Cardin suit. There was a bullet in its head. Its severed penis was stuffed into its mouth. The dirty work of the Corsican Mafia. That was the police's first thought.

Three days later, the plot thickened when the mutilated corpse was identified as that of Stevan Markovic, a Yugoslavian living in Paris. But he wasn't living near this nor any other garbage dump. He had been residing in a huge apartment on the very fashionable avenue de Messine, close to the parc Monceau, where much of *Belle de Jour* had been shot. The apartment belonged to Alain Delon. It turned out that Markovic, thirty-one, whose photographs revealed a stunning resemblance to the stunning Delon, then thirty-two, was the actor's bodyguard, body double, man Friday, and, until recently, inseparably close friend.

The plot was thickened even further by the fact that Delon's previous and equally handsome bodyguard, Milos Milosevic, had also been found shot to death under similarly mysterious circumstances in Hollywood two years before. And one more troubling detail was that Delon's very dearest friend and inspiration for his many roles as the "beautiful gangster" was François Marcantoni, the current *capo di tutti capi* of the Corsican Mafia and an old acquaintance of that longtime Corsican groupie Madame Claude. A recent letter from Markovic was soon produced by his brother Aleksandar, stating, in Serbian, "If I get killed, it is

100% the fault of Alain Delon and his godfather François Marcantoni." The text of the letter told Aleksandar that it would serve as a kind of "certificate of insurance from Lloyd's" in case something befell him.

Although the French slang for bodyguard is *gorille,* or gorilla, the cousins Milosevic and Markovic were infinitely more Tarzan than ape. No movie star was more narcissistic nor more beautiful than Alain Delon. Accordingly, he wanted a companion in his own image. He ended up with two of them. Nor were these reflections of himself mere employees. Delon embraced them. "They weren't ready to receive that sort of different life," Delon admitted to the *Times* of London several years after the scandal. "My real fault was to give them that sort of life. Because . . . they were just like me, when we were together. But not outside, and that was my biggest fault because it spoiled them too fast."

Delon himself had risen fast, too. Trained as an apprentice butcher, he might have ended up working in the kitchen of a place like La Tentation de Saint-Antoine, the pig-feast restaurant where Catherine Virgitti scouted girls for Madame Claude. Instead, his mother, a pharmacist, sent him off to war in Indochina in 1953 at age seventeen, which gave him the taste of the outside world that transformed him. "You could play at being a man," Delon told the *Times.* "You even had a gun." One thing that didn't change was Delon's twin fascinations with criminals and movie stars, the former from playing ball in the yard of the Fresnes prison near his home in suburban Paris, where his father ran a movie house—hence the latter interest.

Delon had met Marcantoni during his military training in Toulon, near Marseille, prior to shipping out to Asia. Toulon was such a tough town that it had a section where the gangsters lived that was called "Chicago." Marcantoni's brother had a bar there called Le Dauphin. Marcantoni himself ran a nightclub down the Riviera coast in Cannes called Jimmys, which inspired the name Jimmy'z of Régine's seminal Paris club, where Delon would become a fixture. A deep and lasting friendship emerged and endured Delon's early discovery by a film agent in 1956, when Delon was working as a waiter in Les Halles, selling onion soup to tourists.

Delon met and hired Milos Milosevic in 1963, the same year he met his wife, Nathalie, a *pied noir* (white North African) blond goddess so much in the Madame Claude mold that after Mireille Darc, Nathalie Delon was viewed by the gossipocracy as the girl most likely to have gotten started as a Claudette. But this was sheer wishful thinking; there was no proof whatsoever. After breaking up with Nathalie over her affair with Stevan Markovic in 1967, Delon began a romance with Darc herself, which would last for the next fifteen years. Small wonder Delon was Madame Claude's favorite actor. They had a lot in common, Corsicans and blondes.

After three years trying and failing to become a Hollywood star, Delon went home, but Milosevic stayed. He was doing better socially than Delon professionally. He had affairs with a battery of starlets, lastly Barbara Ann Thomason, the estranged wife of Mickey Rooney and ex-mistress of Cary Grant. Milosevic and Thomason were both found shot through the head in Rooney's Brentwood home while Rooney was in the hospital. Without a suspect, the LAPD quickly closed the case. Milosevic would have never abandoned the needy Delon to fend for himself. Before his death, he had introduced Delon in Paris to his cousin Stevan, whom Delon bailed out of jail when Stevan was under suspicion of a jewel robbery. The two became inseparable, a French version of the Losey/Pinter film *The Servant,* where a valet takes over the life of his master. Within a short time Stevan had purloined his master's wife and moved in with her. Nonetheless, Delon continued to support Markovic.

During that period, Stevan Markovic decided that he *was* Alain Delon. He wore his clothes, he ate at all his favorite haunts, he danced at Régine's and Castel, and he slept not only with his wife but with everyone else, as well. He also hired a number of Claudettes to party with him at his well-known *partouzes,* or sex orgies, as well as at lavish dinners. What the revelers did not know was that Markovic was filming everything. He believed in insurance policies, and celluloid didn't lie. Markovic's guests were the Delon/Claude beau monde, and at least at one of these revels included none other than the soon-to-be First Couple of France, the Georges Pompidous.

Grainy naked pictures of Claude Pompidou began circulating around Paris. Aleksandar Markovic testified he had sat with the Delons and the Pompidous at one of his brother's dinner parties. Delon was called to the quai d'Orsay. He denied everything and was not charged. François Marcantoni was another story, under the Napoleonic Code guilty until proven innocent, the reverse of the English and American systems. He was arrested and held in police custody for eleven months, until December 1969. The police couldn't prove a thing against Marcantoni. They never could.

During Marcantoni's incarceration, Georges Pompidou was fighting for his reputation and his political life. Imagine the grand Claude Pompidou in a kinky ménage with Serbian thugs. That's where Madame Claude entered the picture. In rebuttal, the Pompidou press machine implied that the pictures weren't of Claude Pompidou, but of a Madame Claude look-alike who resembled Claude Pompidou. Madame Claude had a whole stable of Claude Pompidou look-alikes. That was her prime type, wasn't it? Madame de la République was thus linked to the future First Lady of the *république.* Her girls should only do so well, Madame Claude later reflected.

Meanwhile Georges Pompidou was blaming the whole affair on Charles de Gaulle. The president was humiliated not only by the student riots of the violent Paris spring but also by the fact that Pompidou was being given all the credit as the peacemaker, the man who quelled what might have been the second French Revolution. De Gaulle's thanks was to dismiss Pompidou as his prime minister. Pompom was bruised but not beaten. In January 1969, he announced that he would be a candidate for the presidency, challenging de Gaulle in 1972, when his second seven-year term would expire. De Gaulle was furious at Pompom's lèse majesté. That same month, Claude Pompidou's name was headlined in connection with the Markovic investigation. Then the naked pictures were leaked to the press. Claude or Claude, it didn't matter. How could Pompidou satisfy a country when he couldn't even satisfy his own wife? Such was the implication.

This time, however, de Gaulle may have gone too far. The same unrest that had produced the riots began to bubble up. Who cared about Pompom's private life? The French were a nation of sophisticates. Jobs and tranquillity were what mattered. In April, de Gaulle used his favorite popularity test of a referendum to gauge public support of his new ideas to improve things in France. This time, the first time, a de Gaulle referendum was defeated. The general stepped down, a broken man who would die a year later.

In June 1969, Pompidou ran for president and won by a landslide. The Markovic case gradually faded away. The murder was never solved. Delon rode off into the sunset with Mireille Darc. Nathalie rode off to the Côte d'Azur with her new best friends, Mick Jagger and Keith Richards, to record *Exile on Main St.* at what Elton John would later sing about as a "honky château." And Madame Claude came out of her first real brush with scandal completely unscathed, her mystique and her mystery at new heights from her sexy connection to France's two biggest men, its president and its top movie star. She—and France—had survived the sixties. *Vive la madame!*

Chapter 7

AN AMERICAN IN PARIS

If you were a woman in the 1970s, going to work for Madame Claude was like going to work for Goldman Sachs today. It meant you had it made, that you were going to get rich, unless you really screwed up. That was the dream job for a girl, provided you could handle it. Not many Americans could. But I could. I loved sex. I loved money. And I loved older men, all kinds of men. I didn't need a rock star to make my dream come true. And I wasn't grossed out by Arabs, who had become the ticket to ride then. As a little girl, my grandmother used to tell me stories about Rudolph Valentino, 'The Sheik.' Forget that he was Italian. I thought he was an Arab, and that sheikhs were cool. Whatever, it worked for me. And even though I grew up in Georgia, I was fascinated by Africa and Africans. I was going to be a missionary for my church. I read *National Geographic*. And I hated Lester Maddox [the ax-wielding racist governor]. That worked for me, too."

The speaker is Holly, now in her late sixties and happily married to a Georgia construction mogul she met when she was his nurse, after she changed careers from sex to medicine in her thirties. She still looks like Audrey Hepburn, a look she has cultivated since she saw *Breakfast at Tiffany's* as a girl—hence her *nom de boudoir*. She was entranced by Holly Golightly in fiction, just as she was entranced by Xaviera Hollander in nonfiction. *The Happy Hooker* was the bestseller that changed her life, validating and glamorizing the secret life that Holly had been leading as a prostitute since she was a teenager.

In 1973, in the midst of the Arab oil embargo, she decided to go to Paris and try to work for Madame Claude, to put some icing on a cake that had been less Gaston Lenôtre than Hostess Twinkie. Despite her self-declared fascination with the Third World, she wasn't interested in becoming another Margaret Meade or Albert Schweitzer. Nor was she looking to become a Grace Kelly and marry a prince. She was beyond Cinderella fantasies at this stage of a tough life. She didn't expect Claude to be her fairy godmother. She was already a working girl. She was looking to get rich.

"It was like a gold rush for hookers," Holly said, describing her odyssey. "They all descended on London and Paris, because that's where the money was, the big money. The money was where the Arabs were, and now that the oil crisis had made them richer than rich could be, they wanted to go somewhere to spend it, and that was London and Paris. The Arabs never liked New York, because to them New York was a Jewish town, and in the early seventies New York looked finished. President Ford to city: 'Drop dead.' I'll never forget the headline. It was like Ford to hookers: Drop dead, too.

"The stock market was dying, and it was Wall Street that paid our bills. Instead of jumping into bed, they were jumping out windows, like in the big crash. The Arabs were the new Wall Street. They were the top customers, if you could get to them. They liked L.A. better than New York, but who wanted to sit, even in a Bentley, waiting for hours in a gas line? No, they went to Europe, and why shouldn't I? I was sick of waiting for my phone to ring, so I got on a half-empty Pan Am 747 bound for Orly. There was no Charles de Gaulle then. Maybe there wouldn't ever be. Nobody was traveling. The world was frozen."

The Arab takeover of all things luxury, including call girls, came in the wake of the 1973 Yom Kippur War, in which Egypt and Syria attacked Israel, which fought back and won with massive American military assistance. The other Arab countries of the region, sick of losing to Israel, decided to use their secret weapon, an oil embargo, declared by OPEC (Organization of Petroleum Exporting Countries) against all the countries that supported Israel. The embargo did not include England and France, which may have helped explain why the rulers of OPEC chose those two nations as their favorite playgrounds to spend their suddenly massive windfalls of petrodollars. Almost overnight, the U.S. stock market plunged, losing nearly half its value, as the price of oil quadrupled from three dollars a barrel to over twelve.

The cost of all the things the newly superrich Arabs loved most, things like the Ritz, Cartier, and Madame Claude, multiplied accordingly. Europe, which had been a deal since the end of World War II and had spawned the *Europe on $5 a Day* series (it quickly became *Europe on $50 a Day*), was, at the top levels that made Europe "Europe," priced out of the market for all but millionaires. To say that England and France catered to rich Arabs, at the expense of Israel, was an understatement. Meanwhile, the bet was that rich non-Israeli Jews would never boycott the splendors and glories of England and France because the Arabs were getting most-favored-nation status. Oil money talked—loudly and globally. In the postembargo new world order, L.A. became Tehrangeles, London a foggy new Mecca, and Paris Babylon on the Seine.

Holly had been born into a world of tasteful status, where money was no object. She spent her early years on Manhattan's Upper East Side, attended the Convent of the Sacred Heart, a school that educated a number of Kennedy women, and spent weekends on her paternal grandfather's Greenwich estate on Round Hill Road. Unfortunately, marital stability did not exist in her family. Her grandfather ran off with a young cover girl. Her mother died when she was eight. No sooner had her mother fallen ill, her faithless father divorced her and ran off with a much younger English winner of minor beauty pageants, who had no interest in keeping Holly and her older sister around to spoil her fun. She sent them off to everything she could send them to— schools, camps, religious retreats.

"I spent all my free time in the Catholic church," Holly recalled. "I had nowhere to go but down, into trouble." At ten, Holly had her first sexual experience with her female bunk mate at a camp in Maine. Boys would have to wait until she was fourteen. Her sister was molested by her grandfather; after she told Holly about it, Holly was never sure whether she had repressed the memory of a similar experience on her part. Whatever stability Holly had known was obliterated when her father decided to relocate to Atlanta in order to take advantage of the sixties property boom there.

"The minute the plane started descending and I saw those endless flat pine barrens, I knew I would have to get out." Her sister quickly did, marrying at sixteen. The family's Peachtree Road plantation-style mansion was lost in a property recession. What was supposed to be *Gone With the Wind* became a Dixie version of *Blackboard Jungle*. Holly was placed in public school and lost her virginity to a redneck classmate who was a football star. "Today they'd call it rape. Then it was a date at the drive-in. He carried a gun." She took a drug overdose at fifteen, after which the therapist her father had sent her to advised her that leaving would be her smartest move.

Holly and two girlfriends graduated early from high school, where Holly had somehow managed to get elected class vice president. "I always tried to please everyone," she said. While in school, the girls had become part of the harem of Atlanta's top drug dealer, a young, cool operator "who was just like Johnny Depp in *Blow*." He sent them to New Orleans, where they shared a tiny apartment in the French Quarter and went to work for a bounty hunter the dealer was friends with. "Pretty teenage girls could find out anything. I was a good spy. Once I put a pillow under my dress and pretended I was knocked up and went to see the family of the guy our boss was looking for. They wanted me as their daughter-in-law, and told me where he was." In a short time, Holly discovered that the bounty hunter was less a hunter than a trafficker. When the girls saw that their ultimate destination was to go to work in a brothel across the Mississippi River owned by crime boss Carlos Marcello, long a suspect in the JFK assassination, her two friends left, on the proverbial midnight train to Georgia. Holly, intent on escaping her family, went to work as a waitress in the coffee shop of a cheap motel. Only when a nice female customer took her aside and said, "Girl, you do not belong here!" did Holly realize that it was time for a change.

Holly's Dickensian odyssey next took her back to New York and her maternal grandfather, who represented the poorer side of her family, though nowhere near as poor as the checkered existence she was leading in New Orleans. He owned a garage in Washington Heights, next to Columbia-Presbyterian Hospital. He had a black secretary, who turned out to be his mistress, and was jealous of Holly's presence. Holly soon found out why when her grandfather kept entering the bathroom whenever she was in the tub and wanted to help bathe her, "like he did when I was a little girl." Holly realized now that *both* of her grandfathers may have molested her.

Holly found the first job she could, as a showroom model on Seventh Avenue. She might have been a Ford model, but her parents had refused to pay for braces. "I figured out how to smile but never show my crooked lower teeth." As it turned out, no one, except Eileen Ford, and eventually Madame Claude, was noticing her teeth. She was tall and willowy, with prefect C-cup breasts, which was unusual for such a slender torso, and something even Audrey Hepburn could not boast about. "I never really dreamed of being a Ford model. I couldn't stand still, didn't have the discipline. Modeling wasn't that big a deal in the sixties. Call girls made more. If you wanted a straight job, it was better to be a Pan Am stewardess, or Braniff. 'Fly me.' That's what the really hot girls wanted to do, travel, see the world. I obviously wasn't made for a straight job.

"Men were hitting on me all day long," Holly recalled. "I thought the fashion business was supposed to be gay. But not the buyers, not the guys who owned the stores. They were all sex fiends. Most men were. If they had sexual harassment back then, I could have spent the rest of my life in court and made a fortune," Holly said, looking back. Then she described her pivot. "One day, the ad director of the coat company I was modeling for told me he wanted to introduce me to a very rich man. All he said was, 'You be nice to him, and he'll be nice to you.' I wasn't shocked.

"After New Orleans, I knew about hooking. It was a way of life. So many girls did it on the side. Only a fool would give it away. Maybe in college, being the sixties, but in the big city, you had to make a living any way you could. The guy turned out to be great. He owned a fabric company. He lived in UN Plaza, which was brand-new then and the best address in New York, down the hall from Truman Capote, who was my idol. Johnny Carson lived there, too. The guy bought me my first Hermès scarf. He gave me one hundred dollars every time he saw me. Never more than an hour. I thought I was rich."

One wealthy man led to another, through word of mouth. "I didn't really need a madam," Holly said. "I had plenty of guys who 'helped me out.'" Among the men she met was the notorious wiretapper and private eye Bernard Spindel, who had spied for, or spied on, a wide range of celebrities, from Marilyn Monroe to Teamster boss Jimmy Hoffa. Holly seemed to have an affinity for detectives, and vice versa. In what seemed like a sexual chain letter, Spindel introduced Holly to Sy Alter, the bodyguard and girl wrangler of the billionaire playboy A&P heir Huntington Hartford. Spindel had been tapping the conversations of Hartford's soon-to-be ex-wife, with singer Bobby Darin and other men, for upcoming divorce proceedings.

Alter then introduced Holly to Hartford, then in his late fifties, who took her to his Paradise Island Ocean Club, the out-of-this world resort that he had conceived as a Bahamian version of the French Riviera's Hôtel du Cap. The hotel's gardens were modeled after those of Versailles, and the grounds were highlighted by a reconstructed French monastery brought to the new world, à la San Simeon, the home of William Randolph Hearst, on whom Hartford, a fellow megaheir and Harvard man, tried to model himself.

Holly was in good company. Hartford had hosted Winston Churchill and Aristotle Onassis on Paradise Island. The Beatles' *Help* was filmed there, as well as *Thunderball,* with Sean Connery. Nonetheless, the resort failed, losing Hartford thirty million dollars. He didn't care. He had lost far more, in movies, theater, magazines, a modeling agency, those divorces. He would have been a great catch for Holly. Alas, he rarely saw a working girl like her more than once, unless he decided to marry her. He did, however, later make the connection for her to Madame Claude.

Socially, Hartford was Holly's high-water mark in New York. Hers was a clientele much more out of Damon Runyon than the *Social Register*—garmentos, private eyes, promo men, but not the kind of people she had initially grown up with on the East Side and Round Hill Road. To access that banker elite, she had to connect with madams, and so she did, albeit not Xaviera Hollander, who had yet to publish her book and become famous. Holly began working a few nights a week at one of Manhattan's rare brothels, a York Avenue high-rise penthouse with its own swimming pool, an establishment that was set up by the members of one of the city's most exclusive men-only clubs, like the Knickerbocker, the Union, the Racquet and Tennis (she didn't want to say which), the way Le Chabannais in Paris had been bankrolled by the Jockey Club. But the house, run by a hyperefficient former club secretary named Jan, was a small-scale operation, like Claude's rue de Marignan apartment, with three bedrooms and never more than five girls on the premises.

Big luxury bordellos on the Paris model had thrived in New York up until World War II and had enjoyed a golden era during Prohibition, when they were the top places in the city for famous people to drink the Depression away. New York's answer and precursor to Madame Claude was a Russo-Polish immigrant corset maker named Polly Adler, who ran a series of celebrity brothels and was protected, as was Claude, both by the mob, in the persons of Dutch Schultz and Lucky Luciano, and by Tammany Hall, in the person of playboy mayor Jimmy Walker. Madam Polly's calling card showed nothing but a parrot on a perch and the number LExington 2-1099. Her memoir, *A House Is Not a Home,* was a vicarious thrill in the Eisenhower era of suburban family values, which made sex, and particularly commercial sex, seem as un-American as communism.

Madams still operated widely in New York and elsewhere in America, but very much under the radar, with police payoffs a major cost of doing their illicit business. The price Xaviera Hollander paid for breaking this code of silence was deportation. Silence remained golden. In general, the girls at Jan's York Avenue penthouse didn't match the men. There weren't any of what Holly would later get to know as "Claude types," though at this point Holly had no clue who Mireille Darc was. American hookers, even Manhattan hookers, still *seemed* like hookers. Maybe that was the market here. Maybe the club men had had enough of what Tom Wolfe would dub the "social X-rays," their anorexic clotheshorse wives at home on Park Avenue.

The moneymen seemed to prefer to let their hair down with lustier, bustier borough types, like the Staten Island secretary played by Melanie Griffith in *Working Girl*. Or with southern outliers like Holly, who once overheard Jan describing her as a "truck stop type with a model body." That one stung. There was still too much Lula Mae Barnes in this Holly Golightly wannabe. In her relocation to the South and in her rejection of the family that had abused and neglected her, the girl who might have been a debutante became a Daisy Mae. She still had lots of work to do to take Georgia out of the girl.

Holly began looking for other madams. There were plenty of them. New York in the early seventies was sex-crazy. Between rock 'n' roll and birth control, the sixties had unleashed a tidal wave of sex without responsibility, free love in every sense, except for the madams and call girls, who were charging a clientele for it that was one generation out of sync. People were having sex as if there would be no tomorrow, or as if they sensed that that grim tomorrow, the maelstrom of AIDS that would end this party, was less than a decade away. Rather than just being jealous of the students who were having all the fun, the suits of New York, the Mad Men and the Wolves of Wall Street, simply began paying for it in the greatest frenzy of "buying pussy" since the Roaring Twenties.

That is, until 1973, when the oil embargo drove the stock market into one of its most severe nosedives, one from which it would not fully recover until the presidency of Bill Clinton in 1993. Call girls seemed to be the first item of discretionary spending that got the ax. Sex was a celebratory event. Hours-long lines at the gas stations had created a massive national bummer. The only people who were celebrating, really living it up, Holly quickly deduced, were the Arabs, who had created this windfall of the century for themselves by exploiting America's fatal dependence on oil for its energy needs. Unfortunately, there were very few rich Arabs in New York, other than at the United Nations, and those diplomats were currently lying very low as the villains of this petrodrama.

"I remember seeing pictures in the papers of decadent Arabs in Beverly Hills, living it up. There was this mansion on Sunset Boulevard where some young Saudi had ten Ferraris and these marble Venus statues on the lawn that he had painted in flesh colors, plus their black pubic hair. That drove everybody crazy. There goes the neighborhood. That got me thinking, like prospectors in the Westerns, There's gold in them thar hills," Holly said. "So I used a New York madam to hook me up with Madam Alex in Beverly Hills, who was forever looking for new faces. She ran the show in L.A." Alex Adams was a Manila-born ex-housewife who had run the flower shop at the Ambassador Hotel, where Bobby Kennedy had been assassinated in 1968. She had bought the black book of a Hollywood madam who was transitioning into the dog-grooming business and built it into the preeminent call girl operation in the West.

Out to California went Holly, who soon found herself whipping future Reagan kitchen cabinet member Alfred Bloomingdale, and doing a ménage à trois with pop duo Steve Lawrence and Eydie Gormé at Madam Alex's mansion brothel in the hills above Malibu. "I was pretty open about sex," said Holly. "I would do anything and anyone. I liked challenges. I liked meeting peoples' needs. That's why I eventually became a nurse. But I drew the line at drugs. Alex had a lot of big show business clients, especially the music people, who wanted girls to do coke and other stuff with them. You know, sex, drugs, and rock 'n' roll. I had been down the drug route in Atlanta, and I almost died, so I was totally no way on that. So Arabs were perfect for me, because they didn't do drugs and they didn't drink. Their vices were fucking and spending. That's when Alex decided to send me to Alabama to see Prince Aziz [not his real name], who was going to flight school. Some school, some student. He lived in a mansion like Tara, and had his butler pick me up at the airport in a Rolls. He liked Southern girls, so for me it was like hitting the jackpot. I got two thousand dollars a day. I went back for three more trips. I wept when he graduated."

Prince Aziz would ultimately go on to become his country's minister of defense. A far bigger part of the Arab spending spree in their oil boom than call girls was military, and that is how middlemen purchasing agents like Adnan Khashoggi, who bought them tanks and the jets and all the high technology that petrodollars could buy, became some of the world's richest men, the Gettys of the Gulf. Alex had a pipeline, as it were, to these people, but Holly didn't get along with Alex, a coke-sniffing martinet who took 40 percent and insisted on being paid her pound of flesh within an hour after the girl left the client. Alex, a master baker and decorator, was immensely charming with her clients, listening to the travails of the rich and famous for hours on the phone, something the all-business Madame Claude would never do. Conversely, Alex would never do what Claude did to transform her girls into the best they could be. She saw no need. There was an endless supply of beach beauties and starlet hopefuls in L.A., and, although Alex could be warm and maternal, she could also be high-handed and treat them like scullery maids. She assumed these girls were basically born to be bad and would all try to cheat her, and she never trusted them with clients' numbers or anything else; plus, she maintained a network of ex-cop "enforcers" in case the girls tried to do a private deal with a client or commit some other act of rebellion. Alex's plantation-master mentality was way too Atlanta for Holly. She went back to New York and began planning for Paris.

"This was my first trip abroad. I was twenty-three. I hated Paris on sight. I mean, I should have been thrilled, and I was. It was old and beautiful, just like the musicals I had loved growing up, *Gigi, An American in Paris, Funny Face*. But I was so intimidated.

I didn't speak the language. I was a high school dropout. I had no idea about all this glorious history. I thought Napoléon was something you ate. I checked into the Paris Hilton, just to have someplace safe and familiar where I could order a BLT and a milk shake and drink water straight from the tap. It was right under the Eiffel Tower, so I had the best of both worlds, but I liked the New World better. I was a Georgia girl. But again, I was open to learn.

" 'The Arabs don't speak French, either. So you'll be fine,' said Catherine Virgitti, Claude's right hand and booker, who I would soon meet. She was pretty but mean, like the salesgirls at the fancy French boutiques on Madison Avenue who refused to wait on you unless you were Gloria Vanderbilt. She answered the phones for Claude in at least four or five languages. She was a blonde, a real tough bitchy blonde, wore tight leather pants and an unbuttoned silk blouses and expensive high heels, and somehow rode a motorcycle. She had to be a dominatrix. She probably was great if you wanted to suffer.

"Catherine was acting as my translator, as Madame Claude, it turned out, didn't speak much English. That didn't surprise me. Neither did the shopgirls on Madison Avenue or the captains at the fancy French restaurants like Caravelle and Pavilion that sometimes the rich dress shop owners from Dallas or Saint Louis might take me to when they came to New York. I'd just order steak and french fries to be safe, but my dates weren't any more sophisticated than I was. They liked playing fancy and throwing their money around, which was fine with me. And now I was in Paris, no one spoke a word of English, not a cabdriver, not the café waiter, no one except the nice people at the Hilton.

"I'm glad I had gotten Madame Claude's information before I went, or I'd have been lost. It was hard to get. Madam Alex claimed she didn't know it, nor did any of the New York madams I knew. They had all heard of her, but their attitude was that she was out of their league, and mine, too. Who did I think I was, wanting to work for her? Little Miss Stuck-Up? I tried to get Prince Aziz's number. I figured he would know how to get to Claude, maybe give me a recommendation. But Alex guarded his info, and all of her clients', like the gold in Fort Knox. In the end, I went to Sy Alter, who had set me up with Hunt Hartford. He gave me the number, and promised to call her, but he tried to discourage me. 'You're way too sweet,' he told me, warning me off, trying to be polite. 'She just has a lot of cunty uptight French debs. Hunt never uses her. He hates those types. He outgrew them in prep school.' What he was saying, between the lines, was that I wasn't polished enough for Madame Claude. I felt like saying, What am I, chopped liver? I wanted to tell him about my real background. I might have been a cunty deb, too. What would that have been like? Oh, well. I wasn't. I just took the number and ran.

"The place where I was meeting Claude was the brothel part of her operation. It was full of antiques and paintings that looked like they came from the Louvre. It looked like a fancy hotel, which I guess is what it was. Two giant sporty blondes were there, not at all friendly. 'They're Austrian,' Catherine said by way of explanation. They looked like they belonged on the Olympic ski team. Or in Goldfinger's lair. Catherine gave me some delicious coffee and rolls on fine china.

"I just sat there as she worked the phones in another room for seemingly an hour until Claude came in, reeling off dozens of orders to Catherine in machine-gun French. She was tiny and perfect, beautifully dressed and made up, super hair, the best bleach job I had ever seen. She seemed like a little general, the head of L'Oréal or Lanvin, not a sex broker. When she caught a glimpse of me, standing up politely to say hello, she just stared and didn't say a word, as if thinking, What is *she* doing here? 'She's Huntington Hartford's friend,' Catherine said, beginning to introduce me. Claude, without even looking at me, went into a tirade that sounded as if she was saying how worthless Hartford was, and then said, 'I hope you told her there's nothing here for her.' Before Catherine could say 'But wouldn't you like to meet her?' Claude went into her office and closed the door.

"Catherine tried to apologize. 'She has a lot going on.'

" 'I came all the way . . .'

" 'I know.' Catherine seemed nicer than I had thought. She went into Claude's office and, after twenty more minutes, somehow got her to come out and interview me, with Catherine doing simultaneous translating. 'She has never taken anyone who doesn't speak French,' Catherine said, opening the conversation as Claude primly sat in what must have been some king's throne and just looked at me with nothing but doubt.

" 'Stand up and show her your figure,' Catherine said. 'She has a great figure.'

"As I stood up, so did Claude. In her heels, on tiptoe, she came over and pulled my jaw down, like a dentist, to look at my crooked teeth. Right away she had found my Achilles' heel. 'What good is her figure if her teeth are bad? And her skin . . .' She pointed her perfectly manicured index finger over some blemishes I thought I had covered with makeup. 'McDonald's,' she sneered, making a face. They called Americans 'McDonald's' in France. It was a put-down. It meant tourists. She asked where I went to school, if I had gone to college. I didn't lie. She gave me another hopeless grimace. She asked what countries I had visited. 'This one,' I said.

"Then Madame Claude gave me one of the culture quizzes she became famous for. Did I know who Valéry Giscard d'Estaing was? Of course I didn't. But I tried. Wasn't she this new madam in D.C.? I had heard of a Madam Valerie. . . . Claude cut me off with another one. 'What is a madeleine?' I thought she meant a mandolin. It was the delicious cookie I was holding in my hands. 'Who is Madame Bovary?' she went on. I thought it was one of Alex's rivals in L.A. *Mon Dieu!* Claude said, exasperated with me, as if I was the worst student she ever had. 'The girl has a one-track mind.' I didn't have the answers she wanted. I tried to tell them a little of my life history, how I had come from a good eastern family, how none of that worked out. Nothing impressed her. She made me feel like poor white trash.

"'She doesn't take girls who have already . . . started working.' Catherine looked for a nice way to say it. 'Claude doesn't want prostitutes. This isn't a brothel.'

"Again, I was too polite to ask, after looking in at the two Nazi skiers, 'What the hell is it?' Instead, I just dropped the best name I had. 'I really hit it off with Prince Aziz in Alabama. We had a very special chemistry. I was hoping to meet more guys like him.' Suddenly, both Catherine and Claude's expressions changed. I had said the secret word, like on the Groucho Marx show when the duck would come down and give you a hundred-dollar bill. 'Prince Aziz! How would you know him?' Catherine asked. All of a sudden, they were taking me seriously.

"With the drop of that name, all of Madame Claude's rules ceased to apply. I didn't have to speak French. My past was no problem. I could have been hooking at Times Square, as long as Prince Aziz had picked me up. If he liked a girl, that was all it took. Every other Gulf prince would like me, too. Of course they were going to check me out, call the prince, if they could get past the walls of security, to find out if I was bullshitting them."

Holly was checked out, and indeed she did pass muster. Claude would have loved to have the prince as a client, to take him from Alex. The two titans of the field had never met. East was east, west was west. But Alex, who had a son and a house of cats that she doted on, was much more effusively embracing and maternal, "the mother of all madams," than Claude would or could be, and Alex's men were as loyal to her as men could be—that is, until the next perfect girl came around whom they were dying to meet. Claude's gambit would be to reach out to the prince, remind him of Holly, say she was dying to see him again and was no longer with Alex. Claude was not concerned that Alex would send one of her LAPD goon squad to Paris to wreak revenge, as L.A. or even New York madams might have done if confronted by a similar attempt at poaching.

Normally, Madame Claude would have never taken an American at all, unless she was a gorgeous French-speaking Ford model, which was unlikely. With unusual exceptions like Ali MacGraw, Wellesley '60, gorgeous American models weren't known for being bookish. The only other Yankee option would be a junior year abroad Seven Sisters student at Smith College's Paris campus, Reid Hall, off the boulevard du Montparnasse, who wanted to take a walk on the wild side, which was also a rare occurrence. Claude spoke little English, and, untrusting as she was, didn't like relying on Catherine Virgitti, whom she always suspected of plotting to steal her business, to do simultaneous translation for her. She wanted her girls to be multilingual, as most well-bred European girls were.

Madame Claude was a terrible snob. Like most French members of the aspirational middle class, she was unduly impressed with titles, pedigrees, degrees, and the like. She was also impressed with wealth, whatever the provenance, be it feudal land grants from the Holy Roman Empire, Corsican vendettas, Arab holy wars, or African tribal massacres. When money talked, no one listened like Madame Claude. More than anything else, the Arab wealth explosion was what changed the call girl game. Until the embargo, Claude was at her snobby happiest catering to club men, either from Le Jockey or Le Racing or across the Channel, from White's or Boodle's. She needed the cops and the gangsters, to protect her, and the movie moguls, just because the French were cinephiles who were in awe of the movies even more than they were in awe of the ancient aristocracy. But now because of the dramatic new magnitude of their wealth, the Arabs zoomed to the pinnacle of Madame Claude's wish list, and that of every other madam.

Whomever she was catering to, Claude never stopped hating the idea of prostitutes, just as she never stopped hating herself, or at least the true self of Angers and the rue Godot-de-Mauroy. Like Groucho Marx, she didn't want to be a member of any club that would have her, and in her case, that was her old club of unhappy hookers. Despite the high dudgeon she expressed when anyone dared describe her swans as whores, if anyone was going to take away their "virginity" in the sense of taking money for their favors, it was Madame Claude who had to be the first. Hence her initial revulsion at Holly's history as a working girl.

Holly was different from most Claude girls in that she had no interest in the social aspects of being a Claudette. All her Cinderella fantasies had been destroyed by her miserable childhood. She didn't want to marry a count or a duke, or even a millionaire. That was the end goal of the Madame Claude School of Love. Holly didn't want to marry anyone. When both your grandfathers and your father betray you, you're not looking for Mr. Right. She just wanted to be independent, of all men, of all people. And so did Madame Claude. Actually, Holly and Madame Claude had much more in common than it initially seemed. "We were both kind of feminists," Holly reflected. "Feminist hookers, if you can be such a thing."

The conjugal fantasies of most European Claudettes ran to conventional Western noblemen or tycoons, and maybe to rock stars. Arabs did not enter the picture. These girls were prejudiced, if not flat-out racist. Since part of the Claude program was a version of the Actors Studio, racism threw a major monkey wrench into the Method acting that Claude required. Many girls, like the future art dealer Véronique, didn't want to see Arabs for love or money. Holly, notwithstanding her upbringing in the South, was an equal-opportunity courtesan. She served all customers, and, from her waitress days, knew that the customer was always right. Catherine Virgitti understood that the Arabs needed the best actresses she could find. Accordingly, she was able to convince Claude to give Holly a chance, a chance that Claude otherwise never would have taken.

Because of the language problem, Catherine would be Holly's point person in Paris. That night, to welcome her into the Claude fold, she took Holly out on the town. Holly wasn't aware of Claude's program of testers, but that night was less the beginning of a beautiful friendship than a test in which Catherine played *essayeuse* to Holly's guinea pig. Claude didn't have any Arab or African male testers, so Catherine would have to suffice.

Everything about Claude was business, even when it seemed like pleasure. Pleasure *was* her business; there was no downtime. Claude had Holly sized up for the niche she would service—the Gulf and black Africa. Just as she had pigeonholed Véronique as her token Jew for her refined Lebanese and Persian clients, she pigeonholed Holly as her "missionary" who would bring the Claude gospel to the Third World and to the rich but unsavory fat cats her normal girls did not want to see. She was a commercial sex version of baseball's utility infielder.

Catherine was told not to waste her time trotting out Holly for the titillation of the young swells at Régine's or Castel, whom Claude was certain would not be interested in her. Instead, Catherine took her to "Sappho night" at the avenue Victor Hugo nightclub L'Aventure, which was basically every night at the trendy bôite. Waiting for them was a hot Berber girl from Morocco's High Atlas mountain range who was the hostess at Bébert, a couscous restaurant in Montparnasse. There was also a Crazy Horse Saloon dancer from Martinique on her off night, a big butch Nigerian who managed a bowling alley in Belleville, and a pretty black girl from Vicksburg, Mississippi, who cooked fried chicken at Haynes, the only soul-food restaurant in Paris. The Mississippian was the only one who spoke English, and she and Holly hit it off immediately, like southern soul sisters.

The entourage danced until dawn, then all finished the evening, in a massive tangle of each other's arms and legs, at Catherine's apartment close to the George V and the Plaza Athénée, two grand hotels highly favored by the Third Worlders, and where Catherine told Holly she would be spending lots of time. "This is the house that Claude built," Catherine told Holly, with the encouraging implication that Claude could build her one, as well. Holly's good nature and sexual adventurousness made the evening a success. Catherine was testing her to see how she handled a mix of cultures, though Catherine also had an insatiable need to be with every interesting woman she met, conventionally attractive or not. "She was my first French woman," Holly said. "We had beginner's luck." That connection made Holly nearly as secure as the service at the Paris Hilton. As a stranger in this strange land, it was a good thing to have a friend at court.

"I knew right away that I couldn't live in Paris, even in an American hotel, which I would have had to be making a fortune to afford. It was way too strange, not speaking the language. My first big fight with Claude was over the braces. She sent me to her skin guy, her hair guy, her exercise guy, you name it. She insisted I shave my pussy. Arab men hated hair, she said. Breeding ground for disease. I did it not to argue. Everything but braces. I was game for change, but I wasn't going to sit in Paris for a year or more waiting for my teeth to start moving. I was great at giving head, and I wasn't about to cramp my style with a bunch of metal and rubber bands in my mouth.

"'You don't need your mouth,' Catherine told me. 'All they like is anal.' Great, I thought, just great. What had I gotten into? Well, that wasn't off the menu. There was just a surcharge. And that triggered Claude off, who blew up and said, 'This is not prostitution!' 'Then what is it?' I asked her, and you weren't supposed to talk back to Claude. I pushed it. 'What is it, then, a cultural exchange? Come on, what we're exchanging is money for bodily fluids!' I should've bitten my tongue. Claude flipped. 'Catherine, go take her to the rue Saint-Denis! She'll be right at home there. Until the pimps kill her.' Luckily, Catherine was a peacemaker. She knew my actions would speak louder than my uppity words.

"Catherine got me my first date, with a young Pakistani businessman at the George V. He was very Westernized, had gone to school at an English military academy. I guess that's why he wanted some discipline, but it was nothing too much. I ordered him around. He enjoyed himself so much that he insisted he introduce me to his cousin, who had his own suite on another floor. He was even younger, and even simpler, as he had attended a nonmilitary English school. Neither of them demanded the dreaded "A levels" as they called it, which was an English exam term that was also a shorthand for saying anal sex. Muslim wives have to be virgins, and the only way to have sex and keep your virginity is a rear entry. But in my experience, the men would rather have had normal intercourse whenever they could get it. Whatever, I was prepared for whatever came up, and relieved when it didn't.

"I was at the hotel for less than four hours and came back to Claude with over four thousand dollars, which netted me almost three thousand for myself. Before they divided the take, Claude and Catherine 'debriefed' me. They had wanted me to find out what the boys were doing in Paris. It was a big meeting and party with the top brass of Dassault Aviation. That was all I could get out of them, but to Claude, it was like I was Deep Throat. Catherine told me later that it meant that the Pakistanis may have been in negotiations to spend some of the new oil windfall on the Dassault Mirage fighter jets.

"That information was valuable to Claude's investor friends. Maybe they were all going to buy the stock. It was inside information, though I had no idea how all that worked. I was too busy counting my three thousand dollars, which would buy me a month at the Hilton and the chance to make tons more. Claude

Je suis un Parisien. President John Kennedy on his first official visit to Paris, June 1961, where he also had his first secret encounter with a Madame Claude girl. (© *AGIP/Bridgeman Images*)

Liz and Dick. Richard Burton was Madame Claude's favorite Hollywood star client. He often used Claude as a refuge from his turbulent marriage to Elizabeth Taylor. The couple are pictured here after the brief wedding ceremony in a Montreal hotel, 1964. (*Bridgeman Images*)

Going native. Frank Sinatra (with Robert Viale and others) at Le Pirate, the Riviera nightclub so popular with the jet set and rat pack, a clientele that heavily overlapped with that of Madame Claude. (*Mondadori Portfolio/Bridgeman Images*)

Arms and the Man. Steve McQueen, another Claude habitué, brandishing a toy pistol at a Paris party; 1964. (*Reporters Associati & Archivi/Mondadori Portfolio/Bridgeman Images*)

Belles de Jour. Catherine Deneuve played a call girl in Luis Bunuel's 1967 film *Belle de Jour,* inspired by Madame Claude, while Françoise Fabian (center) would go on to play Madame Claude herself in a film by Just Jaeckin. (*Bridgeman Images*)

Public Enemy. Pierre Loutrel, AKA Pierrot le Fou, one of the notorious Corsican gangsters befriended by Fernande Grudet in the early 1950s, when she was a Montmartre gun moll prior to becoming Madame Claude. (© *Tallandier / Bridgeman Images*)

Role Supermodel. Gorgeous actress Mireille Darc was the slinky blond goddess template for the "Claude Girl." (© *DILTZ / Bridgeman Images*)

Top Cop. Maurice Papon, Nazi collaborator and all-powerful Paris police chief, who was Madame Claude's principal protector; 1962. (© *AGIP/Bridgeman Images*)

First Family. French President Valery Giscard d'Estaing and his wife, Anne-Aymone, who gracefully endured his many rumored affairs before his tax authorities drove Madame Claude into exile in Beverly Hills. (© *AGIP/Bridgeman Images*)

Culturati. Claude's top film producer client, Darryl F. Zanuck; her best woman friend, France's number-one bestselling author Françoise Sagan; Zanuck's mistress and pop singer Juliette Gréco; and Hollywood legend Orson Welles at the Cannes Film Festival, 1959. (© *Everett Collection/Bridgeman Images*)

Big Boys. Boxing champion Georges Carpentier, singer Maurice Chevalier, mogul Darryl Zanuck, and the Duke of Windsor at an opening night at the Lido nightclub, 1959. They all might have celebrated with Claude girls afterwards. (© *AGIP/Bridgeman Images*)

The Emperor Has No Clothes. Jean-Bedel Bokassa, dictator of the Central African Republic, seen leaving the famous Parisian cabaret Regine's, 1974. Claude sent women to spy on him for France. (© *Giovanni Coruzzi / Bridgeman Images*)

Plain Jayne. Jayne Mansfield dancing with Le Tour d'Argent owner Claude Terrail (seen here at the Cannes Film Festival, 1963), who turned fine dining into an aphrodisiac that allowed him to seduce many Hollywood stars, including Marilyn Monroe, Ava Gardner, and Rita Hayworth. (© *AGIP / Bridgeman Images*)

Sister Act. Françoise Sagan and her wannabe writer brother, Jacques Quoirez, who ghostwrote Claude's first memoir and had a free pass with her girls. (© *AGIP / Bridgeman Images*)

A Night at the *Opéra*, 1968. President George Pompidou, who protected Madame Claude and used her for espionage, and his wife, also named Claude, whose height, blondness, and regal bearing was precisely what Madame Claude was looking for in her courtesans. (© *Giovanni Coruzzi / Bridgeman Images*)

Beau Monde. Movie heartthrob Alain Delon, his model wife, Nathalie, and their son, Anthony, in Monte Carlo, 1965. This "royal family" of the French jet set was considered too perfect. Major scandals would ensue. (© *AGIP / Bridgeman Images*)

Body Double. Stevan Markovic, Alain Delon's bodyguard and lookalike, tried to take over Delon's glamorous life, including having an affair with his wife, pictured here in Saint-Tropez, 1967. Markovic was murdered in one of the great unsolved mysteries of the era. (© AGIP / Bridgeman Images)

Jolly Roger. Roger Vadim with wife Jane Fonda, whom he forced into ménages à trois with girls Vadim ordered from Madame Claude. The director was also married to Brigitte Bardot and had a child with Catherine Deneuve. (Bridgeman Images)

The Enabler. White House press secretary and future California senator Pierre Salinger, with Jacqueline Kennedy Onassis, seen leaving Maxim's, Paris, 1974. Salinger arranged assignations for John Kennedy with Claude girls while Jackie went on culture and shopping trips. (© Giovanni Coruzzi / Bridgeman Images)

Musical Chairs. The sexual requests of Aristotle Onassis and Maria Callas were, Madame Claude said, "too depraved" to recount. Here they are at the Lido, December 1966, with the First Couple of French rock 'n' roll, Sylvie Vartan and Johnny Hallyday. (© *AGIP/Bridgeman Images*)

An Offer He Couldn't Refuse. Marlon Brando liked to hire Claude girls and lecture them on human rights; Paris, 1957. (© *AGIP/ Bridgeman Images*)

Soul Brothers. Two of Madame Claude's top clients: the unlikely duo of Baron Elie de Rothschild and Sammy Davis, Jr.; 1967. (© *Giovanni Coruzzi/Bridgeman Images*)

Italian Stallion. Auto tycoon Gianni Agnelli, who gave Madame Claude a Fiat when she was released from prison. (*Bridgeman Images*)

Shah Na Na. Mohammad Reza Pahlavi, the shah of Iran, seen here at the opera in 1961 with his empress, Farah Diba, was Claude's most generous client, lavishing precious jewels on all the many women she dispatched to his palace in Tehran. (*Bridgeman Images*)

The King and I. Yul Brynner, one of Claude's Hollywood favorites, at the Olympia, Paris, 1963. (© *Giovanni Coruzzi/ Bridgeman Images*)

Camelot. Jack and Jackie, in front of Paris' city hall, during their 1961 trip where he betrayed her. (© *AGIP/ Bridgeman Images*)

Amazing Grace. Birgit de Ganay was a regal Grace Kelly doppelgänger who married both a French count and a Greek tycoon. One of Madame Claude's superstars, she shocked *le tout Paris* when she jumped to her death from her avenue Marceau designer apartment. (*Courtesy of Philippe Jadin*)

was pleased, both with the money and with the info. Catherine said she shared it with the French government, which liked to be on top of these things. She thanked me. I was touched. '*Merci et bravo*,' she said. I saw it as a breakthrough."

What Holly would find out later was that Madame Claude, while servicing the rich Arabs, was communicating whatever intelligence she learned through her Claudettes to the Israelis, as well as to Americans. Dassault, the aviation giant, had long been one of Israel's prime supporters, manufacturing the Mystère and Mirage jets that were the mainstay of the Israeli air force and that gave the country the firepower to consistently outgun the Arabs in the numerous wars after Israel's independence.

The company's founder, Marcel Dassault, believed to be the richest man in France, was born Marcel Bloch and was Jewish. During World War II, he was sent to Buchenwald. Released by American forces, and weighing seventy pounds, he changed his name and converted to Roman Catholicism. He remained one of Israel's best friends in Europe. However, after the ignominious Arab defeat in 1967's Six-Day War, Charles de Gaulle, understanding the importance of Arab oil to France, won more than Brownie points with OPEC by imposing an arms embargo on Israel, forcing Israel to rely solely on American aircraft suppliers. Now, however, Dassault, either pressured by the Elysée Palace, or blinded by petrodollars, was possibly triggering Israel's worst nightmare by selling jets to its enemies.

While Pakistan had never been to war with Israel, the countries were hardly friends. The Islamic Republic's new president, Ali Bhutto, was closely allied with Saudi Arabia, and any major arms purchase by any Muslim state in that hotbed was something both Israel and America wanted to know all about. It was also possible that Claude was reporting back to Dassault himself on his new clients. He was precisely the sort of military-industrial elitist that Claude treasured most among her clientele. As Madame de la République, she saw it as a civic duty to keep this elite fully informed about anything that could impact the future of the *république* she proudly served.

"The worst part was the waiting," Holly said, describing the many missions she went on for Madame Claude, whether to the George V or the Saint-Georges in Beirut or the Mamounia in Marrakech or the Nile Hilton in Cairo or the Riyadh Sheraton. "The Arabs are night people, and sex is the last stop on the night train. They would eat at midnight for hours and hours, and, for people who weren't supposed to drink, they seemed to get pretty wasted. Usually, the big event didn't happen until sunrise, though it didn't take all that long. I think they were as tired then as I was. A lot of it was ceremonial, lots of bathing."

There was lots of information acquired between the sheets of the hotels and in the bathtubs of the Levant and the Gulf, and Holly would often spend more time being debriefed by Catherine and Claude than she actually spent in bed with the clients. Most of the information was about what the clients did sexually, seemingly for potential blackmail dossiers, as well as geopolitical information on oil deals and arms purchases. The biggest payday for Claudettes and Madam Alex's "creatures," as she called them, as well as for any other ambitious women, was to go to Tehran and see the Shah. Even more than Khashoggi, Reza Pahlavi was the highest of the high rollers. He often tipped the girls with expensive jewels, which created no end of battles over whether these were commissionable and spelled the avaricious end of many a call girl—madam relationship. "The Shah liked blondes," Holly said. "I sadly missed that boat."

Holly did have the unusual experience of boarding the diamond-encrusted "Good Ship Lollipop" that was captained by Jean-Bédel Bokassa, the president, and later emperor, of the Central African Republic, so named because it was at the dead center of the Dark Continent. Bokassa was up there with Mobuto of the Congo and Idi Amin of Uganda as the most ruthless and bloodthirsty of African despots. The only alleged atrocity about Bokassa that was never proved was cannibalism. He supposedly had two vast walk-in human-flesh freezers, one for white and one for black. For all his decadence and corruption, Bokassa was a great favorite of the French power elite. He called de Gaulle "Papa." Giscard d'Estaing called Bokassa "cousin" and often went big-game hunting with him.

The French fêted Bokassa with honors, with gourmet food, with Madame Claude's girls. He was a frequent guest of honor at the Elysée Palace and was decorated with the Légion d'honneur, whose badge he added to his bulging chest of ribbons and medals. Not bad for a cannibal. Located between the British Sudan and the Belgian Congo, the primitive Central African Republic had long been a French colony and had two things France highly valued. Its biggest lure was uranium, for France's ambitious nuclear program. And then there were diamonds, which proved to be best friends to both girls and boys in the game of nations.

"I would have been terrified if I had known. But I was out of it. I had no idea where the place was, and until I had to go there, I never needed to know," Holly said. "Bokassa had a big château outside of Paris, which didn't seem like a place where you could get eaten. What I didn't realize then was how Claude couldn't have cared less, as long as she got paid. I was expendable. She wasn't grooming me to marry a Rothschild. I would never be a trophy for her, just a cash cow. Which was why I was there, so nobody got disappointed. I wasn't insulted that she didn't think I had the class to marry someone famous or titled. Maybe a little. But I got over it. Not speaking French kind of isolated me from her mainstream, but it may have kept me out of the palace intrigues and the competition among the girls as to who got the top guys."

Holly's first meeting with the dictator, self-styled as the CAR "president for life," was at his Château d'Hardricourt in Yvelines, where the Georges Pompidous had their weekend-escape home.

This evening was arranged through Madame Claude via Albert Jolis, an Antwerp-born, Manhattan-based global diamond dealer who was angling for a concession in the CAR and sought to curry Bokassa's favor. Jolis had been a member of the OSS during World War II; during the Cold War, he was very active in anti-Communist activities, such as supporting Russian dissidents, and was often suspected of working with the CIA. People were never sure where the diamond business ended and the spycraft began. The Claude girls were Jolis's "gift," his tribute to the leader, and exactly the favor the lusty man of war appreciated.

"She sent me and Trinh, this knockout Vietnamese girl who Claude would never send to her 'white' clients, unless they had some kind of Asian fetish, which is big now, but it was unusual then," Holly said, describing the small army of Uzi-toting, commando-dressed African bodyguards who ringed the château. Bokassa bragged to the girls that they had been trained by Israeli security, the best in the business at assassination prevention. "Bokassa loved Vietnamese girls, everything Vietnamese," Holly went on. "The whole kitchen at the château was staffed by Vietnamese. Food was great. He had served in the French army there, and had become a French officer and war hero. Trinh, like me, was a back-street girl in Claude's eyes. She had a cute sing-song accent in English. My southern drawl was worse. I'm sure we were both branded as low-class.

"I got some cover because a few of the top Paris models, like Lauren Hutton and, later, Jerry Hall, had cornpone accents, so it made it a little chic. But never chic enough for Madame Claude to showcase me. Trinh's family were immigrants, her mom cleaned the Métro, but somehow she was tall, so she got in the door that way. Tall was the way to Claude's heart, if she had one. Claude was so mean. She called her 'the laundress.' She probably called me 'the waitress.' Whatever, we were both 'specialists,' not mainstream. Affirmative-action hookers."

Aside from the Vietnamese cooks, Holly described the Bokassa château as staffed with African butlers and waiters and other help, all in livery and white gloves, a surreal scene from *Planet of the Apes,* with an African orchestra playing Strauss waltzes under crystal chandeliers while Bokassa, the two Claude girls, and another half a dozen African beauties who were the dictator's harem sat at a long formal candlelit dining table eating *pho* and *nem* and lemongrass shrimp with ancient silverware instead of chopsticks. The dinner was punctuated by the roar of the lion that Bokassa had illegally imported and kept on the grounds as a mascot.

"He was cute. For a dictator who killed people," Holly said. "He reminded me of Sammy Davis, Jr., that kind of high energy. And he dropped names of all the famous politicians he knew, like a Hollywood person would drop the names of stars. De Gaulle, Edward Heath, Khrushchev, Nasser, Sadat, Ceausescu of Romania. He was little and intense, and he wore his full-dress field marshal uniform, with all the medals, every one with a story. He was really proud of himself. He wanted to belong. I can almost see him standing up and singing 'I Gotta Be Me!' like Sammy.

"Bokassa loved to speak French, and I'm not sure he got that I didn't. He didn't care. He just liked to talk about himself. Trinh helped me understand. He went on and on about all his battles, against the Vietnamese, the bloody 1965 coup, where he became his country's first president, kicking out the Communist Chinese, who wanted his uranium. He said he hated communism. That was clear from how he lived. He showed off a large cross that had been given to him at the Vatican by his good friend Pope Paul the Sixth. But he said his other good friend Colonel Qaddafi of Libya had convinced him to become a Muslim. He was still drinking Dom Pérignon. He said he had at least forty children, and that he loved all of their mothers, wherever they might be. We could never tell whether he was joking or not. He told us how he had just celebrated Mother's Day back in his country. He released all his female prisoners in his jails, and ordered the execution of all men who were in jail for rape.

"Bokassa asked us which title sounded better, president or emperor. We both said emperor. He said he loved Napoléon, like Madame Claude did. Funny, because five years later he made himself emperor in the most expensive coronation in history, which overdid it so much that it got him deposed. After dinner he told us to get undressed, in front of him, and go for a swim in his pool. As we were about to jump in, he warned us to be careful not to disturb his pet crocodile, who slept at the bottom. Then he laughed wildly. Whatever he said, we did it. We did our best not to make waves.

"The only people who had sex that night were Trinh and me. Bokassa and his harem watched. Each of his wives kissed us on both cheeks when we left. He gave us ten thousand dollars. Again, Claude was pleased. In our debriefing she was mostly interested in how he felt about America. He loved Muhammad Ali. Otherwise, we told her he had barely mentioned America, or the oil crisis. With all his Arab friends like Qaddafi, it wasn't something he was worried about. I wish I had had more to report, but that was it. With Madame Claude, you had to be alert, all the time. You learned to look for details."

Holly made numerous trips to Africa, mostly North Africa, Morocco, Algeria, Tunisia, the former French colonies, where France still held sway. The trips always involved oil, politics, or arms, where Claudettes were used as party favors, to lubricate international conferences, to celebrate deals, to curry favor. Usually several girls would go together as an entourage. But because the classic Claudettes were loath to "do" either Arabs or Africans, Holly picked up a lot of assignments in the two years after the embargo, when oil was king. One of these trips was to visit Bokassa again on his home territory, the CAR capital of Bangui.

"I flew on an Air France 707 nonstop from Paris," Holly recalled. "It showed how important the place was to France. But you'd never know it. It was like a dusty, dumpy little colonial town with unpaved dirt roads." The most arresting visual of Bangui were its natives, mostly in tribal costumes, among whom Bokassa's soldiers, dressed up like some splendid Napoleonic regiment, marched in formation. There were also lots of European businessmen in Lanvin suits hustling about, seeking to do business with the palace, of which there were several, one for Bokassa, another for his "first wife," Catherine, and a few other marble riffs on the Taj Mahal, for lesser wives and children. "The only charm, if you call it that, was seeing and hearing French everywhere, and the people drinking coffee and eating croissants outdoors under signs for Pernod and Ricard. It reminded me a little of an African New Orleans, not that New Orleans doesn't have a lot of Africa in it. Bangui was on this big wide river like the Mississippi that was called the Ubangi. In Georgia, they used to call black people 'Ubangis,' and it was hard to get that association out of my mind.

"I was going to tell President Bokassa the Ubangi story, to make conversation, but I held off. It probably would have gotten lost in translation. The party group consisted of me, Trinh again, and five other Claude girls, mostly her bitchy blond types, who started complaining the minute we got off the plane. There was only one modern hotel. It had air-conditioning and a pool, but it was more Holiday Inn than the George V, and these girls were spoiled. They wanted blondes because the occasion was some sort of uranium conference and there were a lot of important Western businessmen who may not have been willing to "go native" with the many black beauties in Bokassa's harem. Most tycoons, except for some kinky Germans, were as conventional in their tastes as the Claude girls who refused to see blacks or Arabs. Fuck them both. Or not," Holly said with a laugh. "I wasn't sure who was paying for this outing, Bokassa trying to sell his minerals, or the Euros trying to buy them. Whatever, it was a big payday for five days in the jungle. I was going to make fifteen thousand dollars. The money was out of this world.

"The African week was a blur of folklore banquets, champagne, and sex," Holly said. "A lot of the guys were serious uranium scientists, chemists, geologists, who I don't think had ever got laid before outside of their wives. They left happy. If there was a deal there that had to be closed, it got closed. But we couldn't learn much from them to report to Claude, because it was all over our heads. I do remember accidentally walking into one room in the main palace that was filled floor to ceiling with piles of brand-new five-hundred-franc notes. They had just come off the printing press, never used. It was like Fort Knox.

"I also met this famous Israeli general, Shmuel Gonen, who had been second in command to Moshe Dayan and then somehow ended up as part of Bokassa's cabinet. A little tough guy who was cute and always wore army fatigues, ready to go to war. He and Bokassa, in his velvet robes and dripping with bling, made an odd couple. Two of the girls talked about how the general, what everyone called him, had bought two modern military transport jets for Bokassa from Israel and filled one of them with Claude girls as a gift." Shmuel Gonem was indeed an Israeli general and hero of its war of independence, wounded five times. He was famous for the quote "We looked Death straight in the face, and it blinked." During the Yom Kippur War, which triggered the oil embargo, however, General Gonen, leading the army, suffered unacceptable losses and was removed from command and left the country in disgrace, going into the diamond business in the CAR, his goal being to make a big-enough fortune to return to Israel and sue the government to clear his name. He died of a heart attack in 1991.

"Bokassa was superhappy himself. When we left, he gave each of us a beautiful little silver box. They all had diamonds in them. It was like with the Shah. I finally got some diamonds. I was so thrilled. That was the thing with Madame Claude. Her girls got diamonds. We had a big discussion on the plane whether to tell her or not. She would want her thirty percent of these. We all agreed not to. And guess what? Everyone lied. When we got back to Paris, everyone thought she was stabbing the other in the back by confessing to Claude. I knew you could never trust another girl, not those girls. There was no honor among thieves.

"But the crazy thing was that Claude was big about it. She told me we had done a great job, that Bokassa was pleased, that the Elysée [Palace] was pleased. We deserved it. She also said it was a tip, and she didn't commission tips, even if those tips amounted to a small fortune, which these diamonds could be worth. Alex would have had you killed for a percentage point. I wanted to sell these stones, cash out right away. But I didn't go to a Paris dealer, because somehow I thought Claude knew all the big jewelers, like Bert Jolis, and somehow they would recognize these and word would get back to her. She could change her mind. So I waited until I went back to New York. I went to Diamond Row, on Forty-seventh Street, and got them appraised. I was so disappointed. The whole box was worth under a thousand dollars. It was nice, but now I could see why Madame Claude could play such a big sport. Either she had a great eye for diamonds or she just knew."

If the moral of Holly's story was that all that glitters isn't gold, it was a story that would repeat itself, with serious consequences for France, in the years ahead. First, Bokassa became a victim of his own grandiosity. For his coronation in the national soccer stadium as emperor in 1977, he sat on a solid-gold throne studded with twenty thousand pearls and wore a five-million-dollar crown and an ermine-lined robe. The massive event, attended faithfully by the French elite and other high-level sycophants from all over the world, was estimated to have cost thirty million dollars.

Because Bokassa loved diamonds at least as much as sex, he demanded from Albert Jolis, whose company Diamond Distributors, Inc. had become CAR's chief concessionaire, a stone that would rival Britain's crown jewels. It had to be larger than a golf ball. Anything less would be disrespectful; Jolis's head would roll. Jolis came up with a carbonado, a very rare and very huge seventy-karat black diamond found only in the mines of the CAR that had the added value of being cuttable into the shape of the African continent. Jolis set the whole thing as a massive ring with a gleaming white diamond in the center, just as CAR was the center of Africa. Bokassa couldn't have been prouder. The dignitaries from everywhere drooled over the priceless treasure. It was the perfect gift for the emperor, a true bling ring.

Two years later, the combined wretched excesses of Bokassa's coronation and of cannibalism became too much for France to tolerate. The emperor was unseated in a coup ordered by his putative best friend, the new French president and fellow elephant hunter, Valéry Giscard d'Estaing. (Bokassa exterminated thirty thousand of the CAR's forty thousand elephants, selling the tusk ivory into an industry of his own.) Seven hundred French paratroopers seized Bangui while Bokassa was away in Libya visiting his other best friend, Mu'ammar Qaddafi. Despite his ordering the coup, Giscard nonetheless welcomed his erstwhile pal back to France and allowed the ex-emperor to continue to live like one in his Château d'Hardricourt. In 1986, a homesick Bokassa returned to the CAR, where he was promptly arrested at the Bangui airport. He was soon tried on fourteen counts of human rights violations, mass murder, treason, and other atrocities. His lawyer, imported from France, was Paris's answer to F. Lee Bailey and Johnnie Cochran, Francis Szpiner, the top gun whom Madame Claude would hire to defend her when she was finally charged with *proxénétisme* in 1992.

The best Szpiner could do for the "black Napoléon" was to

get him acquitted on the cannibalism charges. He was found guilty on all other counts and sentenced to death. Luckily, the new president of the CAR decided to demonstrate his humanity by commuting the death sentence to one of solitary confinement and life imprisonment. In 1993, in his final act in office, this president declared a general amnesty, and Bokassa was released. He lived in the CAR, declaring himself the thirteenth apostle, until his death of a heart attack in 1996. He never tried to sell his coronation ring, reputedly his most treasured emblem of office.

Once Bokassa was safely dead and buried, Albert Jolis came out with the awful truth: He had stung his nefarious patron, not so much out of revenge but because he couldn't come up with a big-enough stone in time for Bokassa's coronation spectacle. That failure alone could have lost Jolis his CAR diamond concession, or his life. The priceless carbonado was actually a cheap boart, or industrial diamond. The whole ring, even with the real diamond in the center, was worth under five hundred dollars. But since Bokassa trusted Jolis and because he wanted to believe he had a crown jewel, he never tried to sell it, preserving what would have been the highly endangered life of Jolis, who died in 2000 of natural causes.

If there were no reprisal to take against Albert Jolis, Emperor Bokassa did get his own fourteen-karat revenge against his treacherous "cousin Giscard," who would be known as the man who also betrayed Madame Claude, the old friend of his class and his regime. On Giscard's many trips to visit Bokassa, starting when Giscard was Pompidou's minister of finance, he was always lavishly gifted with diamonds, just like Holly and the Claudettes, but on a grander scale. The problem was that Giscard never declared these gifts. In 1979, the year Giscard engineered the coup that toppled his friend, the Paris investigative journal *Le Canard Enchaîné* did an exposé on Giscard's diamonds, claiming that the French president had been given treasures worth hundreds of thousands of dollars, not to mention similar gifts to his brother, his cousins, and other top members of his staff.

Giscard's embarrassed response echoed Holly's experience with Madame Claude. The diamonds were so insignificant, Giscard said, that he had put them in a drawer and forgotten all about them. Diamond men and diplomats stepped up to declare, on the president's behalf, that Bokassa never gave anyone diamonds worth more than ten thousand dollars, including the despot's other dear friend Henry Kissinger. Giscard arrogantly attacked the scandal as a calumny, engineered by his enemies on the Left, and counted on the right-wing papers to investigate the story and clear his name. The diamond tale was never laid to rest. Two years later, in the general elections of 1981, Giscard was defeated by leftist François Mitterrand. Meanwhile, both Holly and Madame Claude had left France, Holly cashing in on her own Arab windfall to enter nursing school and Claude to start a new life in Beverly Hills, where the people might be fake but the diamonds were always real.

Chapter 8

THE TURN OF THE SCREW

By 1973, with the rise of the Arabs and Africans as her "cash crop," the saga of Madame Claude became less a story of romance than finance. Cinderella gave way to Shylock, and what started as an unusual variation on a marriage bureau increasingly became a sexual riff on the global management consultancies like McKinsey and Booz Allen, or on the international investigative firms like Kroll. The headmistress who used to be so concerned with the long-term future of her charges was now blinded by the lucre of the short-term score. That was why she took on girls like Holly, "sector specialists," whom she would have never considered in her early days. She was less interested in transforming them than in how the money they might make could transform her. The thrill of Pygmalionization was dissipating, though Claude remained the most critical woman on earth. The change in goals was inevitable. With the oil embargo, Claude probably made more in 1974 than in all her seventeen previous years combined.

Many marriages were still made. Madame Claude's big challenge in the new age of big money was how to monetize her matchmaking. After all, when one of her girls hit the jackpot and married an industrialist, an arms dealer, or a sheikh, her commissionable earning days for Claude were over. The cash cow had been sent to the abbatoir. Claude could be gracious in the old days, when the highest goal for one of her swans was to marry someone with a title, even if destitute. Claude may have lost a girl, but she gained a title, and the bragging rights thereto only enhanced her mystique. That led to the biggest brand in sex, and the biggest business. But Claude could not live on prestige alone. Money was her scorecard, and this was the time to make all she could.

Although Claude scorned pimps and indignantly denied that she was one, she had her own entourage of men who were high-class procurers by any other name. She didn't need men to find her girls. Girls came to her in droves, and there was always Catherine Virgitti to find her hidden treasures. She did need the men, however, to bring her *men,* and none of her male wranglers brought Claude more rich men and more big money than Harry Winston's two top European salesmen, who surely were the most highly commissioned vendors in the history of luxury. The two men, Manfredo Horowitz and Albano Bochatay, both based in Geneva but global in their reach, were each worth more than $100,000,000. Adnan Khashoggi, a close friend of both, may have made more, but his commissions were for arms, not jewels. (He recycled a large part of those enormous commissions with Harry Winston, Cartier, Van Cleef, and other top jewelers.) What they had in common was that they all worked hand in hand with Madame Claude, using her girls to close their deals. As with the dictator Bokassa, diamonds and Claude were a common denominator of what made the rich of the seventies a different category of wealth than had been seen before.

Between them, Horowitz and Bochatay knew every rich man in the world. They would introduce these men to Madame Claude's girls for the one thing these men did not necessarily have. Many long-term relationships, some with benefit of clergy, some without, occurred. All these relationships utilized high-end jewelry as proof of their seriousness, a symbol of their love. In return for introducing them to their husbands and sugar daddies, these girls then turned to Horowitz and Bochatay to solidify and memorialize the rich men's commitment by having the men purchase great stones befitting their love. The two sales-men made huge commissions, which they rightfully and duti-fully shared with the one girl to whom diamonds were the best friend of any girl: Madame Claude herself. Claude made far more on diamonds than she ever did on sex.

Manfredo "Fred" Horowitz, who was born around 1920, was the son of a prosperous Polish Jewish family that had emigrated to the safety of Lugano, Switzerland, and was in the wholesale paper business. A superb skier, sailor, and tennis player, the lanky, aquiline Horowitz was a bon vivant and ladies' man. After finishing university, Horowitz started out before the war work-ing for his parents, which he hated. Then he joined a shipping company, which he also hated. Finally, he answered a cryptic want ad for a "person of trust," which led him to the top jeweler in Geneva. The first year there, Horowitz increased the store's sales by 100 percent. He had found his métier, but he found his bliss when he met Harry Winston.

In 1951, the year of Winston's legendary auction of the dia-monds of the Egyptian King Farouk, a precursor of, and tem-plate for, the high-rolling Arabs of the seventies, Winston was looking to set up an office in Switzerland, which was the center of Europe and a haven for wealth that had been unscathed by the war. Zurich was the richest city, but Zurich was German, which was still a deterrent to Harry Winston. Winston, who was Jew-ish, had rescued the diamond collections of many Jewish refu-gees fleeing from the Nazis. Many packages of diamonds were hastily addressed to simply "Harry Winston, New York City" but somehow found a safe harbor. French Geneva thus became Win-ston's choice, and in Geneva all roads led to Fred Horowitz.

Not that Horowitz was in Geneva that much. He spent most of his winters skiing in Saint Moritz and, après-ski, at the bar and lobby of the Palace Hotel, where the richest people in Europe came to play. Horowitz's best childhood friend from Lugano was the Baron Hans Heinrich Thyssen-Bornemisza, whose father was a shipping and coal magnate on a par with the Krupps and whose brother, Fritz, had been an imprisoned Nazi collaborator. His was one of the great industrial fortunes of the Continent, not to mention his unrivaled art collection. Horowitz would introduce the baron to his last wife, a former Miss Spain and friend of Horowitz's, who would, after the baron's death, move the baronial collection to Madrid. Horowitz, known as "Europe's matchmaker," also introduced his own ex-wife to Muck Flick, another of the industrial superheirs of the postwar "German miracle." The two Flick brothers, Mick and Muck, heirs to Daimler-Benz, were considered world-class playboys, on a par with fellow German Gunther Sachs, heir to Opel, who married Brigitte Bardot. All were friends of Madame Claude.

Flick married the former Mrs. Horowitz, who stayed friendly and grateful to Fred, hence cementing his network by conjugal ties that were even thicker than those forged on the slopes or the clay courts of the Palace Hotel, the winter nerve center of European high society. Furthermore, Fred Horowitz was a great and early confidant of Madame Claude, going back to her start-up in 1957. He seemed permanently surrounded with a retinue of stunning and willing models and ambitious playgirls. To denigrate Horowitz as a mere procurer would be akin to calling Metternich a mere courtier.

Horowitz was a master in the art of connections, and, hence, the art of the deal. He knew the best girls, the best restaurants, threw the best parties, and even had the most lively yacht in Cannes, which he christened the *Diamond D*. Horowitz, of the infinite Rolodex, would thus sell jewels to his rich and titled sports buddies for their wives and their mistresses, both of whom he might have introduced them to. If you needed to buy jewelry, you would go to Fred Horowitz, because you got not only a Harry Winston diamond but also the time of your life.

Fred Horowitz's contribution to the art and science of selling jewels was what became known as the "exhibition." Before the war, great jewels were sold exclusively at deluxe emporia like Garrard and Cartier and Tiffany in the world-class cities of London, Paris, and New York. The client would enter a very controlled and sedate sanctum sanctorum and be shown an array of priceless objects with the utmost solemnity. Horowitz knew how to make the whole process fun by turning it into a party, a special event, held in the ballrooms of Europe's most exclusive caravanseries, with Madame Claude girls lining the bars and salons outside the ballrooms as both distraction and temptation. In summer, Horowitz's prime venues were the Carlton in Cannes and the Hôtel de Paris in Monte Carlo; in winter, it was the Palace Hotel in Saint Moritz, where the shimmering snow backdrop reflected the Alpine light onto Harry Winston's great jewels.

Horowitz would hold court at the entrance to each ballroom, the dashing gatekeeper, with his retinue of towering beauties, and clients, male and female, would pour in, in droves. Harry Winston, as formal and proper as Fred Horowitz was louche, would stand at the periphery of the room, as sort of a Wizard of Oz figure. Winston was the éminence grise of the world of jewels, a Delphic oracle whose opinions were sought by all. He was treated like royalty by royalty, pulled from corner to corner of the ballroom, as if he were doing the diamond waltz, the master of the business yet somehow seeming, as did the equally reticent and reclusive Madame Claude, like a pawn in the Horowitz game of mix and match.

Horowitz was a master fixer and did much of the fixing for both Madame Claude and Harry Winston, a tiny and proper gentleman who, unlike the European playboys and Arab emirs, maintained a fiduciary propriety and a fidelity to his wife of forty years. All the concierges in all the hotels were on Horowitz's payroll. He had spies at all the yacht harbors, and at all the airports, as well as spotters who took down the license plate numbers of all the expensive cars, so that Horowitz could track those they belonged to and where they lived.

Both Fred Horowitz and Harry Winston were in accord that potential clients were most vulnerable, particularly to top-dollar jewelry, when they were on vacation. Horowitz was great at playing to women's lust for diamonds, and to men's lust for women, all to the great benefit of Winston. His dinner parties at the chicest restaurants of the Côte d'Azur, places like Tetou or La Bonne Auberge, were summer's most-coveted invitations. Among his greatest early clients were Agnelli of Italy, Krupp of Germany, and his virtual in-laws, the Thyssens and the Flicks, but the list of names and titles was endless.

Albano Bochatay, younger than Horowitz by a decade and in his early forties in the Madame Claude seventies heyday, had grown up as an unsophisticated "valley boy" from a tiny village in the rugged canton known as Le Valais, home of the Matterhorn but with little in the way of civilization. He left his cow town for Geneva as a teenager, going to work in a jewelry shop called Gübelin, changing his birth name of Marius for the made-up Albano, which had sophisticated Italian overtones. Bochatay was handsome, like the young Roger Vadim, and learned to dress dashingly and sell charmingly.

In 1952, Harry Winston hired Bochatay away from Gübelin on the salesman's twentieth birthday. Bochatay's dream had come true. He had arrived. Winston, who came to Geneva only a few weeks a year, gave Bochatay an office with stunning views of Lake Geneva, but as Winston employees noted, he never looked outside. Instead, he set his desk in front of a wall mirror, admiring himself during his endless phone calls to Arab princes and their retainers, who would become his specialty and the source of great wealth, both for Harry Winston and for himself.

The world of Harry Winston outside of America was divided into three parts: Fred Horowitz had the European tycoons and royalty; Albano Bochatay had the Arabs and, soon, Imelda Marcos; and a third super-salesman, a Tunisian *pied noir,* bridge champion, and math prodigy named Serge Fradkoff, had the wealthy European Jews who had survived the war. Once he cornered his share of the millionaire market, Fradkoff began acting like one himself. He began dressing like Bokassa and buying racehorses, competing with the Rothschilds in derbies across the Continent.

Bochatay, too, had his affectations, but they were all about refinement, not flash. He collected fine art, bought a chalet in Gstaad, married a beautiful French woman, and lived in increasing splendor in a château on Lake Geneva. No salesmen could have ever lived more grandly than Harry Winston's. Each one was said to hate the others. Horowitz moved out of the Winston suite above the lake to his own quarters in Geneva's old city. Harry Winston could barely control the men, but he didn't seem to mind that they were getting rich off him, recalls his son Ronald. " 'They serve their purpose' was all Dad would say about them. They were multilingual, while Dad could barely get through a French menu, so he depended on them."

One of the perks of Bochatay's rise to power was entering the rarefied orbit of Madame Claude. Claude herself spent significant time in Geneva, a short flight from Paris or a four-hour train ride. Although she was not a jewelry collector, she kept her fortune in secret Swiss accounts and had a leading Geneva lawyer, who in 1972 arranged a marriage of convenience between Claude and his gardener. Those nuptials would give her Swiss citizenship, a useful shield against the fiscal inquiries into her affairs that were initiated by the new regime of Giscard d'Estaing, who became president after the unexpected death of Georges Pompidou in 1974, at the very pinnacle of Claude's own success.

Bochatay began taking groups of Claude girls on his often bi-weekly hejiras to Riyadh and Jeddah to help him pass the many hours spent waiting for the early-morning buying appointments with the assorted members of the royal family. The predawn hours were when the royals bought their jewels, and slept with their concubines. The Claudettes Bochatay took with him were less important to his own pleasure than as catnip to the royals themselves. Bochatay wanted to be the Horowitz of the Levant and the Gulf, creating a large new market of lavishly kept mistresses with an insatiable demand for diamonds.

Meanwhile, back in Europe, Bochatay began a long affair with one of Madame Claude's superstars, an imposing Jewish Moroccan from Casablanca, and installed her as a salesperson in the new Harry Winston Paris headquarters in a lavish *hôtel particulier* right next door to the Plaza Athénée. This woman had a huge following in the Paris elite, most of whom turned to her whenever they needed birthday or anniversary gifts to mollify the wives they were perpetually cheating on. Taking a page from the Horowitz playbook, Bochatay eventually introduced his mistress to her future husband, who possessed one of the oldest titles in Europe. Bochatay had brought him into the Winston atelier to select a bauble for his then wife, knowing full well he might be meeting his future one at the same time. This was a world where one hand was washing the other so much that it could have been the basis for a designer soap commercial.

Even in this high-stakes world of cynical wheeling and dealing and self-dealing, there were still women who sought out Madame Claude for the same reason that had made Claude famous to begin with: meeting Mr. Right. "I was turning thirty and so desperate I would have tried anything. Anything was signing up with Madame Claude." So said Isabella, whose English father was a high official at UNESCO and whose Greek mother, whose *marrano* (Christianized Jewish) family had fled Spain during the Inquisition, was a curator of medieval antiquities at the Musée de Cluny.

Isabella had a series of jobs in Left Bank art galleries and antique stores, where she met a lot of Paris's most eligible bachelors, often through their collector mothers. They all liked Isabella and insisted on fixing her up with their sons, whom they wanted to marry off. Born in India, raised in Japan, and educated in an all-girls English finishing school, Isabella was blond, horsey, all in all very Sloane Rangerish, which was the Londonese for the Lady Diana types who populated Sloane Square, the Chelsea epicenter of haute-Brit conspicuous consumption in the 1970s. *Sloane* in London had the very same signification as *sixteenth* did in Paris. Lady Di equaled Claire Chazal. The multilingual Isabella could have passed for either one.

"Every guy I ever dated in Paris seemed to be a Claude client. They'd brag about it. They thought it showed how cool they were," said Isabella. "They would say things like 'You're like a Claude girl who doesn't fuck.' Charming. I figured they could sleep with the Claude girls. I'd keep my mystery, dignity, whatever you want to call it. In truth, I was intimidated. If they had all slept with Claude girls, I'm sure they would find me boring in bed. So I tried to stay out of bed. Eventually when I'd give in, it was just a matter of time before they did get bored. Or disgusted. One man told me this joke: 'The definition of eternity is the time between when you come and she goes.' I wondered what Claude girls had that normal girls didn't. That was the secret of the universe.

"My parents were intellectuals. They were too busy being smart to have sex. My father was English, so he wasn't interested; he gardened for relaxation. And my mother was Jewish and less interested. My two baby brothers were sex maniacs. They spent all their time on rue Saint-Denis, it was great for horny teenagers to have that outlet, and they never got over it.

We weren't rich enough to even think about going to Madame Claude. I had had an awful marriage at eighteen to an Italian whose family was friends with us. He was supposed to become a famous writer, but he didn't. He was dying to sleep with me until we got married, and then he lost interest.

"I should have been terrified about putting myself on the block with Madame Claude, but I was in a panic," Isabella continued. "My shrink told me that it might be a good idea, to confront my worst fears, which he thought were sexual. The fact that my own psychiatrist would not deter me from going to work as a call girl shows how famous Madame Claude was in Paris, how respected. It was as if I had told him I was thinking of going back to school and applying to Sciences Po. Another shrink would have said, 'You must be crazy.' Maybe he was a client. Everybody was.

"So what the hell? It wasn't hard to get to her. I knew two dozen men who knew her. I almost felt like *I* already knew her. The trick was to keep it secret. That would have been the end of me. I used a gay *antiquaire* friend who sold things to Yves Saint Laurent's lover and business partner, Pierre Bergé, and other major collectors. He was normally a terrible gossip, but he had shared some of his own secrets with me, and I trusted him. He was part of that Saint Laurent crowd that knew everyone, and he was *très sympa*. He called her and said she was very excited to meet a "high-class" girl, that we were hard to find these days. I suppose women's lib was killing the hooker business.

"She invited me to meet her at her apartment. It was a typical sixteenth building on rue Cortambert. I noticed it was between two churches. Maybe I noticed because I was feeling guilty. I had bought some incredibly expensive lingerie, because the guys had told me that she made you strip and then she made you wash yourself in the bidet in front of her. I knew the whole drill. Everyone in Paris did. You weren't to dare show any pleasure, or she would reject you on the spot. What kind of woman would masturbate on a bidet in front of Madame Claude?

"I almost backed out. It seemed so absurd. And then I met her. She was very nice, perfectly put together, maybe fifty, but with great work. I wanted to ask her who in case I needed some. At thirty you start worrying. It was a tasteful apartment. There were no other girls there, no help, just her. My friends used to talk about her brothel on rue de Boulainvilliers, but this must have been where she lived. There were some gorgeous antiques my mother would have loved. That's what I talked about, nervous when the inquisition would start.

"But it never did. 'You're perfect,' she said. I was never so flattered, or relieved, in my whole life. 'I assume you have no secrets, do you?' I was loaded with secrets, but what she meant was that did I have some awful scars or sagging breasts or something she couldn't see that might turn men off. My main secret was that I would be doing this, and I didn't want anyone in Paris to know. I was totally candid in telling her that I was using this as a dating service to meet a great husband. 'It happens all the time,' she said.

"She mentioned Fred Horowitz, who was famous for introducing people, and the name of a very rich German who was now in the market for his third wife. I was, she said, just his type. He was obviously a client, as she knew him well. That's why she was being so nice to me. This was an easy score. I knew precisely who he was and rejected him out of hand. My mother's family died in Nazi concentration camps in Thessaloniki, and this guy's fortune was based on Jewish slave labor in the camps. My mother wouldn't care if I were a Claude girl, or even a street girl, but she would die if I married a Nazi. Madame Claude tried to convince me to give it a chance, but no sale.

" 'Then I'll send you to New York. Have you ever lived in New York?' Claude asked me. I had only been to America a few times with my parents and my ex. I hardly knew it. 'They'll like you in New York. You'll play the Jewish-mother card. You won't believe how well it works.' If you read the French or English papers,

New York was on its last legs, covered in graffiti, racked with crime, broke and looking for a bailout. 'The rich are always rich,' Claude said to me. 'And New York, the good New York, is obsessed with France. You will do well. Just be as French as you can be. And, I just thought of it. I have this boy in Rio. Have you ever flown the Concorde?'"

In less than two weeks, Isabella was flying down to Rio. The sharp-tongued but otherwise sedate gallery girl was now looking at herself as a female James Bond, eating caviar and sipping champagne on the brand-new Air France Concorde, which had just gone into service a few months before, in January 1976. The supersonic plane stopped briefly in Dakar en route to Brazil, in half the time the 707s had been taking. "I looked around the plane and realized, apart from the air hostesses, I was the only woman on board. Everyone looked like a millionaire, and they probably were. The cabin smelled just like the toiletries counter at Old England (Paris's premier men's shop). This was the real jet set. All I had to do was keep flying this route and I was bound to get lucky," Isabella said, recalling her excitement as well as her trepidation. "I was off to meet a gangster."

If the object of Isabella's assignation, and her anxiety over it, had a criminal past, it was buried in several generations of upwardly mobile money—and reputation—laundering. Her blind date in Rio, call him "Paulo," was a highly observant Orthodox Jew, at twenty-six an unlikely mob scion. His family was in the magazine and advertising business, the Brazilian counterparts of the Bleustein-Blanchets of Publicis. But while the Russian Bleusteins had made their grubstake in the furniture trade, the Polish forbears of Paulo had made a far dirtier living in the sex trade, heading a Jewish crime syndicate that would enshrine the word *polacas,* which technically meant "Polish women," as Portuguese slang for prostitutes, akin to the word *hookers* in America, a reference to the camp followers of the Civil War Union general Joseph Hooker. Just as the Corsican-run fleshpots and streetwalkers of Paris had evolved into the refined academy of femininity that was Madame Claude's, the Jewish-run white slavery operation in Brazil had evolved into an empire akin to Time, Inc.

Paulo's great-great-grandfather had been a white slaver of the most vicious sort, a kingpin in the trafficking operation known, with the falsest of altruism, as the Warsaw Jewish Mutual Aid Society. When Polish consuls in South America objected to the taking in vain of the name of their capital city, the organization became known in official police files as "Zvi Migdal," the name of one of the founding traffickers. By the 1930s, Zvi Migdal operated over two hundred brothels, with over thirty thousand women in Argentina alone, and had also branched out into neighboring Brazil. The victims were poor Eastern European Jewish girls from the shtetls in the bleak and barren frontier known under the tsars as the Pale of Settlement. These women were duped into thinking they were getting passage to the sunny New World and jobs as housekeepers, or to arranged marriages.

Instead, these poor Jewish women were raped and brutalized on the transport ships, auctioned like slaves to powerful pimps, and impressed into brothels. Ironically, as with Madame Claude girls, many of these poor trafficked women rose above their circumstances and married their clients. The *polacas* evolved into the cultural subspecies known as the JSAP, or Jewish South American Princesses. Paulo's mother and four sisters were prime examples of the type, and because they controlled the media, they were splashed all over the news as the continent's arbiters of style and taste. The main difference between them and their American counterparts was that the South Americans tended to be much more religious, and much more committed to marrying within the faith. Hence Madame Claude's dispatching of Isabella, in hopes that her somewhat tenuous religious commonality with

Paulo might yield more than an extremely expensive (fifteen-thousand-dollar-plus Concorde fare) one-weekend stand.

If only. When Paulo arrived at Isabella's suite at the Copacabana Palace Hotel, the backdrop for the Astaire-Rogers debut film, *Flying Down to Rio,* he was a head shorter than she and dressed in black, in a Cardin version of a Hasidic Sabbath suit. He didn't even want to have sex. He at least had a good sense of humor about his orthodox restrictions, explaining to Isabella that his rabbi had said it was permissible to have sex with nonwives—that is, call girls—if they were either foreign or in a foreign country, hence his delight with the Madame Claude operation. Nevertheless, he didn't want to push the issue too far. He had been trained as a lawyer and had a legalistic, if not Talmudic, view of all codes, moral and otherwise. Like Bill Clinton and Monica Lewinsky, he had ordained that sex for him did not include manual or oral release. Because Paulo joked that he was also a germophobic hypochondriac, Isabella was exempted from the joys, or trials, of oral gratification. They had no sex at all, but they still had fun meeting each other under these unusual circumstances.

"He was so uncool that I decided I really liked him or was willing to give him a chance," Isabella said. "I think he liked me, too, because he invited me to meet his parents as his date at this charity ball that had grown out of a prostitute benevolent shelter (to protect girls trafficked by his antecedents) into one of the country's leading women's rights groups. I laughed and thought, Who was I to be carrying the torch for women's rights? Claude had told him all about my mother's background, a Sephardic Jew from Spain who ended up in Salonika. He said a lot of the Jews at the ball had roots that went back to the Inquisition in Portugal. My excuse for being in Rio was a cross between cultural and commercial: I was looking for colonial antiques. Long story short was that his parents liked me but didn't think I was Jewish enough. I had never been bas mitzvah'd. I didn't speak Hebrew. I probably was too blond. A few years later, I learned that Paulo married his second cousin. I still had a great trip and couldn't believe I was getting paid to go on these blind dates where I was theoretically looking for love."

Madame Claude was correct in her prediction that Isabella would be popular in New York. Unfortunately, she was so popular among a certain circle of Ivy League–educated Jewish lawyers and bankers on Wall Street that she earned a nickname from the famous Woody Allen short story, "The Whore of Mensa." She flew to New York once or twice a month and held court for the madly Francophile investment-banking crowd. A "dream date" for the Goldman Sachs–First Boston elite who had Madame Claude's number would be to have a gourmet *grand cru* dinner with Isabella at La Côte Basque and then retire across Fifty-fifth Street to her suite at the St. Regis for some "French lessons," as the players coded it.

The problem for Isabella was that none of these propositions led to a single proposal. The French were indeed more "sophisticated" about how they met their wives. The Americans were much more uptight that a Madame Claude introduction, as exclusive as it was, still was something of a scarlet letter that could never be expunged. For all their achievements, the summas, the Rhodes Scholarships, the partnerships at twenty-eight, these golden boys were still too insecure to believe that a *call girl*, however elegant, could truly love them for anything but their money. If Isabella had worked the town another year, she might have made the match she was searching for. But in 1977, Madame Claude left Paris secretly and abruptly. Isabella never spoke to her again and was much too much a lady to try to arrange her own dates. "I could never do the business part myself. That made it all too real," Isabella said. She went back to the gallery scene and, holding out for someone too good to be true, never married.

Why did Valéry Giscard d'Estaing turn against Madame

Claude? As president, Giscard, as he was known, was the heir to, and continuation of, the de Gaulle–Pompidou regime, which had not only tolerated Claude but made great use of her, both for fun and for profit. To suggest that Giscard was a symbol of a New Puritanism would have been to underrate him and to underrate France. No French president, with the possible exception of Félix Faure, who died in bed with his mistress in 1899, had so many rumored hot affairs as Giscard, including a notoriously abortive one with a Madame Claude girl that allegedly was what brought down the house.

The most captivating of Giscard's alleged romances was with Catherine Bokassa, the wife of his supposedly dear friend. Catherine, who was born in Chad and married Bokassa at fourteen, was naturally regal, a genuine African queen whom, according to Bokassa's memoirs, which were, not surprisingly, blocked from publication, Giscard had gotten pregnant and forced to have an abortion. This romance was given as the true reason why Giscard, a true Frenchman motivated by romance as much as by diplomacy, spent so much time with the Bokassas, both in Africa and at their château.

Then there was Giscard's friendship with director Roger Vadim, a perhaps more unlikely couple than Giscard and the dictator. Giscard was as entranced by Vadim's collection of big-game wives and mistresses as he was by Bokassa's elephants and lions. There was also the connection to Madame Claude, who counted Vadim among her stalwarts. He had taken Deneuve, mother of his child, to Claude for character lessons for *Belle de Jour*. He forced Jane Fonda into ménages à trois with Claude girls to Frenchify her.

In 1974, a major scandal almost erupted when Giscard, driving Vadim's Ferrari, crashed it into a milk truck and then got into a fistfight with the truck driver. Vadim was nowhere around, but in the car was a "mystery woman," who was rumored to be Catherine Schneider, the steel heiress who became Mrs. Vadim after Fonda. Giscard's secretary at the Elysée Palace, years later, told a team of Giscard-hunting French investigative journalists, "We crushed it very quickly. Neither the gendarmerie nor the police spoke. In France, if there are no photos, if there is not the name of the girl, it does not exist."

There were also rumored liaisons with the actress Marlène Jobert, the mother of current star Eva Green; famed photojournalist Marie-Laure de Decker; and even Lady Diana, about whom Giscard wrote a shocking novel, *The Princess and the President,* which some readers thought was a steamy roman à clef and others ridiculed as the self-indulgent wishful thinking of a sexual obsessive.

Wanting to present himself as an aristocrat, descended from Charlemagne, Giscard was actually the German-born son of a French civil servant working in the occupied Rhineland after World War I. He married his cousin, Anne-Anymone de Brantes, whose father was a count. And his right hand and the architect of his rise to president was a real aristocrat, albeit a Polish one. Prince Michel Poniatowski came from a distinguished and noble Polish line that included Stanislaw, the last king of Poland.

Because the French were, as ever, "sophisticated," Giscard's deviations from his seemingly ceremonial marriage never seemed to become a political issue until he got into bed, if it were true, with Madame Claude. "Giscard took these affairs very seriously, as seriously as government," said Sylvette Balland, a film producer who became Claude's best friend in her Los Angeles exile and whose publisher husband brought out Claude's second memoir, *Le Meilleur, C'est l'Autre,* in 1986 to raise money after her prison term. Through the ubiquitous Catherine Virgitti, Giscard had, according to Balland and many others, met and fallen hard for the actress Catherine Rosier, who moonlighted for Claude and whose beauty was evocative of that of Giscard's obsession, Catherine Bokassa.

The third Catherine, the ever-enterprising Catherine Virgitti,

noted the resemblance and was said to have had fixed the actress up with the president; sparks flew. Rosier was one of the
rare blacks in Claude's stable. A Martiniquaise model/actress/
chanteuse, she not only resembled Empress Bokassa. She was
also said, by film critics, to strongly resemble Alain Delon, hence
her casting as his opposite by Jean-Pierre Melville in the cult
gangster film *Le Samouraï*.

Another *"samourai"* eventually entered the picture and smashed
the frame. "Everything was fine," Sylvette Balland said, "until
Rosier's large and powerful lesbian girlfriend got jealous. She
broke into Rosier's apartment, caught the two lovers in flagrante,
and physically picked up Giscard from the bed and threw him
into the street without any clothes on. The girlfriend, who was
African, had absolutely no idea who the man was, that he was the
president of France. Giscard was furious that he had lost this
woman whom he was crazy about. He was humiliated by the
sordidness of it all. If this could happen to him, it could happen
to any man. He decided that Madame Claude had to go, that she
was wrong for France. These kind of things should not happen."

First the milk truck, then Rosier—things were spiraling out
of control. The Elysée Palace continued, of course, to do its job
in covering up this and other possible embarrassments. Giscard
was thoughtful, forgoing residence in the palace because of the
scrutiny involved and always letting his aides know where he
might be spending the night in case of a national emergency. But
Giscard, as did any politician, had lots of enemies, and he was
providing them with too much ammunition. He had one big rival on the Left, François Mitterrand, who would have his own
sexual scandal in maintaining two separate families, wife and
mistress, and on the Right, Jacques Chirac, a dedicated Claude
man known as "Mr. Three Minutes, Shower Included."

Going after Madame Claude, supposedly the brainstorm of
Michel Poniatowski, would change the dynamic in Giscard's
favor. Poniatowski decided that Giscard should use Madame

Claude as a symbol of the right wing, old boy Old Gaullists, and repackage Giscard as the modern, progressive voice of the center. After all, Giscard was the champion of the new high-speed TGV. He was a promoter of nuclear energy, to break the country's dependence on oil, and on Arabs. Nothing could seem more reactionary and throwback in the liberated mid-seventies than a madam running a prostitution ring catering to Arabs, African dictators, diamond dealers, uranium speculators, and other fat cats when France was getting skinnier—too skinny for even this never-too-thin country—every day. That was the stuff of Dirty Bertie, the stuff of Le One-Two-Two, the stuff of the Nazis—in short, the wrong stuff. Madame Claude could be further scapegoated as the handmaiden and enabler of the evil Arab-African oligarchy that was causing France's—and the world's—economic troubles.

And so Giscard unleashed the *fiscs,* or fiscal authorities, as opposed to the *flics,* or cops. When it came to the sex part, Giscard knew he lived in a glass house and could not be caught throwing stones. He rejected the notion of pursuing Claude on the grounds of morals, or *proxénétisme,* which implied she was corrupting innocent girls, when in truth she was enabling their sophisticated ambitions. Instead, Giscard would make his case on the much more sympathetic grounds of tax evasion. Claude was rich because of her connections to the French government. Now it was her turn to give something in return. That payback was taxes.

Giscard thus commenced a tax investigation, and not just into Claude but into Madame Billy and a few other lesser rivals, as well. He appointed as his "vice czar" the magistrate Jean-Louis Bruguière, whose brief was to rid Paris of all prostitution rings, high and low. Bruguière would graduate from Claude hunting to go on to a distinguished career as France's leading expert in antiterrorism strategies. Giscard, in throwing a wide net against vice, didn't want anyone to think he was waging a vendetta for personal reasons. "They calculated that Claude had amassed a total income of nearly half a billion francs," Sylvette Balland explained. That translated in 1976 to $100,000,000, after two decades in business, with zero taxes having been paid. The tax bill Claude was facing then was somewhere between ten and twenty million dollars. It may have been a gross overestimation, but it gave the Giscard regime plenty of room to negotiate.

Aside from the restive *fiscs,* there was another strange twist that illustrated contradictions of what seemed to be Madame Claude's charmed life. One of Claude's German *über Mädchen* had begun giving Claude a hard time. When this wonder woman began taking drugs, Claude fired her. After weeks of menacing phone calls, she arrived at the Résidence de la Muette with a Luger. She fired three shots at Claude. One hit her in the shoulder, but Claude was wearing a heavily padded, very chic Courrèges jacket. The bullet did not pierce it. Another shot went over Claude's head, which she credited to the Amazon's being so much taller than she. The third shot went into her right hand, which she raised to protect herself. Two fingers were paralyzed. Fortunately, Claude's dialing finger was not. The matter was kept out of the papers. The German was not charged. She was allowed to go back to Germany and was not heard from again. The *flics,* if not the *fiscs,* were still in Claude's thrall. A public scandal was averted, yet everyone knew what had gone on. This kind of gossip was precisely why Giscard and Poniatowki had sicced the dogs of tax on Claude. Eventually, they believed, she would become a fatal embarrassment to them.

By the end of 1975, Madame Claude was so brazenly public, getting so much attention, that there was an overwhelming sense of overload, that she was too big for her silk breeches. There was her own memoir *Allô, Oui,* and the rival biography, *Les Filles de Madame Claude,* glutting the bookstores. And there was the deafening fanfare of the sale of *Allô, Oui* to the movies. The Madame

Claude story was going to be told cinematically by Just Jaeckin, a fashion photographer turned director who was no man's Godard but who was coming off the soft-core smash *Emmanuelle,* the biggest French global hit since Vadim's *And God Created Woman.* Adding insult to the urgency of putting Madame Claude in her place, which was conceivably behind bars, was the fact that the star of *Emmanuelle,* the "new Bardot," was widely rumored also to be the new mistress of Giscard.

Starring as Madame Claude was the distinguished stage and screen French star Françoise Fabian. The Algeria-born Fabian had crossed Claude's path ten years before when she had a featured part in *Belle de Jour.* Claude then was still on her way up, more the head of a charm school than the head of a corporate colossus that had turned Madame Claude sex into a branded French commodity like Cartier jewels, Vuitton luggage, and Dom Pérignon champagne. The actress, then forty-three, frankly detested the woman she would be playing. *"Une femme terrible!"* Fabian declared. "She despised men and women alike. Men were wallets. Women were holes." She described how they had met to talk about the film at the classic Left Bank bistro Au Petit Marguery, near where Claude had lived when she first arrived in Paris after the war. "There were just the two of us, woman-to-woman. She was very self-deprecating, but she was arrogant at the same time." Noticing how all the diners were staring at the famous Fabian, but no one at her, Claude remarked, "Nobody knows me. But I know everybody."

"She was like a slave driver on a plantation in the Old South," Fabian said. "Once she took a girl on, the makeover put the girl in debt. Claude would pay Dior, Chanel, the hairdresser, the doctors, and then the girl would have to work to pay them off. It was sexual indentured servitude. Claude took thirty percent. She told me she would have taken more but the girls would have lied and cheated if she had tried to do that."

Fabian derided the notion that Claude was a Henry Higgins professor type who transformed her girls into that rare combination of beauty and brains. "Beauty, yes, that was what mattered to her—and her men. Brains were optional," Fabian said. Claude's idea of education was not a degree at the Sorbonne, but a speed read of the monthly magazine *Historia,* a Gallic version of Cliffs-Notes on literature and history. It was a good quick study for cocktail party chatter, but not if the challenging likes of Sartre or Françoise Sagan were in attendance. "She wasn't interested in ideas," Fabian asserted. "She was interested in money. She loved money."

The film *Madame Claude* was released in the fall 1977. In addition to Fabian as Claude, it also starred the Canadian former Disney Mouseketeer turned Ford model Dayle Haddon as the object of Claude's makeover, as well as Klaus Kinski as a tycoon. The film's music was by Serge Gainsbourg. The screenplay was credited to Jacques Quoirez. There was a huge premiere on the Champs-Elysées, with an after-party at Fouquet's. But the biggest impression was made by Madame Claude in her absence. Fearing that Giscard and Poniatowki would score a massive publicity coup by arresting her at the premiere, Claude that day had boarded an Air France 707 to Los Angeles and a new life.

"I never met her face-to-face," admitted Just Jaeckin, then thirty-seven. The film's plot involved a *Blow-Up*–type model-chasing fashion photographer who is dragooned by the CIA into taking incriminating secret shots of Claude girls with rich, famous, and politically strategic men. "She saw a screening in L.A. and called me and said, 'This is how it's really done. How did you ever find out?' She also said, 'Françoise Fabian is exactly me. She's perfect.' Claude loved being played by someone who conveyed high class like Françoise. She liked the film so much that she said, 'I'm going to send you a gift. What is your fantasy?' That gift was to be one of her girls. I told her to surprise me.

"Well, what a surprise. A few nights later, the bell rings and

it is one of the most stunning women I had ever seen. And remember, I'm a fashion photographer and I'm in the movie business. I'm not easily impressed. She was Belgian, charming. We
had dinner, made love, the whole catalog. She had multiple orgasms. She seemed to be crazy about me. But again remember,
I'm a director. I know how actresses fake things. This girl was
great, and we talked all night. The next morning, when she was
leaving, I asked her, boldly, 'How was I?' I would have never
asked if I didn't think I knew the answer. And she just started
laughing at that question. I said, 'Come on, tell me.' So then she
said, 'Like a client.' I was crushed, she was that good. Crushed.
But amazed. I suppose that was why Claude was Claude. I'm
sorry I never met her."

Chapter 9

EXILE ON RODEO DRIVE

$\mathcal{I}$ was as nervous as an otherwise-innocent college girl going to Madame Claude for an interview that might make her rich. In my case, I was a young male writer going to Madame Claude to try to convince her to collaborate on a memoir that, if sufficiently revelatory, might make me rich. She was already rich, so I knew I had my work cut out for me. The two Madame Claude books that had come out recently in France had not been picked up by English-language publishers. Why? Neither *Allô, Oui* nor *Les Filles de Madame Claude* had named any names. The year was 1981, the dawn of the Reagan era of fascination with money and stardom. Madame Claude was at the pinnacle of both, plus sex. This was also the era of the inflated book auction, when paperback sales drove the market. According to my New York agents, what would drive that market crazy was knowing who Madame Claude's supposedly famous clients actually were, and which actresses, princesses, and celebrity wives had met their enviable fates through her.

My connection to Madame Claude was through a Persian banker friend from my previous incarnation as a Wall Street lawyer. His father, a courtier of Reza Shah Pahlavi, who had just been overthrown in 1979, had joined the Persian diaspora to Beverly Hills and had reconnected there with Madame Claude.

She could also have been described as one of the Shah's courtiers, having dispatched by jet weekly "care packages" of her beauties to the ruler. My Persian friend was also transitioning out of Wall Street to the movie business and had joined his family in California. He offered to introduce me to Claude in return for a finder's fee percentage of any book deal that transpired, not to mention a share of film rights.

To me, Madame Claude was no more than a vague abstraction, one more way that the very rich were very different from you and me. She was for movie stars, for tycoons, for the Shah. I had spent lots of time in Paris, where everyone knew her name. "Madame Claude girl" was shorthand for the Ford or Elite model who was inside *Vogue* or *Elle* but rarely on the cover. She was not someone mere mortals were likely to meet, and less likely to afford. She was synonymous with a certain unreachable level of luxury that made Paris *Paris* but didn't make you hate it, didn't turn you into a Communard. Like the Ritz, La Tour d'Argent, Hermès, the Rothschilds, even Marie Antoinette, there was a trickle-down effect from these pinnacles of exclusivity that made Paris, the most elegant and beautiful of cities, into something we all could share and enjoy, just by being there.

The same could not be said for Beverly Hills, where, apart from the perfect weather, all the good stuff was behind closed doors and security gates. The restaurant where I was to meet Madame Claude, Ma Maison, was a case in point. It had an unlisted telephone number, and was probably the most exclusive restaurant in America. It was surely the only temple of gastronomy located in a former garden-supply shed. New York's ultrasnobby La Côte Basque, scene of Truman Capote's 1975 society-eviscerating short story, was open sesame by comparison. Escaping an arctic, slushy New York, I was feeling very L.A. in my rented Mustang convertible, only to find a parking lot filled with Bentleys, Ferraris, and Rolls-Royces. Chilled by the dirty looks of the valet parkers, I found a space on the street a block away.

The intimidation factor at the parking lot was only the beginning. Instead of a Hollywood red carpet, there was green Astroturf. The whole restaurant was a reverse-chic outdoor patio with junky lawn tables and cheap garden chairs, in which were seated some of the world's most famous people, eating haute cuisine prepared by the soon-to-be-famous Wolfgang Puck. I spotted, at least I think I spotted, Orson Welles, Tony Curtis, Johnny Carson, Larry Hagman, Jack Nicholson, Farrah Fawcett, Faye Dunaway, Joan Collins, and a lot of tieless mogul and agent types in Gucci loafers hopping from table to table like grasshoppers. In New York, only Elaine's and the Russian Tea Room had such Hollywood scenes, but they were nothing like this. A haughty maître d', wearing an outfit resembling tennis whites, gave me an interloper stare, without saying a word. I said the right ones. "Madame Claude." His dour face lit up.

And there she was, the real thing herself, a tiny, perfectly coiffed blond woman, dressed in pastel Chanel, looking very properly Paris in the midst of film festival Cannes, which, appropriately, happened to be Beverly Hills's official sister city. All around us were big Hollywood blondes, big jewels, big hair, big busts, the sunshine version of the ladies who lunch. She was different, totally different, quiet and self-contained. My first impression was that she was a banker to the stars, somebody who took care of their fortunes. In a way, I was correct.

To break the ice, I had brought her a copy of *Marilyn Secrète,* the French version of my recent book *Marilyn Monroe Confidential,* which had been a big hit all over the world, in an effort to focus an agenda. "*Une vache,*" Claude said, dismissing in a bovine slur the most famous star in cinema. She continued in French that she could never understand what all the fuss over Marilyn was about. I wanted to riposte with "*La vache qui rit,*" but I got the impression that Claude was bankerly serious and did not go in for cross-cultural jokes or puns. I later learned that America's earthy and lusty sex symbol was the complete opposite of the reserved and refined Claude ideal, that Marilyn would have had no chance ever working for Claude. I learned on the spot that Claude had little interest in speaking English, forcing me to revert to my North Carolina high school French to hang on her every word. If only I'd had a *Larousse*. Whatever the agenda, Claude would be setting it.

I wasn't sure how to ease into the delicate subject of prostitution with the world's preeminent sex broker. Instead, we talked about Wolfgang Puck's food, most of which was being eschewed by Claude, who ordered only a tomato salad and then a slice of melon. She drank only Perrier. There was no wine, no cigarettes. How un-French. She asked me at one point what I thought of the bread. I was honest and said it was much less French than my delicious *tarte aux asperges* and the *caneton en deux façons*. It tasted like cotton. That elicited her first smile.

Claude loved critiquing everything—movies, food, women. The put-down was her rapier. If she had spoken English, she would have loved the *Dean Martin Celebrity Roast* on TV. When we finally got to Dean, many lunches later, she roasted him herself, saying he was too cheap to use her girls. America's cheapskate, Jack Benny, was another story. . . . Claude said that when she arrived in Beverly Hills, she immediately recognized that there was no good French baking in L.A., that this was a niche to be filled. One of her best friends was the famed French patissier Gaston Lenôtre, who shared his oven secrets with her. All confidence, she opened a bakery in Pacific Palisades and called it Le Canard. She promptly went out of business, she admitted, with one parting shot. "*Ils sont sauvages*," she said. "What they want here is Wonder bread and Hostess cupcakes." I would learn that she was having challenges in selling her girls in the L.A. market similar to those in selling her baked goods. At least I could tell the difference. That made her trust me. A little.

Before I could get to the business of this lunch, I knew I had to prove my own bona fides. It was, however, hard to get a conversation going with all the well-wishers dropping by our table, kissing her hand, kissing her cheeks, kissing her ass. With all the stars here, she was the biggest star of all, the secret celebrity the public celebrities wanted to know. She clearly had what Hollywood wanted. The most famous agent in show business, Swifty Lazar, came by, fawning. The tycoon Armand Hammer, of Occidental Petroleum, came by and spoke perfect French. So did George Peppard, who Claude told me was at a low ebb in his career, skidding from *Breakfast at Tiffany's* to junk TV, and having just been fired from the new nightly soap opera *Dynasty*.

Two actresses dropped by, first Geneviève Bujold, who was French-Canadian, then Jacqueline Bisset, the star of François Truffaut's *Day for Night*. Could *they* have been Madame Claude girls? I wanted to ask, but that would have been too aggressive at this point. Bisset was with a well-tanned, gold-chained Moroccan jeans mogul, of which there seemed to be several at Ma Maison this day. Jeans were big business. Guess, Sasson, Jordache, Girbaud—all had ties to *pied noir* North Africa, and now to L.A. How did the Moroccan get a beauty like Bisset? I wondered. "*Le plus gros casquette du monde,*" Claude naughtily replied, referring not to the jeans but to the artillery within.

Then we met the proprietor of Ma Maison, Patrick Terrail, a big, bluff thirtyish Frenchman whose bulging eyes did give him a froggish affect. A graduate of the Cornell School of Hotel Administration, Patrick had learned how to bring modern efficiency to the ancient art of haute cuisine. He made a huge fuss over Madame Claude, as had his uncle Claude Terrail, who owned the Paris restaurant that gave Ma Maison its cachet, its snob cred. Uncle Claude's restaurant was La Tour d'Argent, the most prestigious, expensive, and romantic restaurant in Paris, if not the world, with its bird's-eye view of Notre Dame, its three Michelin stars, its specialty of numbered well-bred ducklings, roasted and ceremonially pressed and mixed with cream and Cognac to create a sauce of the duck's own blood, its celebrity clientele, which was said to frequently overlap with that of Madame Claude. Claude and Claude, the host and hostess of *la ville gastro-sexuelle*. Madame Claude had famously been quoted in France as saying, "The two things people will pay for are food and sex. I wasn't very good at cooking." Claude Terrail had the other side of that coin, and now his nephew Patrick was presiding over a replicant iteration of it in Beverly Hills. He had great food. He had Madame Claude. Plus he had Hollywood and sunshine. What could be better? "This is paradise," I marveled.

"*Paradis du fou,*" snapped Madame Claude, who confessed she was not enchanted with either L.A. or Patrick. "*Claude le deteste,*" Madame Claude added, sotto voce, describing how the Paris Terrail was furious at his beach-boy nephew for taking his name and fame in vain. The Terrails were a hotel dynasty that had owned, among other luxury lodgings, the George V and the San Régis. But the family had its schisms, and one was between Claude and his brother, who was Patrick's father. It was becoming clear that Madame Claude loved to gossip.

Claude Terrail had more than paved the way in Hollywood, Claude told me, finally breaking the ice about her business. He had had affairs with Ava Gardner, Marilyn Monroe, Rita Hayworth, Jayne Mansfield, and then married Hollywood royalty in the person of the daughter of mogul Jack Warner. If anyone didn't have to "pay for it," it was the suave, polo-playing sportsman Terrail. But he paid and paid, hosting orgies in his bachelor pad below the restaurant, which boasted its own shooting range, as well as nude horseback rides on country estates for groups of his fellow playboy friends. But after a few titillating anecdotes, she stopped and made me plead for more. She was a great tease. "Americans," she sneered, "will never understand what I created. A country of Pilgrims."

Claude meant Puritans, but I got her point. Walter Matthau came by and made a joke. The dour visage of Charles Bronson brightened as he walked past and nodded. Orson Welles lumbered out in his caftan and kissed her hand. How the mighty have fallen, I thought, shuddering. Had Claude fallen, as well? But Ma Maison was hardly purgatory, and the wine-guzzling, duck-gorging stars and moguls didn't seem like Puritans to me. I wanted to ask her about everybody here, and everybody in Hollywood. But she was too canny to show and tell. So I told her a little about myself to show her I wasn't one of those Yankee Pilgrims who would make a snap judgment and brand her with a scarlet letter.

Even my little eastern North Carolina tobacco town had its own Madame Claude. Her name was Eunice Pickett McLawhorn. She owned a place called Eunice's Court, a moss-draped motel on the edge of town where nobody I knew had ever stayed. Eunice's had a fancy gate and two armed guards and a mythology that matched the secrecy. It was a real brothel that catered to local politicians, tobacco titans, and the top brass of the military-industrial complexes of nearby Camp Lejeune, Cherry Point, and Fort Bragg. My mother owned the town's fancy women's clothing store, and periodically she would open her store on Sundays (as in *Never On* . . .) to allow Eunice to bring in a dozen of her voluptuous charges to shop for fancy lingerie, away from prying eyes. Madame Claude was fascinated by this snapshot of forbidden Americana. She began warming up.

We found that we had someone in common. Back in New York, I had just been introduced to a beautiful young French actress who wanted to write a book about her long relationship with one of Hollywood's greatest moguls, the recently deceased Darryl F. Zanuck, whose amazing success story had taken him from Wahoo, Nebraska, to writing scripts for Rin Tin Tin to the ownership of Twentieth Century–Fox. The actress lived in splendor on Fifth Avenue, thanks to Zanuck. The story she wanted to tell was that Zanuck had discovered her in a convent in Normandy when he was living in Paris and producing his

World War II epic, *The Longest Day*. He had taken a strictly paternal interest in her, and she wanted to tell the story of the glamorous world he had shared with her. But where was the sex? I had asked her; Zanuck was known as one of the great showbiz swordsmen. No sex, she insisted. That was the charm of the romance. It was all beauty and no beast. And no book, as far as I was concerned.

Madame Claude broke out laughing. Claude laughs! Garbo talks! She wasn't a laughing type. No sex? Ha! Convent? Ha! Ha! This girl was one of her greatest creations, and one of the wildest creatures who had ever worked for her—and now completely denied it. Claude hated being denied. She may have embraced anonymity, but she liked this Beverly Hills version here at Ma Maison. She liked the respect she got. In fact, Claude was going to testify in the actress's pending big-buck palimony suit against the Zanuck estate. Zanuck's son and heir, Richard, whom Claude pointed out to me across the patio, had promised to use his major influence to settle her pending immigration problems in return for her saying, basically, " 'Tis pity she's a whore." That this woman had presented herself to me as a convent virgin just broke Claude up.

Richard Zanuck, Claude noted, was sitting with Alan Ladd, Jr. These were two Hollywood princes, as royal and interconnected as the European princes she had catered to in the Old World. Zanuck was the patron of Steven Spielberg, having produced his first feature, *The Sugarland Express*. "Laddie," as he was known, to separate father from son, had been the patron of George Lucas, green-lighting *Star Wars* when he served as Darryl Zanuck's production president at Fox. French royalty may have had the pomp and ceremony, but it didn't have CinemaScope.

Patrick Terrail, because of this quickly iconic restaurant, had become the fulcrum of the large Hollywood "French Colony," which included resident French stars like *Gigi*'s Louis Jourdan; American stars with French or French-speaking wives, like

Gregory Peck and Kirk Douglas; and Francophone/Francophile European-born film people like Billy Wilder, a young Arnold Schwarzenegger, and, until he became a fugitive in 1977, Roman Polanski. There were "honorary Frenchmen," Americans worshipped in Paris, like Gene Kelly, Jerry Lewis, Alan Jay Lerner, and Orson Welles. There were all the rich new French-speaking Arabs and Persians who had embraced Southern California as the new, war-free land of milk and honey. And here was Madame Claude, in medias res, just as she had been in Paris. Sex was indeed the universal currency. After two hours of chat, she had told me very little in the way of seven-figure revelations. But I knew they were there, and she agreed to see me again. I was in the ring with the champ, still standing after round one.

What I didn't realize at the time was how tenuous the champ's hold on the title of queen of sex actually was. Sylvette Balland, who had come to Hollywood to work in the film business, became Claude's best friend when she first arrived, in 1977. They met at a party given by Patrick Terrail. "She was this sad, lonely little woman," Balland recalled. "I would have not noticed her. Then Patrick whispered who she was. I was bowled over. It was like meeting Al Capone." Before she opened her patisserie, Claude seemed to Balland "adrift in L.A. She had nothing to do but shop. She had a small apartment in West Hollywood near the restaurant [Ma Maison] filled with wardrobes full of glamorous French clothes no one would ever wear in L.A., which is so casual. She had at least a hundred pairs of shoes."

"Claude was a big name-dropper," Balland said. "She showed me pictures of herself as a girl in Angers. She was ugly. Dark hair. Bad teeth, bad nose. Now she was blond and very attractive. She had to tell me that her work was done by Pitanguy in Rio. I doubt it was. Probably by a man in Paris. It was good work, but for her it had to have a big name, or it wasn't good. I got a friend of mine from UCLA to give her English lessons, but she didn't seem that motivated. She didn't like to read, other than

French magazines from the international newsstand on Beverly Drive. And there was no cable then, so she didn't watch TV.

"What she really loved was to clean. I never saw anything like it. I took her to the Venice apartment of my friend Barbet Schroeder [the Iran-born French director of the S&M classic *Maîtresse* and later the Claus von Bülow saga *Reversal of Fortune*]. The place was a pigsty. Artists, you know. But she sort of went into a trance and started cleaning it madly. For hours and hours. And in the end, it was like a new place. Spotless. Perfect. She was obsessed with cleanliness."

"I was one of the first persons Claude called when she came to L.A.," Patrick Terrail said. "I had met her in Paris when I was a teenager. Both my uncle and my father were clients. She was alone and adrift here, not speaking English. I think she came to L.A. because some of her biggest clients lived here and couldn't live without her. Everybody here who had made films in Paris knew her. She had a big base in L.A. They all gave her money. She also had Pierre Salinger, who had become the senator from California. She knew Senator Tunney, too."

Terrail cited two frequent L.A. residents who had mansions all over the globe and whom Claude had introduced to several of their multiple wives. One was Jacques Gaston "Tony" Murray, also known as the "King of Saint-Tropez," where he kept a gargantuan yacht and gave the biggest parties on the Riviera. Murray, who had made his billions in fire extinguishers, pronounced his surname like the Moray eel and added the Tony to give himself a Rat Pack Vegas air. A French Jew whose father died in Auschwitz, Murray had been a Free French fighter pilot during World War II. He was legendary for his bad toupees, but he was so rich that, with Claude masterminding his dance card, looks never mattered. The other Claude benefactor was arms king Adnan Khashoggi, "Mr. Fixit," who seemed to live between his DC-8 airborne seraglio and his $75,000,000 yacht *Nabila* (later sold to Donald Trump). "She told me that she refused to betray Khashoggi to the French authorities," Balland said. "They wanted him, and she covered for him. He owed her for that, and he honored his debts."

To say that Madame Claude introduced these and other men to their wives was not to accuse these wives of having been prostitutes. Claude, the despiser of the *p* word, would have been the first to take offense. Yes, with Claude's male friends, there was money everywhere. Money was who these men were. But who could say where the money stopped and the sex began? However, Claude, knowing Balland was from France and that she knew exactly what Claude was famous for, made no pretense from the beginning of their friendship that the patisserie was anything other than a front. "With the telephone, Madame Claude did not have to be in Paris to be Madame Claude," Balland said. "I soon met two of the girls who were working for her in L.A. One was what you might expect—tall, blond, a model. But the other, she looked like a rat. Then one night she came out all dressed up, and I didn't even recognize her. She was even better than the first girl. Claude liked to transform women like that. That was her art."

Hers was an art that she could not stop from creating, no matter the circumstances. For example, Balland described that at one point in her stay, Claude was arrested by the Immigration and Naturalization authorities and sent to jail for not having the proper papers. She was incarcerated at the Sybil Brand Institute, the female county jail. "It was a very tough place, but she could find opportunity wherever she went," Balland recalled. "There were a number of beautiful Latino girls that she thought had potential. She gave their numbers to her friend Bob Evans [former Paramount studio head who produced *Chinatown* and married Ali MacGraw] as the first person to call the minute they were released. She brought home her prison jersey and wore it over her Saint Laurents. Eight eight eight. *Ocho ocho ocho.* She loved to repeat the numbers. They were good luck in Chinese. She could be very funny, usually in a mean way."

Standing in the way of Madame Claude's "art" was the equally artful Madam Alex, who dominated the luxury call-girl trade in L.A. Madam Alex never went to Ma Maison. She never went out at all. Instead, she held court in her current Xanadu, a Spanish Colonial mansion just up Stone Canyon Road from the Bel Air Hotel. She had a hundred cats, an Olympic-size pool filled with naked models and starlets, and rare China soup tureens filled with cocaine. Alex was a gifted cook, as gifted as Wolfgang Puck. She had lavish lunches and dinners for her clients, most of whom knew one another either from the movie business or the oil business or the arms business and had nothing to hide from the other members of their clubby elite.

Alex was careful not to mix movie people with music people or with businesspeople at her swinging soirees and wild afternoons. Her millionaires were separate but equally paranoid, and she knew how to keep secrets, and to keep the Los Angeles Police Department in her good graces as well, sometimes with sex, sometimes with drugs. In short, she was everything that Madame Claude was not. Claude didn't entertain. She didn't tolerate drugs. She didn't socialize with the men. She just found them their dreams and got out of the way, and then cashed the checks. That may have worked in formal, proper Paris, but it didn't play in wild, laid-back L.A.

Then there were the Claude girls, girls she began importing from Europe. There was always a market for well-bred, well-groomed princess types, but this was more an urban phenomenon for sophisticated cities, where people dressed up and their dates needed to make smart conversation about politics and culture. Alex's army was completely different, blond, busty Malibu beach-bunny types who were often found in the sex grotto of Hugh Hefner's Playboy Mansion, not in the library at UCLA.

Claude's girls were like the women in *The Group* or *The Stepford Wives*. Alex's were like the girls in *Beach Blanket Bingo*. Unfortunately for Claude, formal and fancy didn't play in L.A. She was selling croissants to a bagel market.

Claude's biggest liability of all was not speaking English. Furthermore, even if her lessons bore linguistic fruit, she was not a schmoozer like Madam Alex. Alex would stay on the phone for hours, talking to coke-revved moguls like Paramount's Don Simpson or lonely tycoons like England's takeover master Lord Gordon White, who saw in Alex the caring mother they'd never had. Then again, what mother, outside of Greek tragedy, would soothe her sons' flagging egos by fixing them up with the call girl of their dreams? Madam Alex was all ears. Madame Claude was all business. She may have played mother superior, but she would never be mother confessor. Even a multinational tycoon like Britain's Sir James Goldsmith, who was not only multilingual but kept a whole second family in Paris, preferred the gemütlich ambience of Alex's to the ancien régime cold perfection of Claude's.

I had no idea how badly Madame Claude was doing. One barometer of her troubles was that she had married a gay bartender named Bruce Cook. Cook was a mixologist at Le Dome, the Sunset Strip version of Fouquet's, populated with rock stars and their managers and beautiful girlfriends, many of whom were loyal Alex girls and unrecruitable. Le Dome was owned by Claude's Belgian friend, Eddy Kerkhofs, who also sold Claude his ski house in nearby Big Bear. Both the mountain house and the bartender marriage were intended to keep the vampires of the INS at bay and prevent further trips to Sybil Brand. Meanwhile, word was that Giscard's Paris *fiscs* were bringing pressure to bear on the Reagan administration to deliver Claude to them and to French justice. But she never breathed a word of it to me. Why should she? I wouldn't have cared. For the book project, all that mattered was her glorious past, not her precarious future.

I didn't meet any of Claude's friends, such as Sylvette Balland, whom I did meet decades later in France. I didn't know what Claude's private life in L.A. was like, or if she even had one. She drove a silver-gray Porsche, which was so gleamingly immaculate that she must have taken it to that L.A. institution, the Santa Palm Car Wash, in the Boystown of West Hollywood, every single day. She clearly had time on her hands. A few times, we met for tea in the house she was renting in Coldwater Canyon. It was a fifties ranch house with shag carpets. She apologized profusely as she poured me very fine tea from Mariage Frères, which someone sent her regularly from Paris. She was living "on the run," she said and hoped all her fiscal issues would soon be resolved and she could get back to civilization. Her optimism was not convincing. She reminded me of the scene in *Pépé le Moko,* where Jean Gabin, stuck in sunny, shady Algiers and homesick for Paris, looks at an old Métro ticket and recites all the stations on the line.

Madame Claude and I would get together for lunches two or three times a week, either at Ma Maison or its Italian counterpart, Caffé Roma, in an ersatz souk called Le Grand Passage in the heart of Beverly Hills. Run by two Roman émigrés from the Via Veneto, Caffé Roma had authentic Italian food and a Felliniesque crowd of cigar-smoking playboys of all ages. We met Roger Vadim getting out of his yellow XKE in the parking lot. *Tout le monde* seemed to be in Beverly Hills now, with the Red Brigade terrorists and economic depression and other problems taking the glamour out of Europe. In L. A. all seemed safe, spotless, perfect, like the movies that were created here. As at Ma Maison, Madame Claude was the toast of the restaurant. Across from the outdoor café part of the restaurant was a chic sportswear boutique called Georges Cibaud, which had the most beautiful salesgirls of any store I had ever seen. As it turned out, most of these girls were visiting foreign Claude girls. They were on display there for the Roma men, who might then call Claude to set up an introduction.

Eventually, once she was confident that I wasn't some undercover Interpol informant out to entrap her, Claude let down her guard and admitted to playing matchmaker to the stars. Claude and I would often play a game in which we would scan the Ma Maison and Caffè Roma lunch crowds and I would guess which of these distaff diners had the looks and bearing to be Claude girls. I usually got it right. I was flattered when she praised my *oeil aiguisé,* or good eye.

I was even more flattered when she asked me to become one of her L.A. *essayeurs.* That seemed like even a greater job than being a food critic, a sex critic. Nice work if you could get it. She told me she liked writers for testing the girls, because we were "observant and poetic." Her top tester in L.A. was a transplanted French author named Pierre Rey, who, in his thirties, had been the wunderkind editor in chief of the women's magazine *Marie Claire,* the French *Cosmo.* He was now writing sexy roman à clef novels about Greek shipping tycoons and Palm Beach heirs, both well-known Claude constituencies. I was flattered, again, to be in such fast company, and basically couldn't believe this was happening to me.

Claude didn't give me a checklist, as I would later learn she gave to her Paris testers. She just said, "Take the girl to dinner and see what happens." And so I did. My first date was a blond Greek girl visiting from London who wanted to be a journalist, a more beautiful version of Arianna Stassinopoulos Huffington crossed with Tina Brown. Call her "Penelope." She was an Oxford graduate and could talk *Phaedra* but much preferred to talk Elizabeth Taylor, whom we saw that night at Ma Maison, where the red carpet was rolled out, courtesy of Claude. Earlier over drinks at Morton's, the other showbiz temple of exclusion, we had spotted Rock Hudson. The cultured Greek was starstruck. Hollywood could do that to anyone.

Penelope was great fun to talk to, and had lots to say about herself, and lots to ask about me. She seemed very genuine, somebody I would have loved to date in real life. I realized the reason I wasn't meeting women like this was that they were going off with famous men for five hundred dollars an hour. I tried to suppress any rage at income inequality. I had no idea how to segue into the Claude part of the evening. I assumed I was supposed to get lucky, but what did luck, or charm, have to do with it when the result was preordained? There was no thrill of the chase here, and that lack of tension rendered the expensive culinary foreplay delicious but unerotic.

I didn't want to ask Penelope, "Well, how did you and Madame Claude hook up?" Claude, the elephant in Ma Maison, was conspicuously absent in our dialogue. Penelope seemed no stranger to the escort trade. She was seamless in suggesting that I come up for a drink in her room at the Beverly Hills Hotel. She poured the drinks from the minibar and took the initiative, which was fine, as I somehow felt I was her guest, and not she mine. She had expensive clothes and expensive lingerie and perfume, and there were expensive linens on the vast bed. It was like a ride, an expensive, erotic Disneyland, totally safe but totally inauthentic. She wasn't like any Oxford girl I had ever met.

Only after round one was I relaxed enough to really start asking her what interested me, which was how a girl like her ended up in a business like this. Ice-broken, she now was able to open up. Her father was a black-tie waiter at the White Tower, the world's fanciest Greek restaurant, on Percy Street in London's Bloomsbury, bowing and scraping to the likes of Onassis, Niarchos, and Goulandris, all of whom were Madame Claude regulars.

The Greek had the burning desire to turn the tables, as it were, on the men her father had served so humbly for decades.

In a way, she was radical, radical chic. But she didn't want to beat them; she wanted to join them. Working for Madame Claude would put her on the same level as her father's betters. She might even end up with one of their sons. Sex, not Oxford, where she had won a scholarship, was going to be her ticket to upward mobility. Oxford, she said, could get her a job. Claude could get her a life. I spent a few more hours with her, hard not to be attracted, but, not being the son of a shipowner, hard to look at this as more than a one-night stand in fantasyland. However, once we stopped the Kabuki play of fake perfect millionaire sex and she lowered the mask and let her true self emerge, things became real, and real was great fun.

I reported back to Claude. She quizzed me mercilessly. I'm sure I blushed. She pressed me, saying that the bottom line was would I want to see her again—and again. That's what she wanted, like any good businessperson, repeat customers. I hedged my answer. What a great way to meet beautiful women, I said. No aggression, no rejection, no anxiety, no bad dates, just a graceful cut to the chase. Thanks, Madame Claude. There was a famous Ban deodorant commercial in the sixties: "Ban takes the worry out of being close." So did Madame Claude. All it took was money, big money.

What I wanted to say was that Penelope's only problem was that she was too easy. But I didn't want to hurt her chances to work for Claude and achieve her dream. For superrich and successful men with huge and impervious egos, the money that went to Claude and the girl wasn't a payment; it was a *gift*. If I were a rich man's son, I told Claude, Penelope would be great. "No, no ifs," Claude insisted. "You as you." "Me as me can't afford this playground of the gods," I admitted. "Then work harder so you can," she exhorted. Which finally gave me my opening to pitch the book, as my one way to become a Claude man.

I was surprised how open Madame Claude was to the idea of an American book—if the price were right. She was nonplussed

that her French memoir had not taken off, even with the impri-
matur of the country's bestselling author Françoise Sagan,
through her brother Jacques Quoirez, whom all France knew, on
the cover. I made it simple. She didn't name names. Of course
she wouldn't, she said, offended by the notion and peremptorily
taking the subject off the Ma Maison table. I decided to try to
keep it on. What did I have to lose? A seven-figure advance!

Madame Claude was very much the fiduciary she looked like.
She didn't want to do anything that might damage or embarrass
her clients. And then there were the libel laws and the specter
of lawsuits, not to mention more corporeal reprisals. I didn't
know at the time her deep roots in the Corsican Mafia, or about
Bokassa or anything like that. I didn't know much about her
past at all. That took time and confidence. All she had reminisced
about at first was how she had failed at selling Bibles door-to-
door. She didn't talk about her own early days as a streetwalker,
or the concentration camp before that. But I knew that didn't
matter to the money people back in New York. All they wanted
were names.

I put on my lawyer's hat and tried my best to explain to her
how much stricter French laws were on matters of libel and invasion of privacy than ours. It wasn't that the French were simply "more sophisticated" in their reticence about the private lives
of politicians and other celebrities. It was that Napoleonic Code
of an aristocratic country that better protected and insulated those
at the top from the curiosity of the rabble below. In America, I
said, public figures were fair game, as long as the truth was told.
The law was one thing, Claude conceded. But what about "mo-
rality" asked the woman not normally associated with moral
issues. What about her relationships? Those relationships, I
would learn, were no longer paying the bills as they had in
France. They were no match for the relationships of Madam
Alex. Loyalty to a madam was a hazy, perhaps oxymoronic concept, even if Claude had broken the old mold. Then, and not

before then, did I drop the *m* bomb and tell her the quid pro quo for her disclosures could be a million dollars or more. She liked the sound of that million. It intrigued her. A million dollars for a book was serious money. It was the kind of money Françoise Sagan got, not the relative pittance for *Allô, Oui*. If Françoise, why not Claude?

Again, as cagey mistress of the tease, Claude began dropping names of "friends." She didn't call them clients; she didn't say that money had changed hands. It was no different from all the famous well-wishers at Ma Maison or Caffé Roma. She seemed to know everyone, yet knowing them did not imply that any laws, or even moral codes, were being violated. Once she got that cool million, she promised, is when she'd start telling the stories behind those friendships. We started talking about the friends of hers whom I had met, such as Swifty Lazar. She told me how any man compulsive enough to send his Turnbull & Asser shirts and sheets to be laundered in Paris could, by the same token, send for a Claude girl to unbutton those shirts and share those linens. He was a germophobe, as bad as Howard Hughes, she said, and didn't trust Madam Alex's girls, or any girl, in fact, who didn't use a bidet.

Hughes had turned away from his playboy phase and become too inward by the time she had started her business to have ever been a client, Claude said, almost wistfully. However, she did say she was close to his lawyer, Greg Bautzer, the playboy ex of Joan Crawford and lover of clients like Ginger Rogers and Ingrid Bergman. Claude also talked about Bautzer's other aviator client, MGM owner Kirk Kerkorian, who, she said, was too penurious to hire her girls himself, but whose Vegas aides would fly them over and set him up with them as if they were visiting tourists. The capacity for self-delusion, when it came to romance, Claude said, was unbounded.

Talk of Vegas provided an opportunity to segue into the Rat Pack, and this provided my first huge "get." The nexus here was through the late restaurateur Mike Romanoff, who was the Claude Terrail of Beverly Hills. Terrail had introduced his fellow caterer-to-the-stars Romanoff to Madame Claude early in her reign, and he networked her into Hollywood. Although Dean Martin, as she had told me, was too cheap to use her women, and Peter Lawford was both too cheap and too sexually ambivalent, Frank Sinatra, songwriter Jimmy Van Heusen ("All the Way"), and Sammy Davis, Jr., had been huge fans.

Claude boasted how "liberated" she was in providing women for an entertainer who had been barred from hotels throughout a lingeringly racist America. "Sammy loves my Germans," she said. As for Sinatra, Claude regretted that the Chairman's ring-a-ding style had been cramped by his eagle-eyed new wife, Barbara, a tall, blond ex-showgirl who, in a younger French incarnation, might have fit the strict Claude bill. Claude's attitude toward Mrs. S.'s paranoia was that it "took one to know one." Sinatra had stolen Barbara away from his Palm Springs neighbor Zeppo Marx, whose brother Groucho was also on the Claude list.

Groucho's longtime companion, the decades-younger actress Erin Fleming, had dragged an aging and increasingly frail Groucho to Paris and hired Claude girls to cater to his never-flagging libido. Fleming's hope, Claude said, was that Groucho's sexual appetite would get the better of his coronary elasticity and accelerate her inheritance of his estate. Groucho had eventually accommodated her, dying in 1977, but his sons, presaging the Zanuck playbook, went to court for years to portray Fleming as a conniving gold digger and eventually forced her to return half a million dollars of what Groucho had given her.

Like a chain letter, discussions of Sinatra segued into discussions of the Kennedys. Claude, who generally preferred to denigrate others rather than boast about herself, couldn't conceal her pride in den-mothering John Kennedy. She talked about Pierre Salinger's arranging the president's encounter with a "hot"

Jackie look-alike on his first state visit to Paris, when his sexual relations with the First Lady were at a low ebb. She said he asked for a return engagement in Washington. When "Jackie Chaude" was unavailable for the trip, Claude had to scramble to find a "Jackie Plus Chaude."

There was also Henry Kissinger, whose famous quote that "power was an aphrodisiac" was undercut by Claude's tale that during the Paris Peace Talks to end the war in Vietnam, the CIA had hired a number of her girls to attend social functions and fawn over him, in order to keep his spirits up during the course of the long negotiations. In addition to heads of studios, heads of state seemed to be her specialty.

She talked about the Shah, a good friend who had just died. She clearly missed him. She told me a story of a model she sent to him who, unbeknownst to her, had become a radical Communist and shared the woman's conversation with the emperor on her visit to the palace. "I cannot make love to a Communist," he told her, and packed her off back to Paris, minus the Harry Winston–bought jewels his dates usually got as tips. Claude had a thing for autocratic, luxury-loving despots. Another one she missed was Sukarno of Indonesia. In the early sixties, on his first date with a Claudette, he got so carried away, he stood up Charles de Gaulle at a state reception for him. All Paris had thought he had been assassinated or kidnapped, and Claude barely avoided an international incident.

Yet another strongman still in the Claude orbit was Libya's Mu'ammar Qaddafi. Claude once sent one of her more acquisitive acolytes to him at the Ritz, expecting to be fêted with champagne and caviar. Instead, she was greeted with bottled water and dates. There was also a cassette with Arabic music. Qaddafi gave her a large diamond to put in her belly button and had her dance in front of him all night. The next morning, the material girl was exhausted and disappointed and almost ready to quit, until Qaddafi gave her the diamond as a tip and later enshrined her as one of his favorites.

On the other side of the Mideast scale was Israeli hero Moshe Dayan. Claude was an equal-opportunity madam, working both sides of the Red Sea. Not only did Dayan keep kosher; he kept the faith in every way by insisting on seeing only Jewish girls. Claude said that Jewish girls were always in short supply. They had the motivation and ambition but usually lacked the height that she tended to insist on. She never sent a girl to anyone if there were any chance the client might be disappointed. In her view, all it took was one bad date to lose a client forever. She held off on the general until she found him Miss Right, an ex-lieutenant in the Israeli army who was studying law in Paris. The tall, tawny Sabra was so honored to meet Dayan that she refused to accept any money.

The list of leaders never seemed to end. Claude knew Lord Mountbatten, who was so discreet that the only place he would see her girls was in Baron Elie de Rothschild's private jet, circling the skies above Paris as the two old friends enjoyed a ménage à quatre. While Mountbatten (whose military nickname was "Mountbottom") had long been rumored to have unconventional interests, Claude had no interest in outing him. Once the names started coming, they flowed like a river, though Claude rarely said anything untoward about anyone. The worst tale she told was on Nelson Rockefeller, who liked to pinch the girls in a show of hail-fellow bonhomie that marked his career as a politician. Claude said she had to scold him, like a naughty schoolboy, explaining that after a girl saw him, she was too black-and-blue to see anyone else for at least a week. "Rocky" promised to be more gentle.

I asked Claude about the current Reagan dynasty and his fat-cat Los Angeles kitchen cabinet, which seemed like her natural demographic. She seemed pained, at a loss, and conceded that Madam Alex owned this local elite. Then she turned her defense

into offense by attacking the Reaganites as nouveau riche "shopping center" people and "cowboys" with saloon tastes, by which
I gleaned that she meant glitzy Vegas showgirls as opposed to
understated Givenchy runway models. What about Alfred
Bloomingdale, the most notorious of the Reagan swingers? The
department store heir and creator of the Diners Club credit card
was carrying on a well-known, expensively abusive affair with
an Alex girl named Vicki Morgan, who, after Bloomingdale died
the next year, would sue the estate for palimony, much like the
Darryl Zanuck contretemps that Claude was in L.A. to rem-
edy. "I wouldn't let Nelson Rockefeller *pinch* my girls; why would
I let Alfred Bloomingdale *beat* them?" Claude replied. As far as
S & M was concerned, Claude would allow her girls to be givers
but never takers.

Claude boasted about some of the century's greatest artists,
like Picasso, whom she found hideous but sexy, and Marc Cha-
gall, who used naked Claudettes as his models, and the greatest
musicians, like Dimitri Shostakovich, when he came to Paris
on cultural exchanges. She was tight with his KGB handlers,
tight as well with the CIA. I wonder now how anyone so tightly
connected could have ended up in Sibyl Brand. I suppose all
patronage has to come to an end someday. That's why she was
talking.

There were the usual suspects, the tycoons everyone knew.
They were the hallmarks and bulwarks of her clientele. The style
maven Agnelli dressed her girls in sailor suits for his yacht and
docked in ports on Sunday to take them to Mass. Onassis and
Maria Callas made demands on Claude that she found "too depraved" to discuss. She made fun of J. Paul Getty's cheapness in
making his honored guests use a pay box at Sutton Place, his
English stately home, to avoid leaving the billionaire with
long-distance charges.

Because we were in Hollywood, Claude's name sharing,
which went on over four or five lunches, in drips and drops, in-

evitably returned to the stars. In Paris, she said, she had sent girls to Marlon Brando, though she could never find the truly exotic Oceana types that he preferred. Instead, she would send her brainiest Sorbonne students to Brando, and he would basically lecture them until sunrise about global atrocities and other causes near to his heart. Sex never entered the picture.

Claude loved British actors, who were only a Channel ferry, and later a Hovercraft, ride away from the pleasures of Paris. Topping her list were Richard Burton, whom she said came to her for solace from his epic fights with Elizabeth Taylor, and Rex Harrison, who always insisted, ever politely, on two tall Scandinavians at a time. I asked her if he gave them diction lessons, but my French effort here got lost in translation. She didn't get the *My Fair Lady* reference, though she noted that lyricist Alan Jay Lerner was a big client. The eight-times-married, well-born, and Harvard-educated Lerner fit Claude's French paradigm of clients from privileged backgrounds who went through lots of women, as if by divine right.

Speaking of lots of women, no one had more than Roger Vadim, who headed her directors list. A man who seemingly had loved everyone, Vadim was a vehement opponent of the notion that three was a crowd. I never could understand why he would need more sexual company than his wife Jane Fonda, whom he turned into Barbarella, the sex symbol of the feminist generation. Claude said that, like all directors, he liked scenes and he liked giving orders. Genius auteurs she cited as "her friends" were Billy Wilder, Stanley Kubrick, Bob Fosse, and Roman Polanski, all known for their associations with great beauties. As for comic geniuses, the just-deceased Peter Sellers topped her list as her most neurotic star client.

Polanski, just a few years before I met Claude, had famously fled California and America in the wake of the child rape case. Claude thought he had gotten a raw deal, simply because he was a "foreigner." She was feeling insecure herself because of her own

fragile immigration status. She thought it was unfair that Polanski's great pal and partner-in-seduction Jack Nicholson had been
given a free pass. She called them both *méchants,* or bad boys.
The age of consent in France was only fifteen, which allowed
Lolita-lovers there a much larger playing field. However, Claude
said she was shocked by the wildness, drug taking, and sexual
precocity she had observed among L.A. teenagers, especially the
rock "baby groupies" of the Sunset Strip club scene. She said
French children were "innocent lambs" by comparison.

Where groupies were concerned, Claude's taste in rockers
ran much more to her friend Johnny Hallyday, the Belgian lorry
driver who was now the "French Elvis," than to the real thing,
whom she never met and thought was "coarse." She said she
"knew" the Rolling Stones, through Nathalie Delon, ex of Alain
and the chic, snobby, cold blond French rich bitch type that ex-
emplified the Claude brand. Nathalie had gone off to the South
of France as their muse for *Exile on Main St.,* an album that might
as well been called "Exile on the Promenade des Anglais," because
of its Côte d'Azur provenance. Claude relegated Mick Jagger to
her "tightwad" list and Keith Richards to her "drug addict" no-
fly zone.

My overall impression from all these dropped names was a
great wonder what love, or even sex, had to do with it. The girl
that Claude was selling was basically a luxury "collectible," like
a Warhol painting, a Cartier gem, a Gulfstream jet, a Lürssen
yacht, or a Beverly Hills mansion. She was a dealer and these
famous rich men were collectors. What was the difference between her and Joseph Duveen or Harry Winston? Or P. T. Bar-
num, for that matter. She was selling an experience, sort of like
Patrick Terrail with his restaurant. But he seemed to be working
far harder; it got hot in that kitchen. I suppose Claude's blood,
sweat, and tears were in "creating" the girls, à la *And God Created
Woman,* though the ones I met were found and not made. She

was doing for bedrooms what Hollywood agents did for the screen, discovering and brokering talent.

What fools these immortals seemed to be, spending a fortune on what was basically a vanishing act. Unless they married the girl, which may have been the original goal of Claude's operation, but which had given way to a grand in and out. At least the Warhol they could hang on the wall. But for the men who had everything, the precious memory of an evanescent pleasure must have been worth the price of illusion. That Claude had gotten rich in this game made me all the more impressed with her for pulling it off.

The book we were planning to create had the working title *Sex and Power*. The supposedly radical idea here was that famous people paid for sex. We had proof. We had the names. That these same men squandered even more on art or jewels didn't matter. Sex was different. Sex was sacred. Sex was supposedly the privilege of these gods, and here they were defiling it with money. We were decades ahead of the "Just Like Us" formula that would make *Us* magazine a hit. The low common denominator was "celebrities go to hookers." Just like us. It was a sad story that would be repeated ad infinitum, and always with huge media impact, from John Profumo to Lord Lambton to Hugh Grant to Eliot Spitzer. (But not Bill Cosby or Harvey Weinstein, who may someday wish they had.) But we were going to do it first, and in a mass exposure.

After a few weeks, I had big names to spare, although Claude said she would never go on the record without, at the least, her million in hand. It was now my task to show her the money. It wasn't as easy as I had thought. The long list of names I had assembled, rather than being catnip, was more like Kryptonite. The New York superagent, the one who made the million-dollar-advance call, now had second thoughts. Every famous person he had ever met, or ever wanted to meet, was on that list. This was no way for this socially ambitious man to win friends and influence people. He already had all the money he could ever need or want. The Madame Claude story, in his eyes, was hot all right, but too hot for him to handle.

Still, there were plenty of others in publishing who were more concerned with a place on the bestseller lists than one at Brooke Astor's table. That bible of eighties popularity, *People* magazine, was interested in doing a big piece on Claude in L.A. that could trigger a frenzied book auction. Claude was appalled by the very Barnumesque notion, and by *People* itself. What would brainy, snobby Françoise Sagan say? The last thing Madame Claude wanted was a celebrity circus. Given her continuing problems with the immigration authorities, she wanted to stay under the radar and do nothing to imperil her green card and trigger an investigation or, worse, a deportation. She believed her powerful friends in France were putting the arm on the new left-wing government of François Mitterrand to cut a deal to let *la madame* back into *la république*. The new president supposedly had better things to do than chase after prostitution rings.

Claude seemed to know more about the Socialist Mitterrand than anyone else I had met; she described him, in her vicious style, as a Vichy Nazi collaborator who helped deport thousands of French Jews to concentration camps, a serious charge, which would hit the press over a decade later. Nonetheless, she saw him as her ticket back to France. Claude thus wanted to bide her time. She sensed redemption and return were imminent. She didn't want to offend her host country by going on TV and being introduced as the woman enabler of the adultery of the still-sainted John F. Kennedy. The only book deal she wanted was a cloak-and-dagger seven-figure arrangement that absolutely no one would know about until she were safely back home with the *real* Terrail, at the *real* Tour d'Argent. Despite the Riviera weather, the ersatz of L.A. was clearly getting to her.

Although the book deal did not instantly materialize, Madame

Claude didn't blame me for it. She understood what a hot potato she was. We had become friendly, if not friends. I actually enjoyed her cutting sarcasm—in its limited doses. And I loved her gossip. She was like a living, global Page Six. She told me I was "un-American," which I took as a compliment. Claude continued our lunches, and, in her most magnanimous gesture of all, she continued giving me "testing" assignments, as girls arrived every week from Europe, wanting to meet the rich and famous.

My last blind date, call her "Hannah," was a German model from the ancient Roman city of Trier, in the Moselle Valley, on the German-French border. She was fluent in French, German, and English. She could have been a doppelgänger for the future supermodel Claudia Schiffer, but she was too brainy to settle for living on her looks. A graduate of Heidelberg University, she was in L.A. getting an M.B.A. at USC, locally known as the University for Spoiled Children, but whose film school, alma mater of George Lucas, had turned it into a magnet for foreigners. Hannah was very focused and methodical. Her goal was to become a female studio head, kind of like Sherry Lansing of Paramount, whom I had often seen at Ma Maison.

Hannah thought it would be strategic to sleep with the right people on her way to the top, and that Madame Claude could help her climb the ladder. Connecting to these power brokers through Claude was like being introduced as a family friend, not as a hooker. If Hannah's looks were intimidating, her ambition was terrifying. I had absolutely no business going out with Hannah, much less sleeping with her. But because it *was* business, there I was. I tried to make a joke of it, telling her the one about the ambitious Polish actress who slept with a screenwriter. She didn't get it. I blamed Germany.

I not only had an M.B.A., which gave Hannah and me something to talk about, but I had visited Trier, an amazing city with the best Roman ruins and antiquities outside Italy. Trier had been the capital of Gaul in Caesarean days. Later, it was famous as the birthplace of Karl Marx. There was nothing Marxist about Hannah. She came from a noble Prussian family that was seduced into the Nazi fold by Hermann Göring, a pathological social climber. Her grandfather became Göring's art adviser, which meant to me that he helped loot a lot of masterpieces owned by Jews. I suggested to Hannah that her genealogy, impressive as it was, might not play well in Hollywood. Nonsense, she said. They didn't have problems driving Mercedes and BMWs, so they shouldn't have a problem hiring Germans. Who was I to disagree?

The problem with this fantasy was that it bore zero connection to reality. Whom could Hannah, totally perfect, totally self-contained, totally driven, ever really fall for? Lew Wasserman, the head of MCA-Universal, the most powerful man in Hollywood? Maybe, depending on how far he could advance her career. Mike Ovitz, head of CAA? The only door I could open was the one to Madame Claude; that was my utility. I tried to think about how gorgeous she was, and how lucky I was, and not get too deep into the semiotics of it all. At the end of dinner, Hannah said, "Okay. Let's do it." Those where the last words of murderer Gary Gilmore before he was executed. I could only hope Hannah felt less fatalistic. Hannah did eventually redeem herself. When the conversation turned back to Hitler, which I knew it shouldn't, Hannah proved to be not at all defensive, but remarkably good-natured. She quoted a line from *Animal House,* a comedy, this brainy beauty seriously noted, that was a metaphor for Nazism. "We fucked up. We *trusted him.*" Why hadn't I thought of that?

I never got to give Madame Claude my review. For the next week, she didn't answer the phone, which was odd, because she always answered the phone. Her famous greeting of *"Allô, oui"* was a Pavlovian harbinger of good times. As it turned out, she had been in court, at the palimony trial of her ex-Claudette, whose purported virtue she was going to torpedo on behalf of the Zanuck estate. However, the day Claude was going to take the stand, Richard Zanuck came with some bad news. For all his connections at the top of Sacramento and Washington, even Richard Zanuck could not guarantee that Claude could stay in America. Her green card, through her sham marriage to the bartender, whom she never mentioned to me, was in jeopardy. The Prince of Hollywood could not save the Queen of Sex.

When Claude took the witness stand and was asked whether she knew Darryl Zanuck's inamorata, she replied, "*Je ne me souviens pas*" ("I don't remember"). For every question she was asked, that was the answer: "I don't remember." We spoke on the phone a few more times, but we didn't meet again. I could tell she was shaken by the limits of Hollywood power. Soon her phone was disconnected. She disappeared from Ma Maison, from Caffè Roma. I went by the Coldwater Canyon house. There was a FOR RENT sign. I gave up and went back to New York. I later found out that Madame Claude, like Roman Polanski, had fled the jurisdiction and escaped to her own private Elba, a cattle ranch in the tropical paradise of Vanuatu, a former French colony on an archipelago in the South Pacific. I never saw her again. I knew Claude was anything but sentimental, but I still felt that I had lost a friend.

Chapter 10

THE PRISONER OF SEX

*T*homas Wolfe's *You Can't Go Home Again* might well have been the title of the story of the second half of Madame Claude's long life. That, or *Downhill Racer*. For most of the early eighties, Claude was missing in action, swallowed up by the black hole that was the South Pacific. If she were bored and culturally deprived in Los Angeles, what kind of stimulation could she have possibly gotten in Vanuatu? Maybe she saw this as her Gauguin moment. She had never mentioned that she wanted to paint.

Or maybe Claude liked being a plantation-style cattle breeder, a female version of Emile de Becque in *South Pacific*. Cattle, which had been introduced to the island from Australia in 1774, was the volcanic Vanuatu's most valuable industry, and Claude, who loved business, was always something of a horse trader. Alas, aside from possibly finding an exotic native for Marlon Brando, who had his own Pacific island escape, there was at best primitive phone service and no opportunity for Claude to practice the art at which she excelled beyond all others, the art of the telephone, the art of the date.

In 1985, after an exile of almost eight years, Claude, then sixty-two, decided to go back to France. She ostensibly had plenty of money. Cattle ranches, even in Vanuatu, were not an impulse purchase. There were also the secret bank accounts in Switzerland and Singapore and the safety-deposit boxes full of diamonds from the Shah and others. She still had her fancy lawyers in Paris and Geneva. They told her the coast was clear, that François Mitterrand had no interest in perpetuating anything at all from his predecessor and Gaullist political opposite, Giscard d'Estaing, much less his witch hunt against his erstwhile procuress. Claude agreed with their advice not to make any triumphal gestures that would evoke de Gaulle's return to Paris after the Nazis were routed.

Instead of coming straight to Paris and taking one of her rightful A tables at Brasserie Lipp or Fouquet's, she decided on a stealth reentry, purchasing a charming farmhouse in Cajarc through Jacques Quoirez, near his family's barony in the Lot, the southwest region famed for its truffles, foie gras, and goat cheese. Because it was the home turf of both Françoise Sagan and Georges Pompidou, the area had become extremely rustic chic, the French version of Litchfield, Connecticut. Claude would join the Lot country squirearchy for a while, until she could decide when and how to reinstall her telephones.

She didn't get the chance. Within a few months, there was a surprise raid on the farmhouse and Claude was arrested and charged with those long-simmering counts of tax evasion. The *fiscs* were now asking for eleven million francs in back taxes. Luckily for Claude, assuming most of her assets were hidden abroad, Mitterrand's Socialism had plunged France into a severe economic crisis. He had even nationalized the Banque Rothschild. Paris was feared to become Moscow-sur-Seine. The franc, which was roughly equivalent to a quarter when Claude fled to L.A., was now worth less than a dime. Still, she owed over a million dollars. She said she didn't have it. One of her top clients had been the Geneva-based American financial wizard Bernie Cornfeld, whose once high-flying mutual funds company IOS had been taken over by the vastly more crooked financier Robert Vesco, now a fugitive from American justice in Costa

Rica. It was thought that Claude, emulating the high rollers she served, rolled the dice herself. She had entrusted most of her fortune to Cornfeld, who made his own fortune on guaranteeing outrageously high returns. When Cornfeld finally fell to earth, Claude's money was lost. To jail she went, and the French press went wild.

Claude gave them plenty of "Let them eat cake" ammunition. The Cahors female penitentiary "was the most luxurious prison on earth," said her friend Sylvette Balland, who had also returned to France from Los Angeles to marry a Paris publisher. She was one of the first people Claude reconnected with. "More like a Relais et Châteaux. It was a seventeenth-century castle. She had a private room, a beautiful view of the forest, her own maid and hairdresser, and they brought her meals from the best restaurant in Cahors." Her first meal, the papers of Europe breathlessly reported, was mackerel, symbolic of Claude's other, unflattering name, *mère macquerelle,* or lady pimp. She stayed in this luxury lockup for four months, then settled her tax bill for centimes on the franc, a tiny percentage of the amount the *fiscs* had demanded. The press groaned that the fix was in, just like old times.

Keeping her farmhouse in Cajarc, Claude now returned to Paris and took a luxury apartment in the Marais, close to Balland, who was on the Ile Saint-Louis. Balland's new husband then published Claude's new book, *Le Meilleur, C'est l'Autre,* which she wrote while in the castle prison. The book was not a confessional, but, rather, a Helen Gurley Brown *Cosmo*-style guide to meeting rich men and having fabulous orgasms. She even included a long appendix in the back enumerating vitamins, minerals, and other homeopathies that would enhance a woman's beauty, health, and love life.

Claude then took a job, her first in three decades, as a saleswoman at a chic sportswear boutique on the Left Bank's rue Mazarine. No one who knew her could believe she was playing it straight, and she was not. The store was a similar operation to Georges Cibaud in Beverly Hills. That is, a great place for Claude to find *jeunes filles* who were pretty, stylish, and, most of all, ambitious, so that she could restart her legendary operation. "She was the worst salesgirl in history," Balland admitted. At least where vending *vêtements* was concerned. "Her attitude was not that the customer was always right. No, it was that the customer was always *fat*!" Madame Claude was even more obsessive than the duchess of Windsor that a woman could never be too rich or too thin.

"She was so nasty, even when she was trying to be nice," said Susi Wyss, recalling a 1986 lunch at the Left Bank bistro Au Petit Tonneau with Claude and their mutual friend Françoise Hardy, the sixties *yé-yé* girl who had now become a much sought-after astrologer. "She hadn't seen me for a decade, and the first thing she said was, 'Lose ten pounds and have a *lifting*, and I can still find you a rich man.'" Wyss had become a genuine character in the Paris celebrity firmament of the seventies and eighties while Claude had been away. An American-born, Zurich-raised daughter of a maid and a baker, Wyss had married a French art director and raised a now-grown son in South Africa before returning to Paris, getting divorced, and beginning a new wild life, at thirty. A shorter version of Jane Birkin, with the added surprise of a D cup, Wyss was discovered by Helmut Newton, always in search of busty models in flat-chested France. Then she also began posing for Salvador Dalí.

Newton made Wyss part of his glamorous entourage and took her on shoots to Saint-Tropez. There she caught the eye of the decadent, drug-addicted, but supercharming Italian prince Dado Ruspoli, who began a chain letter that included several Rothschild branches and three generations of Gettys, J. Paul senior, junior, and the third. Wyss continued to service the latter even after a drug-induced stroke left him speechless and in a wheelchair. "I loved him and I loved challenges," Wyss said. On her own, she hung out at the Cannes Film Festival, meeting and seducing Francis Coppola and adding him to her belt of conquests of Hollywood's new generation. She claims, with no disputes, to have slept with the entire cast of *Easy Rider*, except for Jack Nicholson.

Wanting to "try everything I had missed," Wyss also became a call girl. Her first client was Lord Lambton, prior to his British sex scandal, who was introduced by the Gettys and whom she was hired to "punish." She claimed to have done a threesome with Lambton and Christine Keeler, who had starred a decade before in the Profumo scandal. "That was real history," Wyss proudly noted. She said Claude had wanted her to work for her but that she had turned Claude down. "I needn't need anyone to find me business."

Once Claude fled to L.A., Wyss filled that vacuum by becoming a madam, as well. She hooked up with Jacky Cohen, the man-about-the-world personal procurer of Gianni Agnelli. Cohen had a side deal pimping for the Shah of Iran. Wyss thus began taking Claude's place in sending top models to Tehran. "Sure, she was jealous," Wyss said, "but she was jealous of everything. She wanted everyone to fail except herself. She hated me for being so free. She hated me for loving and being loved by men. I'm sure she was a lesbian, but too repressed to do anything. But I could make her laugh, which wasn't easy. So she liked being around me. I did stuff she could only dream of. And I could tease her and say, 'I may not be perfect, but at least I didn't go to prison.' She could take it. She could give, but she could take. I liked that about her."

Wyss developed another subspecialty of rock stars, hence her friendship with Françoise Hardy. Claude, for all her fame, had never inspired a song, such as Iggy Pop's ode to Wyss, "Girls." After five years of turning tricks, Wyss hung it up after one call girl's day of days, a super/quadrifecta where she slept, for cash, first with Yves Montand ("a two-minute man"), Omar Sharif ("so

handsome and sweet but a lousy lover"), David Bowie ("I worshipped him"), and finally a top executive of Mercedes-Benz,
who gave her ten thousand francs for anal sex ("he came in one
minute"). "I had nowhere to go but down after that, so I quit."

Unlike the ravenous Wyss, who made close friends of most
of her clients and, in her eighties, still gives coveted-invite dinner parties in Paris for the children of Rothschilds and rock stars
she has known, Madame Claude could not give up the ghost of
her former glory. She could never be content to become an ex-
madam. The new times were against her. Her old clients were
getting older, some dying off, some no longer able to cut the
mustard, as Marlene Dietrich famously sang. On the younger
front, AIDS was rampant, literally killing the joy of sex, as was
feminism. Women who before might have coveted the lush life
of call girls now found it safer and smarter to get increasingly
available real jobs in banks and corporations.

In France, prostitution, for centuries a key part of *la vie,* was
losing its luster. In the land of sexual freedom, if not license, condoms, long discarded because of the Pill, were now completely
de rigueur. Pigalle had become a dead zone. The bargain beauties
of the rue Saint-Denis were increasingly few and far between,
replaced by poor women from France's old African and Carib-
bean colonies who knew no better and only added to the grim
disease statistics. Claude's attitude was that she was never a part
of the prostitution netherworld, but, rather, the fantasyland of
the haut monde. In her mind, France needed her, now more than
ever.

Instead, France got Claude's former right-hand woman,
Catherine Virgitti, to whom Claude sold her business when she
decamped to Los Angeles in 1977. Contrary to endless rumors,
there was, according to Virgitti, no actual black book, nothing
tangible at all, other than Claude's "brand." Still, the price of the
mystique was so high that Virgitti cut a deal to make payments
to Claude over a period of years. She was, in effect, taking a

mortgage on a legend. Virgitti is adamant that, contrary to all the rumors that she had "stolen" Claude's business when Claude left Paris, they had a fair deal, and a big one. Sadly for Virgitti, the payments she was making were forced to end after little more than a year. The Giscard regime was no more kindly disposed toward Virgitti than it was toward Claude. Showing to France he meant business where sex was concerned, Giscard put Virgitti out of business. Arrested by the newly "purified" Vice Squad, Virgitti was convicted of *proxénétisme* and sent to Fleury-Mérogis, just as Claude would be. However, Virgitti was released after two short months. "I was very close with Giscard's secretary," Virgitti, now seventy-two, says with a Cheshire cat grin.

The feline analogy is apt. Ever since her early release, Virgitti has traded one cathouse for another. Abandoning the glitter of Paris, she moved to the bourgeois suburb of Levallois-Perret, where she has operated Ecole du Chat, a rescue service for cats, as well as for rabbits and other domestic animals, for the last forty years. Virgitti, quite petite for a Claude girl, bears a striking resemblance to today's Julie Christie, a similarity that was not lost on Warren Beatty when, in 1977, he made a hard play for Virgitti, then the new queen of Paris sex and a major status symbol, which always had a special allure for this most status-conscious of Hollywood stars. He took her dancing at Matignon, the new nightclub on the Champs-Elysées that was trying to turn Castel and Régine's into the same sort of history as Madame Claude. "The sex was so fantastic, I simply couldn't bring myself to charge him," mused Virgitti, who claimed that she never once fell in love with any of her many famous clients. "I never met a better lover," said Virgitti. "The rumors were true."

Virgitti's specialty was inculcating the children of the rich and famous into the art of love. She proudly boasted of demolishing the virginity of Rothschild and Niarchos scions, among many others, as she did with the Bleustein-Blanchet heir, an affair that became a book and a film. "Those boys were so darling," she said, albeit, like Edith Piaf, without any regret. If she couldn't become Madame Claude, Virgitti decided to become Doctor Dolittle, and she has succeeded in creating a life that has meaning and service, of a different kind. Despite close to a decade of working together, Virgitti said she was never able to get close to Claude. "She never let down her guard to me," she said, "maybe because she knew how much I wanted to be her, to run her show."

The only vulnerability on Claude's part that Virgitti recalled was her nostalgia over a love affair with the über–rocket man Werner von Braun, a client who became the boss's pet. They had met through another top client, Curt Jurgens, who had played von Braun in the 1960 Columbia biopic *I Aim at the Stars*. The movie star–handsome von Braun had married his first cousin, and had become a born-again Christian who was good friends with both Billy Graham and Martin Luther King, Jr. However, as the Adonis of both the Nazi and then the Yankee space programs, he still apparently had lust in his heart, which found its outlet in Madame Claude.

"She had so many mythical, heroic stories, I never knew what to believe," Virgitti said. The one romance she did witness was anything but mythic. This was René, the parasitical printer whom Claude tried in vain to turn into her majordomo, similar to the director turned butler played by Erich Von Stroheim in *Sunset Blvd.* "Beside the awful girl he left Claude for, he was sleeping with all our girls," Virgitti recalled. "Claude knew it, but she pretended he was faithful, and none of us dared to contradict her. That one time she was as deluded as her clients."

The idea that Claude was the top informant for both French and foreign intelligence was, to Virgitti, largely a myth of Claude's creation, not so much for self-aggrandizement but as a deterrent to the Corsican Mafia, which might otherwise have muscled in on the Claude honeypot. The very notion that Claude was in bed with the law served to keep the outlaws at bay. "She was brilliant in business," Virgitti conceded. "No one could have done what she did. Certainly not me. Not even me." Virgitti saw Claude as an enabler, in the best sense. "She never forced any girl to do anything that could hurt her. If someone felt the slightest discomfort about a situation, the Claude rule was to walk away. Just walk away. Money be damned. She could be impossible, but she made impossible things come true. So many of her—our, I like to say—girls did so well. She changed a lot of lives, all for the best."

Unlike the case with Catherine Virgitti, neither love nor law could impel Madame Claude to tear herself away from being the headmistress of her own feline academy. In her mid-sixties, and long before sixty was the new forty, she forged ahead, doing what she knew how to do better than anyone else. "I had hoped to make enough money in a short period of time to permanently leave this narrow-minded country," Claude wrote in *Madam*. Feeling betrayed by her imprisonment, Claude declared her honeymoon with France was over. She decried the "shopkeeper mentality of the French people, beret-baguette-pension, nothing more."

Claude also decried the equally sorry state of French prostitution, which she blamed on the dramatic rise of drug use in all levels of society, particularly her upscale talent pool. "My girls were not as well-behaved as they used to be" was how she put it. Still she remained possessed by the Pygmalion imperative and could sound as driven as Dr. Frankenstein, and as scarily messianic as Hitler, about her mission and duty to create her own distaff master race. In *Madam,* she wrote, "I was still itching to play Pygmalion. To be able, in a few minutes, to detect in someone the slightest defect, in physical or character traits, and to draw up a suitable transformation program still delighted me. I felt the pleasure an artist feels. The great eye required to create my women is nothing less than the great nose for the creators of perfume and the great palate among chefs and winemakers."

Claude's main confidence that her star could rise again was that she still had her European Old Guard who knew that she was, like them, pure class, and in a class by herself: Rothschild, Agnelli, Niarchos (Onassis had died in 1975), Thyssen-Bornemisza, King Juan Carlos of Spain. The Spanish monarch, like Giscard, had had an obsession with Lady Diana that he sated by having Claude find him look-alikes, as she did regarding Jackie for John Kennedy. Only Claude had the sexual Rolodex that could accommodate such requests. She might have tens of girls now instead of hundreds, but what she would offer would be, as always, the cream of the crop for the cream of world society.

One enemy Madame Claude did not anticipate, which was an even bigger threat to her resurrection than either AIDS or feminism, was technology. In pioneering the call-girl profession, Claude had astutely played the telephone like a Stradivarius, riding the crest of the wave of advances in mass communications as France went modern. Now Claude's favorite instrument, the thing that put her "*Allô, oui*" into the lexicon, was going to put her out to pasture. Enter the Minitel, a boxy little terminal that was the forerunner of the personal computer. This was the pre-Internet invention, launched by France Télécom in 1982 and hooked to people's phone lines, that took the voice out of communications.

In an era where, even in libertine France, commercial sex was becoming something to be ashamed about, the Minitel became a huge hit, because it took the shame out of trolling for eros. Its ostensible utility was to book theater tickets, make travel reservations, and scan the media for news flashes. But what the French not so secretly loved it for was as a way to shop for sex without walking the streets—or knowing someone like Madame Claude, which was an impossibility for mere mortals. That the Minitel caught on only in France (and officially died in 2012 with the triumph of the World Wide Web) was often attributed to the unique relationship between the French and prostitution. France made a hard push to sell the Minitel to both the United States and England. Both turned it down flat, long before the Internet was a viable alternative. It seemed too French, too naughty, to these puritan countries that didn't adopt bidets, either.

The sex lines of the Minitel became known as the Minitel Rose, or pink Minitel, and the bills consumers would run up on its chat lines were legendary. Here, for the first time, was virtual sex, immediate and, in an age of heightened hypochondria, disease-free. It was like the Immaculate Conception. Men clearly liked talking about sex, as Madam Alex learned in accruing her fortune. The terse and laconic Madame Claude would never learn this lesson; her old-fashioned oligarchs obviously preferred to be seen (by Claudettes) and not heard. The rest of the sex-buying universe who could not afford Claude did get a rude awakening when their Minitel bills arrived and they saw that talk was not cheap.

On the other hand, the Minitel Rose entrepreneurs became the new Mesdames Claudes. For one, Xavier Niel, the billionaire who co-owns the newspaper *Le Monde,* owed his success to the sex lines, concocted as a teenager and sold for millions at age nineteen. Niel used this sex stake to create Free, France's leading mobile phone service.

In this French dawn of high technology, Mitterand decided to go after Madame Claude and make an example of her symbolic link to a decadent past. The new Mitterrand administration prided itself on its cutting-edge modernity, its TGV trains, its Jean Nouvel architecture, which was symbolized with his futuristic Institute du Monde Arabe, shaking up the Left Bank more than anything since the Eiffel Tower. President Mitterand was pleased that the Arabs were spending their oil fortunes on something other than Madame Claude. To him and his regime, nothing was more retro, minus the Parisian charm, than madams and brothels. Accordingly, he dispatched the Vice Squad, long the most corrupt organ of the Paris police, to get its own act together and lock the madams up.

In 1992, the Vice Squad got the Moby Dick of prostitution on the hook. What would prove to trigger Claude's Waterloo was her relentless quest for perfection. She had rejected a candidate for being overweight—by eleven pounds, to be precise. Claude was always precise. The girl had thought she was perfect. They all did. The very act of applying to become a Claudette was in itself a vote of self-confidence. But Madame Claude said no. No was no. Her amour propre shattered, the rejected girl went to the quai des Orfèvres and offered to become an informant, collaborating with the Vice Squad, now formally known as the BRP (Brigade de Répression du Proxénétisme).

"I knew her legend growing up," said Martine Monteil, then the first female head of the BRP and a far cry from her police predecessor, the corrupt and sinister Maurice Papon, who was one of Claude's original and most instrumental enablers. "I knew all the famous people. I knew how she had been protected by the state." Monteil would forever be known in France as the woman who busted Madame Claude. Then in her forties, Monteil was a real-life French version of Angie Dickinson in the seventies TV series *Police Woman*. A little taller and a little younger and Claude might have tried to recruit her to be on the other side of the law.

Blond, skinny, and stylish, Monteil had come from three generations of law enforcement. She had attended law school and was working her way up the vice ladder. She had graduated from the lowest rung of drug dealers to the second rung of pimps. She was aiming for the top shelf of organized crime. Monteil had taken a vow, where Claude was concerned, to operate by a new set of rules. "They had played a little game with her over taxes before," Monteil said. "No one dared to bring criminal charges against her. She had been sacred. But now she was not."

After two months of electronic and old-fashioned stakeout surveillance, Monteil, with the help of the still-angry Claude reject, was able to do what the French justice system had failed to do for nearly forty years: arrest Madame Claude, then sixty-nine, and bring her to court on charges of being a procuress, in the

ugly words that Claude despised above all others, a "lady pimp."
Accompanied by a squad of *flics* as well as *fiscs,* Monteil, war-
rant in hand, rudely interrupted Claude *chez elle* while she was
in the midst of an interview with a Crazy Horse Saloon showgirl who wanted to become a billionaire's private dancer. This
dancer might have been rejected as well, because Alain Bernardin, the Crazy Horse's impresario, was as fussy about height as
Madame Claude, who equated size with spectacle. Because of
the low ceilings and high stage of his club, Bernardin was as in-
transigent that his girls be under five-six as Claude was that hers
be over five-nine. However, since good call girls of Claude's old
school were increasingly hard to find, she might have become a
bit more elastic with her impossible standards.

"She was very haughty and arrogant," Monteil recalled. "I could
see how entitled and protected she felt. She had no idea that this
was coming." Monteil said she won Claude over by allowing her to
put on her game face. "She was dressed very casually, in a jogging
suit. I told my men to stand by. I gave her time to dress, put on her
cashmere blazer, do her makeup. She appreciated that a lot. At the
quai, we shared a pizza together while we waited for her to be
arraigned. The ice cracked a bit." Claude was not spared the indig-
nity of incarceration because of her age, or her fame. She lan-
guished in jail for two long days and nights, until she got her lawyer
to bail her out. He was the redoubtable Francis Szpiner, the
mouthpiece of many of Claude's great clients, including the dictator Bokassa, as well as several other African heads of state.

Even the great Szpiner could not keep his new client out for
long. Given the Napoleonic Code's "guilty until proven innocent"
presumption, after two months of freedom, Claude was sent to
prison to await what was heralded to be the hottest trial since
the Dreyfus affair. This time, she did not get a converted château,
but, rather, the women's wing of Fleury-Mérogis, the largest prison
in Europe and by far the toughest pen in the country, the French
equivalent of Alcatraz, Sing Sing, or Joliet.

The "trial of the century" six months later turned out to be all flash and no pan. And no names, either. Not one. "The Financial Brigade dropped their case," Monteil said. "Claude didn't have much money to collect. Her investments had turned out bad. If there was money in hidden Swiss or New Hebrides accounts, they couldn't find it. They thought she had spent it all. She pleaded poverty. She was a good actress. The authorities believed her. On the *proxénétisme* charges, the judge gave her a fine of one hundred and fifty thousand euros, which was a lot for a pimp, most of whom were small-time crooks. He also imposed a three-year sentence, but Claude got credit for the time served, and they let her out for the rest because, one, she hadn't physically harmed the girls like the tough male pimps, and, second, Fleury was full. The cells were overbooked. What were we going to prove with this polite seventy-year-old woman?"

Claude's attitude toward the proceedings, set out in her 1994 memoir *Madam,* was that she was being tried not for the tiny operation she was trying to run now to earn a living, but for the legendary empire she had abandoned fifteen years before. She claimed that Monteil and the Vice Squad had come after her only when alerted to her existence by one of her petty, and equally small-scale, rival madams. "The first time this woman called the police to inform on me, they responded, 'Madame Claude? Impossible! Madame Claude is dead.'"

But the informer called again. The second time, Claude wrote, the police told her, "'You must be wrong. Madame Claude lives in the United States.'" Claude believed she was completely under the radar. She also took the opportunity to bitterly denounce her fellow Frenchmen, "as World War II proved, the biggest collaborators of all. Instead of democracy and liberty, the only value shared by Mr. Everybody is his or her self-interest." Claude attacked the police as inept, inexplicably unaware of her 1985 imprisonment in Cahors. The record had been expunged, but still. The rival madam then pulled up the news articles and sent them to the cops. *Voilà!* This third time was the charm. Martine Monteil was put on the case, she found the angry reject, and, like British fictional supercop Bulldog Drummond, she "got her man," who this time was a woman.

In *Madam,* Claude was indignant at the injustice of French justice, trying her for her epic past and not her pedestrian present. Why, she asked, should she pay the price for her long-past success? The *fiscs* had settled with her for that back in Cahors. That book was closed. She cited evidence of "hundreds of other madams" operating in Paris who were treated leniently with small fines and no jail time, even when these minimadams allowed, as Claude described one operation, patrons to make love "without condoms and without bidets. 'But we have scotch,'" one madam had said.

Yet this madam was free, spreading AIDS and lesser venereal diseases, Claude railed, while she, who only wanted to find a girl a propitious, healthy, and rich companion, was railroaded to the lowest circle of hell that was Fleury-Mérogis. In *Madam,* Claude's description of her life behind bars was a combination of *The Gulag Archipelago* and a preview of *Orange Is the New Black.* She made the women's branch of Fleury-Mérogis sound as depraved and depressing as the tuberculosis sanitarium she went to after her stay in the concentration camp, which she had etched so indelibly in her 1975 *Allô, Oui.*

Claude outlined the demographics there as 70 percent drug addicts, 50 percent HIV-positive, and 10 percent insane, all housed together in a giant petri dish of contagion. What bothered the fastidious Claude more than the disease was the filth. Claude recounted her constantly changing cells and how the hardest thing to clean were the mattresses. She traded her allotted cigarettes, which she did not smoke, for a disinfectant product that did not work because it had to be diluted so as to not poison the inmates who drank it. The female wardens, Claude wrote, were meaner than the *Kapos* of Ravensbruck. Noting how clean her cells were, they would rip the sheets off her bed and throw them on the floor with her uneaten food.

The only edible items were the cookies and chocolate from the prison commissary, so Claude lived on sugar. She became friends with a gourmet Basque terrorist who had developed a relatively healthful mix of cookies and yogurt. These two outliers had "Homeric discussions" about politics, so fierce that the wardens would think they were fighting and broke them up. Because most of the women there were drug dealers and drug addicts, Claude, at the beginning, became fascinated by the roots of addiction and the way many of these addicts had taken to desperate prostitution to support their unquenchable habits. As Martine Monteil noted after Claude's trial, there were two kinds of prostitution, "the prostitution of misery," which Claude now encountered at Fleury-Mérogis, and "the prostitution of bourgeois luxury," the Claude brand, which she denied was prostitution. "They both will go on forever," the Claudebuster had to concede.

Ever the advocate of self-improvement, Claude bragged in *Madam* that she was one of the ten or so of the five hundred female inmates who took advantage of the government-mandated "continuing-education" programs that were offered to the "girls of Fleury." Claude learned Spanish, took literature courses, enjoyed the weekly screening of the latest film. Even in jail, the French were cinephiles. Otherwise, she lay in her cell and dreamed of the past.

Contrary to the image of Claude being a perpetual prisoner of her telephone (in the days before mobiles), she described in *Madam* a travelogue of her global peregrinations, in which she accompanied her girls on some of their more exotic out-calls. Wherever she went, she was always thinking about riches. On one trip to the Arabian Peninsula, she wrote, "the king told me, 'I will offer you a gift that has not been received by any European woman.' Immediately the image of a black pearl necklace entered my mind."

The king had Claude wait for hours until nightfall, then put her in a caravan of Land Rovers, which took the royal retinue out into the desert, where, under a brilliant full moon, the king's cavaliers performed camel races and feats of falconry. No woman had ever before been invited to these male exercises, the king said, flattering her. Claude felt totally let down, though, lady that she was, she never showed her disappointment. "Deep down inside," she wrote, "I could not help feeling regret over that black pearl necklace, my inaccessible dream." Opening her eyes from this dream in the cell of Fleury must have been the rudest of awakenings. "Seventy is not the right age to end up in prison," Claude wrote. After six months, the ordeal was over.

"The government feared a scandal, so they let her out as fast as possible. They didn't want to be accused of abusing an old person," said Sylvette Balland, who was one of Claude's rare visitors at Fleury-Mérogis but who fell out with the madam when Claude accused her of stealing her jewels from her apartment when she was incarcerated. "The only other person with a key was the widow of Jacques Quoirez, but Quoirez was off-limits. She couldn't blame her. So she blamed me." Balland recalled that Gianni Agnelli did send, anonymously, a new little Fiat for Claude after she was released. King Juan Carlos wrote a character reference. Otherwise, aside from Françoise Sagan, who said on TV, "Why bother this old woman?" none of Claude's famous friends lifted a finger to help her. "She was radioactive. No one would dare admit to knowing her."

"She was a little old lady, white hair, frail, barely able to walk, leaning on a cane, with a plastic bag filled with her belongings," recalled film producer Philippe Thuillier, who picked Claude up in the Fleury-Mérogis parking lot on New Year's Eve, 1992. The mighty had never fallen so low. Thuillier was an enterprising young producer who had worked out a deal with the TF1 network to help defray part of Claude's court fine and get her freed in return for her sitting for her first-ever television interview upon her release.

"She hadn't eaten; she looked terrible, especially since at the trial she'd had her hair perfectly blond, [and] she was so chic. Now she really looked like Auschwitz," Thuillier said. He took her to recuperate at the seventeenth arrondissement apartment of Ingrid, a Dutch Claudette who happened to have the body of a stripper but the soul of a nurse. Together, Thuillier and Ingrid brought Claude back to health, fed her, took her to Carita for lavish beauty treatments—in short, got her ready for her TV close-up.

The makeover worked brilliantly. The documentary was a big ratings hit and spawned a new memoir, which Thuillier helped ghostwrite for Claude, and even her own sexual version of a Jane Fonda workout video. Claude also did something at seventy-three she would never have allowed any of her swans to do: She sat for French *Playboy*. The photographer, Christophe Mourthé, a high-end specialist in erotica, had a farmhouse with his wife near Claude's in Cajarc. He was a neighbor and had become a friend. "I had this idea because she was the queen of sex life in the sixties and seventies to put her on a throne, and in lingerie." It was black lingerie, to boot, which Claude had interdicted for her girls. Swans were white. Black was for whores. But there Claude was, slim and regal and back to blond in a black sheer teddy, flaunting Cyd Charisse legs in high heels, sitting on a throne. She was the hottest grandmother one could imagine. Never in her days on the pavements of rue Godot-de-Mauroy could she have ever looked this alluring.

Claude knew it. In an interview she gave after the shoot, she said she broke all her own rules to prove how hot a seventy-year-old could be. That was big news from someone who had famously said that no woman over forty should let herself be seen naked. In the interview, she said, "When we are born, we have the body our mothers gave us. At sixty, we have the body we deserve." She was obviously patting herself on the back for her good habits and iron discipline. "It is very difficult to photograph a woman of my age without clothes without making me look ridiculous. It is a challenge I wanted to overcome."

Claude, being her bottom-line self, declared that the shoot was no public-service announcement. She would never let her girls "give it away," and neither would she. "I am not an exhibitionist," she declared. "I did it for the money"—specifically 50,000 euros to help pay off her 150,000 euro court fine and secure her continued release. Her bitterness was impossible to conceal. "Fifty thousand was nothing for my friends in the old days, when they counted in millions." But those rich friends were not there, so she had to rely on herself, as she always had.

Claude's parting shot was to the "journalists who wanted to write my obituary. Now they will have a beautiful photo to illustrate their story." She called the photos a "*bras d'honneur*," polite French for "fuck you" to the powers of state who had exploited her for their own riches in her heyday and had now forsaken her in her time of need. The unkindest cut of all in what would have been a newsstand sensation was that French *Playboy* tried to renegotiate the deal. Instead of fifty thousand euros, they wanted to pay her a fraction of that. They thought she was desperate. Claude may have *sat* for Mourthé's shoot, but she wouldn't *stand* for what she viewed as *Playboy*'s bait and switch. She refused to take the deal, refused to sign a release. The glorious photos never ran until decades later, and she was too old and sick to savor the notion that looking good was the best revenge.

"We made her a media star," says Isabelle Morini-Bosc, the stylish actress-reporter who conducted the record-breaking television interview with Claude for Thuillier. "She liked playing the frail old woman, but the minute she needed a cab, she dropped the cane and ran like an Olympic star." Morini-Bosc, who had the self-absorption attendant to an acting career, may have had high self-regard before she met Claude, but not after.

"She began by criticizing me. Right off the bat. My curly hair was too short, my breasts were too small, my ears too big. She offered to send me to her plastic surgeon to get bigger lips, a bigger ass. I admit that she did have good work done herself, great nose job, good lips. But any fantasy I had of being able to be a Claude girl—every actress in France likes to measure herself that way: Could I or couldn't I—Claude knocked right out of me. I could be okay *au caisse,* which meant 'at the cash register,' but *jamais en lit,* 'never in bed.' She was saying I may be smart but I wasn't sexy, I wasn't hot. I mean, her ideal look was the blond pageboy and perfect tits of the girls at the Crazy Horse. I was the opposite, and she wouldn't let me forget it."

Despite the flagellation, Morini-Bosc and Claude became friends in Claude's final stage of stardom. "She destroyed everyone, so I decided not to take it personally. She even ridiculed her great lawyer Szpiner. He was very tiny, and she'd make fun of his size. As a lawyer, people had to address him as "*maître*," or master. She did a *jeu de mot* and called him "*mètre*," as in one meter, or three feet, tall. Basically she was calling this legal giant a midget. She gave no respect.

"Claude would see a famous or titled woman across the restaurant or in a magazine and go into her catalog of everything the woman had done, the doctor, the surgery, the price. Once she was browsing through *Paris Match* and she saw a spread on Julia Roberts, at the height of her fame, and she spent half an hour doing an inventory of what was wrong with her. But Claude could be nice, in her mean way. I was in a loveless marriage, to a boring engineer, and Claude listened to me go on and on. I was a kid. It was the thing to do. It was a mistake. She said she was even worse off. She had had no love in her life at all. Two fake marriages, to a hippie Swiss gardener and a gay L.A. bartender, that was all she had to show, worse than me. Once she told me, 'I could be interested in a woman like you.' I couldn't believe it. I was touched, but nothing happened. She was in her late seventies."

Most of the time Morini-Bosc met with Claude, it was at *diner à trois* gossipfests with Thuillier, who was by no means immune from Claude's incisive wit. "When Philippe finally came out of the closet, Claude gave him a hard time for hiding it for so long," Morini-Bosc said. 'I *knew* you were gay from the start. I could have helped you.' Nobody knew this, but Claude discreetly, superdiscreetly, arranged men for men, men for women, women for women. But she only bragged of her hetero business. The rest was supersecret. It was easy to get the handsome young guys, the ones she got from Règine's, to do rich women. And her big *essayeurs,* the stars like Hallyday, Delon, Michel Sardou, she made them all *pay* to do those tests. Are you kidding? If you were rich, you had to pay. The only one who got a free ride was Jacques Quoirez. He was like her brother.

"She could be like a naughty child, an enfant terrible. Once Philippe arranged a dinner for us at the Fermette Marbeuf with Michèle Cotta [the powerful journalist of *L'Express* and the daughter of the mayor of Nice]. Cotta was rumored to have been the mistress of both Mitterrand and [his successor] Chirac. Both men were Madame Claude customers, especially Chirac. I begged her before the dinner not to speak her opinion, which she had said to me, that Chirac had no taste in women. Claude was indignant. 'How dare you tell me how to behave! I am a LADY!' So I relaxed and assumed all would go well. Within five minutes of sitting down, Madame Claude announced to Michèle, 'Well, I hear you had a thing with Chirac. You know I gave him my very worst ladies and he loved them, badly of course. He was done in fifteen minutes.' Philippe and I were mortified. But that came with the territory. You never knew what she would say. It was exciting, like a horror movie.

"Claude loved telling stories about Giscard, her nemesis, the man who really ruined her life. If he had left her alone, she would be the richest woman in France. She still had love letters he had written to one of her girls. She liked to read them to us. One told how he was jerking off to her picture while talking to Gorbachev on the hot line. Even until her late seventies, I believe she was still fixing men up, the ones who were still alive. She couldn't stop. It was a compulsion. I remember her asking me, very seriously, to let Agnelli know she was back in business."

"If she had her way, she would have turned me into a gigolo," said Jean-Noël Mirande, a print journalist and television presenter who made friends with Claude when she became his neighbor in Montmartre after getting out of jail. He was in his thirties. It was a little like *Harold and Maude,* except that Mirande was tall and handsome. For Claude, being back in Montmartre was a nostalgia trip. She had been so happy there, being poor and young and hanging out with Corsican hoods, from whom she had her introduction to the oldest profession. "She was always on my case: 'Why aren't you successful?' I tried to tell her that journalists shouldn't be held to banker standards, but she didn't want to hear that. 'Then do something else.' 'What?' I asked. 'Be a gigolo.'

"Claude knew a number of rich women who had been her girls. She had made them rich. Now they were getting older and less attractive to their husbands. She introduced me to a few of them at Les Deux Magots [a famous Left Bank café], showing me off to them. I was her solution as the way to make their husbands jealous and desire their wives again. I'm not even sure I was supposed to sleep with them. Just be a showpiece, maybe the same way they were when they worked for Claude. Whatever, I said no. It wasn't me. And she gave me a hard time for being a fool."

Claude and Mirande lived in the Villa Dancourt, a Deco complex on a gated and private street. It had history. Josephine Baker had lived there. A current neighbor was Michou, the celebrated drag queen who owned a cabaret on the rue des Martyrs that was a must for tourists who wanted to experience "naughty Paris." Mirande loved going out with Claude, "surrounded with a group of available boys," whose good looks and manners she was as insistent about as those of her swans. They went out all the time, to the Comédie Française, to Charles Trenet concerts, to her new favorite restaurant, Le Petit Ivan, a *borschteria,* where she admired the beautiful Russian girls who were just coming to dominate the emerging Internet call girl business in Paris, to Brasserie Lipp, where the autocratic owner, Monsieur Cazes, still loved her and gave her the best table in his intimidating house. "She knew everyone, all the top men and women, even if they would not acknowledge her. 'Oh, there's the old minister of the interior. He used to come every Thursday at three.' It had to hurt her when the girls she created came in and cut her dead, but she never showed emotion."

The Claude alumnae were doing so well, so scandal-free, that the rare fall from grace among their soigné ranks occurred with a resounding thud that echoed through global high society. Such was the 2010 suicide of Birgitte de Ganay, a Grace Kelly doppelganger who also married, and divorced, both royalty, the Count Michel de Ganay, and plutocracy, the Greek shipping heir Elias Mavroleon. Following a botched facelift, an abortive romance with another tycoon who refused to keep her in the style to which she had become accustomed, as well as a cocaine addiction she could no longer afford, Birgitte, 61, plunged to her death from her fifth-floor apartment on the Avenue Marceau, where she had often and lavishly entertained the likes of Lee Radziwill, Karl Lagerfeld, and Yves St. Laurent.

The Danish born high fashion model had come to Paris in the early seventies and, like so many of her elegant type, hooked up with Madame Claude, who in turn hooked her up with the *beau monde.* As one more never-too-thin model who turned to cocaine as the ultimate diet drug, Birgitte had become addicted, although it was something she was deeply ashamed of. She told her neighbors that the young African drug couriers who would show up at the Marceau apartment at all hours were the sons of diplomats and dictators to whom she played "auntie." The constant nosebleeds, she declared, were from chronic sinusitis. If only she could find a great ear, nose, and throat man, she lamented. Likewise, Birgitte dissembled being a Claudette, claiming that she and Claude were ships in the night in Paris, with Birgitte just arriving as Claude was fleeing Giscard. However, the playboys of Paris told a different story, always putting Birgitte in the pantheon of Claude's all-time greatest hits. Her death involved less schadenfreude than shock. No one seemingly had more to live for.

Claude herself, despite being out of the action she once was the center of, continued to enjoy her later years. She could be generous, effusively so. "She loved going shopping, and not just for herself. Shoes were her big thing. Once I saw some Tod's loafers I said I liked. She bought me five pairs," Jean-Noël Mirande recalled. The friendship continued when Claude moved first to a leafy Paris suburb, which she hated, then to Nice, where she had a number of rich friends to socialize with. She rented a beautiful apartment overlooking the sea, bought a sporty white Austin convertible with an automatic transmission, and began keeping cats. She also managed to assemble, mostly through the boutiques and beauty salons she frequented, an entourage of very pretty boys who doted on her. "She was a big celebrity in Nice," Mirande said.

Still, Claude's Riviera relocation had an ulterior motive, as noted by her other close male friend, Philippe Thuillier. Her only relative, her long-estranged daughter, Anne, lived in Nice, working as an administrator in the Saint-Roch Hospital. The family tie seemed like a logical good connection to have as Claude entered her eighties. It didn't work. Mother and daughter could not make peace. The private eye Thuillier hired succeeded in finding Anne. The two women tried to establish a weekly rendezvous, but they got into an awful row over who would choose this day of atonement. If Claude couldn't dictate the day, the experiment in reunion would be over. So it was.

Mirande, like Thuillier, visited Claude in Nice and received a red carpet, with Lucullan meals and many gifts. "There were only two things she complained about," Mirande said. "One was her hearing, which was a big issue for someone who made her fortune on the phone. She couldn't stand wearing a hearing aid. The other was her daughter. She said she regretted terribly that she and her daughter could not get along. We went to a little church, and she lit a candle for her. That was the only time I ever saw tears in her eyes.

"Normally, she was impossible. Tough as nails," Mirande said, echoing everyone who knew Claude. "She told this story about this pretty guard at Fleury-Mérogis. She asked the guard why she was so mean to her. The guard said, 'Because you make more in a day than I make in a year.' And Claude said back to her, 'Well, why don't you come over to the other side?' The guard was so flattered by the mere possibility, she gave Claude special treatment."

Mirande also remembered Claude insulting everyone, wherever she was. Her edge was not dulled by age. "We were in Nice with this famous actress. She was only in her forties. And Claude said, 'You're finished unless you get a face-lift. Those forehead wrinkles will kill your career.' She was fearless. But she could be sweet. Although I didn't see her at the end, the last five years or so, we did talk on the phone, until we got to a point where she couldn't hear anymore. She always asked me about my mother, who was getting old, too. Her interest was genuine. She wasn't being polite. She didn't know how."

"Claude gave me one gift in all the years we knew each other," said Isabel Morini-Bosc, who stayed in touch until the end. "One gift. It was an ugly ivory elephant, made out of a tusk. It was too big for a charm bracelet, and too small for a necklace. Plus, it was so insensitive. Claude knew my big passion was saving elephants and other animals. I'm still not sure if that was her cruel way of being kind. The last time I saw her, years later, she had mellowed. She said, 'If I had met you when you were young, and you let me do you completely over, maybe'—and she said—'maybe—you could have worked for me.' And, you know, that was the best compliment I ever had."

EPILOGUE

When Madame Claude died at ninety-two, in 2015, it seemed both ironic and tragic that the woman who had brought so much pleasure to so many was mourned by so few. Here at the cremation of the woman who had conveyed the joy of sex to a veritable pantheon of the greatest men of her time were five gay men, three of whom were hairdressers. Even her daughter did not come to say good-bye. Granted, Claude had outlived most of her grand clients, but many of the swans she had created and transformed into the wives of the global aristocracy were still around and likely breathing a "Ding-dong! The witch is dead" sigh of relief. A relationship with the world's top madam was a friendship that dared not speak its name.

Madame Claude nevertheless demands to be acknowledged and remembered as the greatest impresario in the history of romance. She assembled a corps of goddesses worthy of Florenz Ziegfeld and Louis B. Mayer, but, unlike those showmen who sold their fantasies to the masses, Claude sold her fantasy to the one-tenth of 1 percent. She turned sex into the ultimate luxury good, and put her name on it, even if it was the one great brand that could never be flaunted.

Empowerment or exploitation? That is the question. No woman I spoke to for this book who had worked for Madame

Claude voiced any sentiment that she had been exploited. Nor did any of Claude's male clients, including a number of enlightened liberals, well aware of the chauvinism of their glory days, express concern that Claude had done her charges anything but proud. Yes, Claude may have gotten rich off her swans. But so did so many of the swans. What people talked about were the big marriages, the big careers, the inordinate number of success stories. No one cited any tragedies. Then again, I had once asked my cardiologist about what is known as the "French paradox," in which the French gorge themselves on impossibly rich, fatty foods and unjust desserts yet never seem to get fat like Americans do. "You don't see the dead ones," he told me.

The only people who branded Madame Claude as an exploiter were the French law-enforcement authorities who sent her to prison for *proxénétisme*. Traumatic as that was for a woman of seventy, six months and a few hundred thousand dollars in fines was a relatively small price for the millions she had earned and for the free pass the French Establishment had granted her. Nobody would ever say Madame Claude was an ordinary procuress, much less the kind of tough-thug pimp who would entrap, rob, and brutalize defenseless women the law was originally designed to prohibit. Madame Claude never recruited. She didn't have to. The women, in droves, sought her out. They were all highly ambitious. The dreams Madame Claude made come true weren't just the sexual fantasies of her male clients but also the Prince Charming fantasies of her retinue of beauties. Madame Claude was harder to get into than Harvard.

Despite her name, *Madame* Claude was not really a *madam*, not in the traditional sense. The capital *M* and the *e* at the end make all the difference between a lady and a tramp. In France, *Madame* is a sign of great respect, as in Madame de Pompadour, the first lady of the court at Versailles, or Madame Curie, the first lady of French science. In America, by contrast, the first reaction to the word *madam*, particularly employed in any sort of sexual context, is a knee-jerk revulsion, with images of coercion, trafficking, drugs, disease, downfall. Madame Claude could be as tough as the drill sergeant in Kubrick's *Full Metal Jacket*. She was ruthless about her women's looks, but equally ruthless about their manners. She objectified women, but in the sense of an artist, to turn them into objects of beauty, the best that they could be. Most important, her great joy and her great art was in *creating* her women, not destroying them. Where the law was concerned, a more appropriate designation for Madame Claude would have been to borrow the Tour de France bicycle race's *hors catégorie* designation: "outside of competition."

In the literary/cinematic hall of madams, Madame Claude is a veritable guardian angel compared to John Steinbeck's murderously malevolent Catherine Trask in *East of Eden*. She falls closer to the entrepreneurial frontier brothel keeper played by Julie Christie in Robert Altman's *McCabe & Mrs. Miller*. However, her closest analogue may be in real life, with the late Jean Harris, the prim and proper headmistress of the ultraexclusive Madeira School, who murdered her famous lover, the Scarsdale Diet doctor, Herman Tarnower. Madame Claude didn't have famous lovers, and she never murdered anyone. Her business was her obsession. That's why she was so successful. All she did was work. That's also why she died alone.

In today's Paris, the Giscardian modernist reformers who drove Madame Claude out of the country and out of grace seem to have gotten their way. The old Paris of Irma la Douce is no more. The rue Saint-Denis, once Paris's high street of sidewalk soliciting, has been totally Disneyfied and gentrified. Pigalle, the "pig alley" of postwar GI tall tales, has become as hip as Manhattan's Lower East Side. Paris, at least touristic Paris, seems to have gone the way of Rudolph Giuliani's cleaned-up Times Square. As in America, the madams and brothels of yore have evolved into the Internet, with a thank-you nod to the pioneering Minitel. Prostitution has become a subset of online dating.

There's nothing exclusive about it anymore. The French barely seem to be involved in it. The high-end, model-type call girls who can be found on "leave nothing to the imagination" websites are almost entirely from Russia and the former Iron Curtain countries. A sequel to *French Women Don't Get Fat* could be *French Girls Don't Hook.*

Of course, sex is always there, if under the surface. Just as America has its periodic celebrity prostitution scandals, France, too, has its own, most recently in the escapades of International Monetary Fund chairman Dominique Strauss-Kahn, whose sexual obsessions are widely thought to have cost this otherwise-brilliant politician the presidency of the *république*. If Madame Claude, who never suffered a public client scandal on her long watch, had still been in action, she might well have saved Strauss-Kahn his ignominy and France's her own. Likewise, the epidemic of high-profile sexual harassment lawsuits in America might have been mitigated if the testosterone tycoons had had a Madame Claude to provide discreet and appropriate outlets for their obsessions. With the typically American "I don't have to pay for it" cowboy swagger belied by the secret multimillion-dollar out-of-court settlements, hiring Claude girls to entertain the big bosses would have been vastly cheaper, whatever the price.

But Claude, alas, is gone. There was never anyone quite like her before, and the world has changed in ways that make it highly unlikely that her tour de force of eros will ever be repeated. Having come to power in the postwar era of rapid technological change, Claude rode that wave to the bank. But the telephone that had been her chariot eventually became her hearse. Madame Claude's personal touch, her unerring sense of who was right for whom, can never be replicated by a computer; no method of encryption can match her sphinx-like discretion. Madame Claude's great innovation was in turning sex into a branded luxury good, but who wants to buy luxury on the Internet, and, off-line, who is there to sell it? The rise of feminism and equal rights have also contributed to the death knell of the supermadam. There are countless more ways to wealth and power than to marry it or sleep with it. Yesterday's Claude girl is today's Stanford woman.

Madame Claude was a study in fascinating contradictions, unique to her generation and her place in postwar Europe. She craved old-world aristocracy, yet she was equally hooked on cinematic gangland. One day her object of desire might be a Rothschild, the next a Corsican hit man. Her brilliance was her ability to play both arenas. She could be a terrible snob, an insufferable elitist, but those are typically French character traits, a legacy of the days of Marie Antoinette. The faults of Madame Claude can be traced to being born a poor girl in an aristocracy that was struggling to become a democracy. After all, it had taken a revolution, and it still was far from done. Madame Claude simply accepted the stereotypes of her age and took them to their outer limit. Today's women may resent her. They argue that she died alone, that she sold love but never felt it. But as Fernande Grudet, Madame Claude enjoyed her grand passions, and when she assumed her new identity, she equally enjoyed her remarkable success. Hers was undisputedly a life in full. The luxury brand she created may be gone, but the legend she forged will go on forever.

ACKNOWLEDGMENTS

This is by far the most challenging book I have ever done, in terms of getting people to go on the record. Americans in particular were almost universally paranoid about the sexual and moral implications of admitting to know Madame Claude. Never have our Puritan roots been so obvious. I consequently spent the greater part of a year of research in Europe, where guilt by association gave way to the status of inclusion in what was one of the century's most unique elites. So many people did step forward, and I want to thank all of the following, as well as a long roster of remarkable players in this high stakes game of love and money whose kind assistance dared not speak its name.

I'd like to give special thanks to Anne Marie Spataru, my brilliant and unshockable translator-in-chief, to my editor, Charles Spicer, who was bold in his willingness to venture where self-styled angels feared to tread, to his right-hand, April Osborn, and the staff at St. Martin's Press, as well as to its legal eagle Henry Kaufman, who doesn't miss a trick, and to Mai Pham of Bridgeman Images, whose assistance in assembling the photos was invaluable in creating this blast from the past. A huge Michelin star to Mathilde Beziau and the brilliant staff at my Paris home, the classically sublime Grand Hôtel du Palais Royal.

And then, in alphabetical order: Judith Aubrey, Robert Benamou, Raoul Bonnafe, Roberto Borjas, Tony Bourbon, Henry Buhl, Martin Caan, Isaac Cronin, Jan Cushing, Olivia de Havilland, Simon de Pury, Yves Dessca, Dr. Cornette de St. Cyr, Daisy Donovan, Dominique d'Orglandes, Francesca Drommi, Joanne and Gerry Dryansky, Louise Duncan, Pepita Dupont, Carrie-Lee Early, Françoise Fabian, Natasha Fraser, Gisele Galante, Kitty Go, Jean Pierre Godeaut, Paola Gradi, Sylvie Granotier, Allen Grubman, Chiara Donn, Dr. Neal Handel, Chilla Heuser, Nandu Hinds, Winter and Fred Hoffman, Isabelle and Marc Hotimsky, Christopher Hyland, Just Jaeckin, Dany Jucaud, Stephane Lambert, Emily Lodge, Karen Lubeck, Patrick Marant, Vanessa Marsot, Veronique Maxe, Boaz Mazor, Christopher Mooney, Xavier Moreau, Capucine Motte, Albert Nahamias, Mathew Negru, Jenny Newell, David Niven Jr., Cathy Nolan, Isabella and Roger Ohan, Patrick Orban, Dr. Luc Pandraud, Didier Papalou, Suzy Patterson, Jean Pigozzi, Michael Pochna, Kathleen Quinn, Beatrice Reed, Arthur Sarkissian, Conchita Sarnoff, Chris Silvester, Tex Stadiem, John Sutin, Taki Theoradacopoulos, Michael Thomas, Philippe Thullier, Myriam Toledano, Kathy Treyboux, Ruta Vaisnys, Catherine Vergetti, Dimitri Villard, Jean Louis Vuilleme, Denis Westhoff, Ronald Winston, and Susi Wyss.

INDEX

Dollar Diplomacy: Did the CIA Use Madame Claude to "Entertain" JFK?

Jorbi eget elit enim, et consequat tortor. Praesent vitae nulla dolor, convallis mollis eros. Maecenas in erat eu lacus placerat adipiscing quis in nisi. Nulla facilisi. Suspendisse vel urna nisi, in egestas ante. Suspendisse laoreet neque id turpis consectetur molestie. Nam vel augue sed enim mollis blandit. Aliquam imperdiet lectus lobortis nisi euismod consequat consectetur eu diam. Morbi orci nisl, imperdiet sed convallis vitae, ultrices vitae lacus. Aliquam ornare, urna id imperdiet dignissim, augue felis fermentum erat, et gravida massa odio ut tellus. Integer sodales mollis enim, in rutrum augue scelerisque sed. Fusce et lobortis ipsum, as dictum massa vitae metus tempor id pretium sem fermentum. Donec faucibus nisi nec nunc sagittis in volutpat mi imperdiet.

Praesent id egestas lorem. Proin sit amet nibh et lectus luctus eleifend. Aliquam lacus nibh, scelerisque vel convallis ac, pulvinar eget purus. Quisque vel ligula tortor. Morbi fringilla dapibus urna, vel mattis nulla cursus non. Mauris ac convallis felis. Fusce cursus nisl dui. Integer aliquet, diam ac pellentesque vehicula, felis lacus molestie lectus, eu semper

Integer aliquet, diam ac pellentesque vehicula, felis lacus molestie lectus, eu semper tortor arcu vitae orci. Cras eget tellus eu mi condimentum blandit. Cras ornare turpis et neque tincidunt congue. Cras convallis lorem nec urna rhoncus a faucibus mauris tincidunt. Nam augue purus, porttitor sed volutpat vel, pharetra nec sem. Nulla facilisi. Nam vel turpis semper elit porta aliquam ut ... eu libero a dui ... Suspendisse

am lectus nulla, venenatis ut hendrerit euismod, consectetur eu tellus. Aenean vitae justo libero. Donec at felis non lacus ornare tincidunt nec hendrerit sem. Duis fringilla laoreet nisl vitae rutrum. Curabitur quis metus sit amet augue lacinia commodo. Etiam a ante ut velit iaculis aliquam. Suspendisse pretium, orci quis dignissim ultricies, sapien nisi tristique ipsum, at accumsan nibh quam non arcu. Vivamus metus odio, vehicula ut feugiat in, placerat quis mi. Morbi ut lacinia odio. Cras convallis diam quis ligula tincidunt porttitor. Morbi laoreet tristique odio sit amet lobortis. Praesent id egestas lorem.

Proin sit amet

Madame Claude in Beverly Hills

Aliquam quam enim, aliquet sit amet egestas nec, convallis quis leo. Pellentesque odio diam, blandit iaculis tempor et, mollis vel lorem. Pellentesque ullamcorper dui mi. Donec venenatis velit id nisi ultrices eu gravida ante consequat. Vestibulum ante ipsum primis in faucibus orci luctus et ultrices posuere cubilia Curae; Curabitur viverra metus vitae purus facilisis sed gravida nulla aliquet. Etiam tempus volutpat id mattis quam pellentesque sit amet. Praesent vel felis elit, et lobortis sem. Fusce metus mi, sollicitudin vitae turpis in, quis commodo est. Sed at dolor ac ante laoreet ultricies. Nulla faucibus convallis sem malesuada ornare. Duis commodo blandit neque, et hendrerit leo ultricies nec. Donec eget libero leo. Quisque id vehicula libero. Aliquam erat volutpat. In adipiscing semper ligula convallis mattis. Etiam tempor auctor convallis. Suspendisse non augue orci, id faucibus est. Nulla enim magna, eleifend at mollis et, mattis ac est. Pellentesque vel vulputate risus. Fusce a leo in elit tempor consequat eget at nibh. Suspendisse ac massa at diam vehicula fermentum. Praesent hendrerit mollis porta.

Duis bibendum dolor eget erat posuere posuere. Integer vel leo quis urna accumsan vestibulum. Suspendisse dictum tempor adipiscing. Duis id rutrum odio. Cum sociis natoque penatibus et magnis dis parturient montes, nascetur ridiculus mus. Nulla lobortis varius erat, congue gravida urna laoreet adipiscing. Nam vitae nisi in sem consectetur vestibulum id vitae arcu. Suspendisse potenti. Fusce tristique mollis diam, at fringilla eros facilisis eu. Nullam euismod purus in erat ultrices ac congue dui lobortis.

Integer pharetra vulputate semper. Sed porttitor, lacus id feugiat consectetur, nisi lectus pharetra lectus, sit amet ornare magna eu at massa. Proin at arcu porta tortor hendrerit congue vitae nec dolor. Pellentesque pellentesque sapien et lacus feugiat nec tristique ipsum dignissim. Ut vitae aliquet neque. Aenean ultrices mollis lectus, at imperdiet eros vehicula fermentum. Vestibulum et justo nec ipsum varius rhoncus. Integer at ipsum tellus, vel eleifend odio. Ut eu nulla ante. Nunc placerat ullamcorper tortor, eget placerat risus rutrum id. Vestibulum fringilla lectus non nulla suscipit eget.

Adipiscing Augue Lectus

Le Sexe, C'est le Vrai Pouvoir par Madame Claude

Cu his modo definitiones, amet, appellantur conclusionemque per eu, te pro tamquam omnesque delicatissimi. Ea sit velit sadipscing. Qui ea equidem nominati petentium. Sea ad cometetur adipiscing, te nec salutandi periculis conceptam, alia scripserit ne pro. Ei ius elit singulis.

In mea nominavi dissentias. Cu habeo graece constituam cum, propriae adipisci volutpat cu nec. Mei no minimum rationibus, pro no stet etiam pertinax. Minim scripta quaeque mel eu, case admodum has an. Per malis philosophia id.

Putant regione quaerendum mea id, recusabo efficiantur ut pri. Denique appellantur vituperatoribus et vis, tacimates mnesarchum honestatis ei cum. Ne sea decore scripta omnesque, scripta luptatum conclusionemque est id. Id quo case quas velit, menandri antiopam eu duo. Nam id postea temporibus, et splendide intellegam pro, id atqui ancillae vim, qualisque ne mea.

Cu his modo definitiones. Ne duis dolore eos. Accommodare conchdaturque pri no, sale inimicus electram ne pri. In nec quando possim efficiantur, id etiam mollis

Mad... in B...

A... ...

Dollar Diplomacy: Did ...adame Claude to "Er...

...bi eget elit enim, et ...nsequat tortor. Praesent ... nulla dolor, convallis ...llis eros. Maecenas in erat ...

Praesent id egestas lorem. Proin amet nibh et lectus luctus eleifen Aliquam lacus nibh, scelerisque vel convallis ac, pulvinar eget pur Quisque...

Mada... in Be...

liquam quam en...